CONTRIBUTIONS
TO
ECONOMIC ANALYSIS

148

Honorary Editor:
J. TINBERGEN

Editors:
D. W. JORGENSON
J. WAELBROECK

NORTH-HOLLAND
AMSTERDAM · NEW YORK · OXFORD

SOCIAL
INSURANCE

SOCIAL INSURANCE

Papers presented at the 5th Arne Ryde Symposium
Lund, Sweden, 1981

Edited by

LARS SÖDERSTRÖM

Department of Economics
University of Lund
Lund, Sweden

1983
NORTH-HOLLAND
AMSTERDAM · NEW YORK · OXFORD

ISBN: 0 444 86724 4

Publishers:
ELSEVIER SCIENCE PUBLISHERS B.V.
P.O. BOX 1991
1000 BZ AMSTERDAM
THE NETHERLANDS

Sole distributors for the U.S.A. and Canada:
ELSEVIER SCIENCE PUBLISHING COMPANY, INC.
52 VANDERBILT AVENUE
NEW YORK, N.Y. 10017

Library of Congress Cataloging in Publication Data

Arne Ryde Symposium (5th : 1981 : Lund, Sweden)
   Social insurance.

   (Contributions to economic analysis ; 148)
   1. Social security--Congresses. I. Söderström, Lars,
1940-   . II. Title. III. Series.
HD7090.A76 1981   368.4   83-11671
ISBN 0-444-86724-4 (Elsevier Science)

Printed in The Netherlands

INTRODUCTION TO THE SERIES

This series consists of a number of hitherto unpublished studies, which are introduced by the editors in the belief that they represent fresh contributions to economic science.

The term "economic analysis" as used in the title of the series has been adopted because it covers both the activities of the theoretical economist and the research worker.

Although the analytical methods used by the various contributors are not the same, they are nevertheless conditioned by the common origin of their studies, namely theoretical problems encountered in practical research. Since for this reason, business cycle research and national accounting, research work on behalf of economic policy, and problems of planning are the main sources of the subjects dealt with, they necessarily determine the manner of approach adopted by the authors. Their methods tend to be "practical" in the sense of not being too far remote from application to actual economic conditions. In addition they are quantitative rather than qualitative.

It is the hope of the editors that the publication of these studies will help to stimulate the exchange of scientific information and to reinforce international cooperation in the field of economics.

The Editors

THE ARNE RYDE FOUNDATION

Arne Ryde was an exceptionally promising young student on the doctorate programme at the Department of Economics at the University of Lund. He died after an automobile accident in 1968 when only 23 years old. In his memory his parents Valborg Ryde and pharmacist Sven Ryde founded the Arne Ryde Foundation for the advancement of research at our Department. We are most grateful to them. The Foundation has made possible important activities to which our ordinary resources are not applicable.

In agreement with Valborg and Sven Ryde we have decided to use the means of the Foundation mainly to arrange a series of symposiums, as a rule one every second year. Our intention is to alternate between pure theory and applications. The themes of our previous Arne Ryde Symposiums have been: Economics of Information (1973), Econometric Methods (1975), Theoretical Contributions of Knut Wicksell (1977), Economic Theory of Institutions (1979).

Björn Thalberg

PREFATORY NOTE

This volume contains a selection of the papers presented at the 5th Arne Ryde symposium on August 27-28, 1981. Some of the papers not included are being published elsewhere. The topic of the symposium was "Social Insurance". As one could tell from the response to our call for papers, a meeting on this topic was highly timely. Social insurance has become an increasingly important subject, and is now a major concern for economists all over the world. We hope that this volume will prove itself useful to future research in this area.

We wish to thank all those who made this volume possible. Particularly, we would like to express our gratitude to Carl Hampus Lyttkens, who has taken care of much of the administrative work for both the symposium and this volume, to all those who acted as referees on the papers, to Ragnar Söderberg Foundation for its financial support, and to Pia Åkerman who prepared the manuscript for press.

The organizing committee
and editorial board

Lars Söderström
Ann-Charlotte Ståhlberg
Bengt Jönsson
Göran Skogh
Eskil Wadensjö

CONTRIBUTORS

Frans A.J. van den Bosch, Erasmus University, Rotterdam, The Netherlands

Richard V. Burkhauser, Vanderbilt University, Nashville, Tenn., USA

Per Gunnar Edebalk, University of Lund, Sweden

Åke Elmér, University of Lund, Sweden

Han Emanuel, Social Security Council, The Netherlands

Robert G. Evans, University of British Columbia, Canada

Robert H. Haveman, University of Wisconsin-Madison, Madison, Wisc., USA

Mats Lundahl, University of Lund, Sweden

Barry J. Nalebuff, Harvard University, Cambridge, Mass., USA

Peder J. Pedersen, University of Aarhus, Denmark

Carel Petersen, Erasmus University, Rotterdam, The Netherlands

Bernhard M.S. van Praag, Leyden University, The Netherlands

Joseph F. Quinn, Boston College, Chestnut Hill, Mass., USA

Ann-Charlotte Ståhlberg, University of Stockholm, Sweden

Hal R. Varian, University of Michigan, Ann Arbor, Mich., USA

Bengt-Arne Wickström, Noregs Handelshøgskole (The Norwegian School of
  Economics and Business Administration), Bergen, Norway

Barbara L. Wolfe, University of Wisconsin-Madison, Madison, Wisc., USA

Peter Zweifel, Institute for Empirical Research in Economics, Zürich,
  Switzerland

CONTENTS

ARNE RYDE SYMPOSIUM ON SOCIAL INSURANCE
L. Söderström (editor)
© Elsevier Science Publishers B.V. (North-Holland), 1983

INTRODUCTION

Lars Söderström

Social security arrangements are not peculiar to the welfare state. They are found throughout the world, simply because no society can manage particularly well without them. Harvest failures and other disruptions to the means of subsistence are widespread. Moreover, no individual can ignore the risk that, due to, for example, illness, he or she may encounter difficulties in utilising the means of subsistence that are available.

The solution to this problem rests with associations for mutual assistance. The family, village and other similar forms of natural community provide examples of this type of association. Although these natural communities were perhaps not primarily created in order to provide security, they are undoubtedly a major influence on individual security in the majority of societies. In relation to families, this is particularly applicable if several generations are living together. In this case, the association provides a flexible organisation for smoothing out the different phases of the life-cycle - childhood, working age and old age - at the same time as it provides considerable opportunities for mutual assistance in the event of illness etc.

Cooperatives for mutual assistance are common among different occupational groups. The usual arrangement is to form a benefit society. Members commit themselves, subject to certain regulations, to contribute towards the formation of a common fund from which they are entitled, according to certain criteria, to receive benefits. These benefits are usually paid in cash although they can naturally also take the form of medical care etc. which is partly or wholly paid by the benefit society. The insurance companies are of a more distinctly commercial character although in principle they operate in the same way as the cooperatives.

There are roughly speaking three ways in which the Government can be used to supplement and improve private insurance arrangements in society. Firstly, government authorities can endeavour to promote conditions of general stability. Policies to reduce cyclical fluctuations and to facilitate structural adaptations in the economy would come under this heading. At a more fundamental level, the Government's promotion of stable conditions extends to policies that improve law and order within the country or reduce the risk of foreign aggression. It goes without saying that a failure of preventative measures in either the former or latter category could have very serious repercussions from the point of view of individual security. It is equally evident that measures of this type are of major importance.

Secondly, the Government can encourage the growth of private insurance schemes. This could include measures which promote stable family conditions and the establishment of associations or companies providing insurance services. An incentive may be provided in the form of a subsidy which can be used to influence the pattern of insurance arrangements. This type of social security policy measure has actually been in use ever since its inception in Germany in the 1880s. With regards to the insurance system, financial assistance has been limited to the "recognised" benefit societies. In order to receive recognition, certain requirements have to be met regarding, for instance, the legal rights of members and the degree of access to membership. Similarly, in relation to family assistance, the stipulation can be made that those, for example, who cohabit should have certain reciprocal legal ties and maintenance responsibilities. These conditions may be subsequently extended to cover a period when cohabitation has ceased to exist.

Thirdly, the Government may itself administer different types of social security schemes. This may be conducted on a normal insurance basis by means of premiums, funds and benefits. However the Government is able to offer a wide range of other opportunities. For instance, the "insurance" can be arranged as a general tax-financed, minimum income guarantee. Rights of taxation and note issue remove the need for funds. However, with regards, for instance, to the effect on savings, the use of the premium reserve system may still be desirable. As in the case of private social security schemes, a public system may take the form of cash payments and benefits in kind such as medical care and labour market training.

The traditional motives for state involvement in social security provision is to deal with problems such as the "free rider", adverse selection and collective risks which would otherwise have occurred in a private system. The "free riders" evade responsibility for the costs of social security provision. They place themselves outside the private system calculating that they will still be able to receive the benefits that they require. They rely on the willingness of others to provide charity. Adverse selection is due to the fact that the financing of private insurance schemes has to be placed on a proper actuarial basis. As a result, certain individuals will be required to pay premiums that are excessively high. They are quite simply unable to afford social security. Cooperatives or insurance companies that try to provide assistance in the form of subsidies to high risk groups must cover these subsidies by raising their premiums for other policy-holders. Consequently they run the risk of being forced out of the market. Collective risks affect many policy-holders simultaneously with the result that individual cooperatives or insurance companies find it difficult to cover these risks. As a result, they are excluded from private insurance schemes.

A solution to these problems does not require any substantial intervention on the part of the government authorities. A minimum strategy could comprise the following elements. Firstly, everyone is required to have a certain minimum insurance provision. For example, it could be required that everyone over 18 years of age must have a life-long insurance contract which provides a basic old-age pension, a right to substantial medical care as well as a right to receive a certain amount of compensation for a loss of income due to illness or unemployment. The requirement for compulsory basic cover eliminates the "free-rider" problem. Secondly, subsidies are paid to those individuals who are unable to pay the proper actuarial price for basic insurance cover. It is primarily the high-risk 18 year olds who require financial assistance although benefits may also have to be made a-vailable to those individuals who later on in life find themselves in con-tinuous financial difficulties. Thirdly, individual cooperatives and insur-ance companies can be offered the opportunity to reinsure themselves with government authorities against the collective risks contained in the basic insurance cover.

This solution to the security problem provides every citizen with a fixed life-long insurance contract. Most of the financing requirement can be met from normal once and for all fixed insurance premiums. However the latter can be adjusted to take account of the individual policy-holder's ability to pay. There is nothing to prevent an individual being allowed to postpone part of his payment obligations, during, for example, a period of educa-tion. A planned repayment schedule can be drawn up to take account of any debts that arise. Debts that are still outstanding can for example, be wholly or partly written off at the time of retirement.

Alternatively, a comprehensive or partial basic insurance cover can be pro-vided by means of compulsory government insurance schemes. This is essen-tial if one wishes to use the insurance system as a more powerful instru-ment of distributional policy. In this case where insurance provision is financed out of taxation, individuals may be required to pay a higher pre-mium than would be justified on purely actuarial grounds. However there is no particular advantage to be derived from this arrangement. Distributional policy goals can be equally well achieved by other means. There is also a substantial social cost associated with social benefits that are financed out of taxation. Taxation disturbs the structure of incentives in society. This gives rise to an "excess burden" since individuals choose to work, invest or consume either more or less or in a different manner than they otherwise would have done. The social cost of taxation naturally depends on both the composition and level of taxation. However, it is evident that these social costs are frequently substantial. This is undoubtedly a ques-tion which merits considerable political attention.

The earliest example of a state insurance scheme in this century is the Swedish pension scheme from 1913. It was envisaged as a contributory re-tirement pension scheme financed out of deductions from wages. However, it did in fact become largely financed out of general income taxation. Nowa-days, state insurance schemes are found in many countries. A common feature of these schemes is that they are mainly financed by means of more or less proportional taxes levied on wages. If, as is generally assumed, these taxes are then shifted on to wage earners, at the same time as a system of progressive taxation exists elsewhere in the economy, the burden on wage earners will become fairly regressive. The situation is comparable with one where insurance premiums are tax deductible. An individual who has a mar-ginal income tax rate of 40% will pay 60% of the premiums whereas someone with a marginal income tax rate of 70% will only pay 30% of the premiums. Hence it is an open question as to whether the normal type of state insur-ance gives rise to any advantages in terms of distributional policies. Estimates that have been made on the basis of Swedish conditions indicate that it is the average-paid worker who mostly benefits from an insurance system financed out of taxation. In comparison with a system where premiums are charged purely on actuarial grounds, average wage earners receive a basic insurance cover at a subsidised price. Naturally, like everyone else, they will also have to bear the social costs of taxation.

During recent years, there has been a rapid growth of interest, in a number
of countries, in the question of social insurance systems. Several factors
account for the increased attention that this subject has received. Undoubtedly, the most important factor is the stagnation that has been experienced by Western economies during the 1970s. As a result of the lower
levels of economic growth, the resources available to finance the social
security system have not been as forthcoming as had been anticipated.
Expenditure on medical care, old-age pensions etc. account for in many
cases, 30 percent of national income. Countries that have chosen to finance
these expenditures out of taxation have been subject to a rising burden of
taxation and in some cases, a budget deficit. The social insurance system
is now frequently described as being in financial crisis although the economic problems are not solely of a financial nature. In response to the
optimistic climate engendered by economic growth in the 1960s, a series of
fairly generous improvements were made in social security policy. There is
a suspicion that these reforms have undermined economic performance by
removing the motivation for the classical virtues of work and thrift.
Indeed in some quarters, it has been alleged that the social insurance system has been responsible for the weak economic growth of the 1970s.

It is evident that the social insurance system has now established itself
as an important area for economic research. The considerable degree of
mobility that characterises a modern industrial society requires the existence of a well-functioning safety net for its citizens. The major point at
issue concerns the type and level of provision that is required for this
safety net. The cost of unsatisfactory solutions can easily become excessive. Consequently, the effects of different arrangements must be carefully
studied. International comparisons and serious econometric studies should
be able to provide important contributions in this field. However, it is
also of great importance at the present stage to increase public understanding of the purpose and function of a social insurance system in society. In particular, it is essential to emphasize the long-run nature of social insurance. It is first and foremost a question of evening out the differences in consumption opportunities over an individual´s entire life-
cycle. What is the economic significance of using a premium reserve system
as compared to a distribution system for the purposes of this adjustment
process? What role is played by collective risks in terms of inflation or
sudden changes in the average life-span? How is the supply of labour affected by these different solutions?

There is a long list of important questions and the field is open for a major programme of economic research. This volume provides a number of contributions which I hope the reader will find stimulating. The material is
of a heterogenous nature. Firstly, there are two purely theoretical essays
which illustrate different aspects of the demand for social insurance.
Nalebuff-Varian demonstrate that risk-sharing offers one means of raising
productive efficiency. Wickström discusses the possibility of a general income guarantee as an alternative to insurance and shows that a generally
higher level of income is found in the case of insurance. This is followed
by two essays of a more descriptive character. Lundahl shows that the use
of "prestige goods" in primitive economies can be interpreted as a form of
social security provision while Edebalk-Elmér provide an account of the
equivalent arrangement in a leading, modern welfare state, namely Sweden.
The financing of medical care is subsequently dealt with in two essays.
Evans discusses Canadian conditions while Zweifel focuses on the Swiss ex-

perience in this field. Both studies indicate the weaknesses of conventional solutions in the area of health insurance. Indeed Evans considers that the use of the standard concepts of insurance theory can be positively misleading. In her essay, Ståhlberg examines one of the questions which has hitherto attracted the greatest interest, namely the effect of government pension schemes on private savings.

Interest is subsequently focused on the relationship between social insurance and the labour market. Two essays clarify certain conceptual problems related to disability. Van Praag-Emanuel discuss the concept of non-employability and van den Bosch-Petersen analyse hidden unemployment among invalids. Using data from the US economy Haveman-Wolfe and Burkhauser-Quinn show how the supply of labour is effected by pension schemes. This is also an issue that has attracted a good deal of attention. Finally, Pedersen examines the question of whether and to what extent more generous levels of unemployment insurance have led to higher rates of inflation.

ARNE RYDE SYMPOSIUM ON SOCIAL INSURANCE
L. Söderström (editor)
© Elsevier Science Publishers B.V. (North-Holland), 1983

SOME ASPECTS OF RISK SHARING
IN NONCLASSICAL ENVIRONMENTS

Barry J. Nalebuff
and
Hal R. Varian*

1. INTRODUCTION

One of the most fundamental lessons economists have learned in their study of markets for sharing risk has concerned the benefits of diversification. Indeed, diversification is the major route through which risk sharing arrangements work to improve the overall allocation of risk bearing. In the absence of an insurance market each member of society may bear the risk of his house burning down; when an insurance market is available, each member of society can exchange this "concentrated" portfolio for one that offers a share of everyone´s risk of a fire. This "diversification" can lower each individual´s risk and thereby bring about a Pareto improvement in social welfare.

Any phenomenon this general and far reaching deserves to have some exceptions. In this paper we shall describe two interesting classes of exceptions to the diversification credo. Each involves, of course, a variation on the classical postulates. But the variations seem to us to be quite plausible; and the circumstances where diversification is harmful may be more common than hitherto believed.

2. ECONOMIES OF SCALE

In the usual analysis of the benefits of markets for sharing risk, the primary benefit of the risk sharing arrangements is a utility benefit. The chief benefit of an insurance market, for example, is usually taken to be the peace of mind it affords. Similarly, with a stock market an entrepreneur is viewed as desiring diversification of ownership due to the increase of expected utility resulting from the reduction of the risk he has to bear.

Little attention has been paid to the <u>productive</u> benefits of risk sharing arrangements. It is our thesis that in many cases there can be considerable increases in technological efficiency resulting from markets for risk sharing; these technological benefits may be the essential motivation behind many existing arrangements.

For example, consider the history of the stock market and the corporation as economic entities. According to most accounts these economic arrangements arose not as a way of diversifying existing risk, but as a way of reducing the risk of new investments to tolerable levels. The profitability of the East India trade was apparent to all; but the risks were equally apparent. Only by spreading these risks via stock markets and insurance markets could the massive investments needed to launch such trade expeditions be financed.

The case of ocean voyages brings out an essential feature of the productive benefits of risk sharing arrangements that we wish to discuss; namely, the importance of economies of scale. The technology of ocean trade involved a definite element of increasing returns to scale: a voyage halfway across the Atlantic was worth nothing; a voyage across and back could be worth an immense amount. But in order to exploit these economies of scale some method of reducing risk was needed.

Let us try to formalize this argument by means of a simple example. We use x to denote the amount of some input and w its price. In the example given above we might think of x as the size of the ship constructed as outfitted by some entrepreneur. The value of the output of this enterprise is given by

$$f(x)\epsilon + \delta \qquad\qquad\qquad (1)$$

where ϵ and δ are independent random variables with $E\epsilon = 1$ and $E\delta = 0$. Hence $f(x)$ measures the expected value realized by a ship of size x.

Let us suppose that $f(x)$ exhibits increasing returns to scale as illustrated in Figure 1. What will be the efficient pattern of production for this technology? What size voyages should be undertaken?

If we ignore the uncertainty aspect of the problem, it is clear that the optimal size voyage is at x^* as illustrated in Figure 2, that is the point where average product equals marginal product. But will this level of output be achieved by the functioning of a private market?

In the absence of markets for spreading or diversifying risk the optimal scale may well not be attained. Suppose for example that a single entrepreneur determines output so as to maximize expected utility of profit. Let $u(W)$ be the entrepreneur's expected utility function of wealth; we assume it has the conventional properties of monotonicity and risk aversion ($u'(W) > 0$, $u''(W) < 0$ for all W). Then the maximization problem becomes:

$$\max Eu\ (f(x)\epsilon + \delta - wx) \qquad\qquad (2)$$

The first and second order conditions for this problem are:

$$Eu'(W)\ f'(x)\epsilon - w) = 0 \qquad\qquad (3)$$

$$Eu'(W)\ f''(x)\epsilon + Eu''(W)\ (f'(x)\epsilon - w)^2 \leq 0 \qquad (4)$$

Note that the second order condition is composed of two parts: the first

Figure 1. Production function with increasing returns

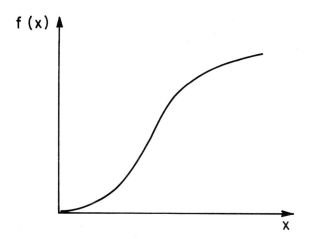

Figure 2. Optimal scale of production.

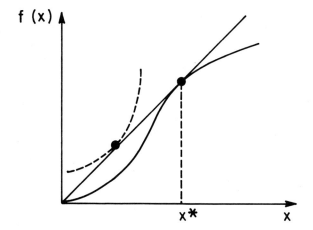

term is the technological effect - its sign depends on the sign of $f''(x)$ at the optimal scale of production. The second term is the utility effect; under the assumption of risk aversion it is unambiguously negative.

It can easily happen that the second term dominates the sign of the expression and that the preferred operating position occurs where $f''(x)$ is positive - that is, in the inefficient region of the production function. This is illustrated in Figure 3.

Figure 3. Interior solution

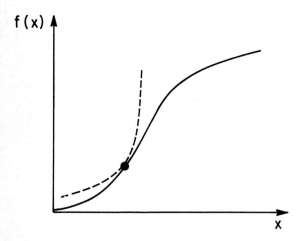

Here the riskiness of the investment has induced the entrepreneur to choose an inefficient scale of operation. He deliberately keeps expected output low so as to reduce the level of risk he bears.

This type of inefficiency can be eliminated by various sorts of risk sharing and risk pooling arrangements; indeed, it is this opportunity for profit that stimulates the development of such institutions for minimizing risk.

Let us distinguish two logically separate roles for risk minimizing institutions. The first is that of risk sharing. This is simply the fact that coalitions of entrepreneurs can form to share the risk of some single investment activity. The second is that of risk pooling. This refers to the fact that when several investment activities are available that are not perfectly correlated one can reduce overall risk by investing in each of the projects; that is, part of the risk involved is eliminated by portfolio diversification.

In actual economies both effects are present, of course, and the literature on risk bearing often treats the two phenomena interchangeably. However, they are quite distinct concepts.

Let us first consider risk sharing. We will first discuss the special case where $\delta \equiv 0$, and later examine the more general case. We suppose that entrepreneurs can pool their resources and each can purchase a share of the investment being considered. That is, each entrepreneur can provide $s_i wx$ of the costs involved and then reap $s_i f(x)\varepsilon$ of the output produced.

Hence the maximization problem facing such a shareholder is simply to determine how much of the risky investment to purchase.

$$\max_{s_i} Eu(s_i f(x)\varepsilon - s_i wx) \tag{5}$$

Note that we are not considering any diversification behavior on the part of the shareholder; we are only concerned with the risk sharing aspect of the problem at this stage.

Of course, the shareholder cannot determine the optimal level of shared investment in the activity until he knows at what level the activity itself is going to operate. This decision has to be made jointly by all of the shareholders involved. But we can at least ask what level any given shareholder would prefer if he had the dictatorial power to arrange this decision.

Accordingly, we differentiate shareholder i's expected utility function with respect to s_i, his share of the profits, and x, the scale of operation. We find the first order conditions:

$$Eu'(W) (f(x^*)\varepsilon - wx^*) = 0 \tag{6}$$

$$Eu'(W) (f'(x^*)\varepsilon - w)s_i^* = 0 \tag{7}$$

Multiply the second equality by x^*/s_i^* and substract it from the first to get:

$$Eu'(W)\varepsilon(f(x^*) - f'(x^*)/x^*) = 0 \tag{8}$$

or,

$$f'(x^*) = f(x^*)/x^* \tag{9}$$

Note that this result is _independent_ of the utility function involved; hence all shareholders will unanimously agree that the investment should be operated at the technologically efficient level where marginal product equals average product.[1]

Note further that this result has nothing to do with diversification; it is purely concerned with risk _sharing_ arrangements. Unfortunately, once we leave the world of multiplicative uncertainty this simple result vanishes. Suppose for example that we return to the case where output can be written as $f(x)\varepsilon + \delta$. In this case the first order conditions take the form:

$$Eu'(W) (f(\hat{x})\varepsilon + \delta - w\hat{x}) = 0 \tag{10}$$

$$Eu'(W) (f'(\hat{x})\varepsilon - w) \hat{s}_i = 0 \tag{11}$$

These conditions can be combined to give:

$$Eu''(W) (f(\hat{x})\epsilon - \hat{x}f'(\hat{x})\epsilon + \delta) = 0 \qquad (12)$$

or

$$Eu''(W) \epsilon(f(\hat{x}) - \hat{x}f'(\hat{x})) = -Eu''(W)\delta \qquad (13)$$

Since $E\delta = 0$, the term on the right is simply the (negative of the) covariance between marginal utility and δ. The concavity of $u(W)$ implies that this term is, therefore, positive, which in turn implies:

$$f(\hat{x})/\hat{x} > f'(\hat{x}) \qquad (14)$$

Marginal product is less than average product at the optimal level of operation for individual i. Thus, each investor will prefer that the investment be undertaken at a scale that is too large from a technological viewpoint. Of course, investors will typically disagree about what exactly the "optimal" scale should be, since this will generally depend on their expected utility functions. However, they all agree that the technologically efficient scale is too small!

This simple example provides the motivation for a more general argument that production scales are too large. In the presence of risks that do not grow proportionately with size, there will always be an incentive (due to risk sharing) to develop a project beyond the technologically efficient size and own a relatively smaller share of the output. If $s_1 > s_2$ and $f(x_1)/x_1 = f(x_2)/x_2$ then $s_1(f(x_1) - wx_1) = s(f(x_2) - wx_2)$ implies

$$Eu(s_2 (f(x_2)\epsilon + \delta - wx_2)) > Eu(s_1(f(x_1)\epsilon + \delta - wx_1)) \qquad (15)$$

as the additive risk (δ) is less important when the fraction of ownership is smaller. (This result follows from stochastic dominance.)

Let us turn to a description of the risk <u>spreading</u> effect. We suppose that there are several ex ante identical investment activities described by production functions of the form $f(x_i)\epsilon_i + \delta_i$, $i=1, \ldots m$. We further assume that all of the random variables ϵ_i and δ_i are independently distributed across projects. In this case, it will pay each individual investor to diversify his portfolio across the m firms. A typical individual's portfolio would satisfy the maximization problem:

$$\max Eu \left(\sum_{i=1}^{m} s_i (f(x_i)\epsilon_i + \delta_i - wx_i) \right) \qquad (16)$$

$$\sum_{i=1}^{m} ws_i x_i = B \qquad (17)$$

Except for the budget constraint, the first order conditions for this problem are similar to (10) and (11) with $\hat{x}_i = \hat{x}$ and $\hat{s}_i = \hat{s}$. The analog of (13) is:

$$Eu''(W)\epsilon_i(f(\hat{x}_i) - \hat{x}_i f'(\hat{x}_i)) = -Eu''(W)\delta_i \qquad (18)$$

Now if the individual's optimal portfolio is highly diversified, and all of the risks (ϵ_i, δ_i) are independent, then wealth will be nearly certain.

Hence

$$Eu^{-}(W)\ \delta_i \simeq u^{-}(W)E\delta_i = 0 \qquad\qquad (19)$$

Thus, we find that the optimal level of investment is again technologically efficient: average product equals marginal product. This time the fact that diversification is possible plays an essential role in the argument.

Note also that this result is <u>independent</u> of the form of the utility function. Each shareholder agrees about the scale of operation of each of the investments.

The argument is depicted in Figure 2. Since the risks are all independent by assumption, the per capita production set society faces is simply f(x). To operate most efficiently given this technology it pays to operate each investment at the optimal level x and simply vary the number of investments to achieve any point along the indicated straight line. If the returns to scale are sufficiently great, the increase in technological efficiency from the improved institutions for risk bearing could be quite large.

3. ECONOMIES OF SPECIALIZATION

Our next example of the productive benefits of risk sharing can be cast in an agricultural framework. Suppose that we have a large number of identical farmers who can devote their resources to farming corn or wheat. Let us suppose that there are some sort of economies of scale (or other economies of specialization) so that the individual production possibilities sets are concave, as in Figure 4, rather than convex as is usually assumed. In the case illustrated, the farmer can specialize in wheat and produce 100 bush-

Figure 4. Social production possibilities

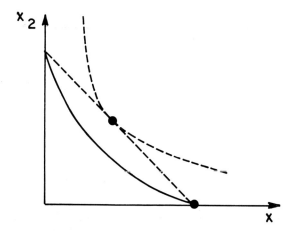

els of wheat, or specializes in corn and produce 100 bushels of corn. But
if he produces both wheat and corn he ends up with only 40 bushels of each.
Thus, the individual production possibility sets exhibit diseconomies of
scope or economies of specialization.

Society's (per capita) production possibilities set is quite different: it
is the convex hull of the individuals' production sets. If we want to produce an average of 50 bushels of wheat and 50 bushels of corn per farm, we
simply have half the farms produce wheat and half produce corn. If we want
75 bushels of wheat and 25 bushels of corn per farm, we have three fourths
of the farms produce wheat and one fourth produce corn, and so on. For society as a whole any combination along the indicated straight line is
feasible. Where society chooses to operate is, of course, determined by the
tastes for wheat and corn; one example is given in Figure 4.

But will the private market induce producers to operate in this efficient
manner? In the absence of uncertainty - or when markets exist which can
eliminate uncertainty - the answer is yes. If the relative prices of wheat
and corn are 1:1, specializing in wheat or in corn is equally profitable
and either option is more profitable than diversification. The market induces the optimal technological choices even in the presence of
nonconvexities.

When uncertainty is present the situation is considerably different.
Suppose, for example, that the price of corn, p_C, and price of wheat, p_W,
are random variables. Let c be the amount of corn produced by an individual
farmer and w(c) the corresponding maximal amount of wheat; i.e., w(c) is
the boundary of the production possibilities set.

If a farmer behaves as an expected utility maximizer his problem is:

$$\max \ Eu(p_C c + p_W w(c)) \tag{20}$$

This has first and second order conditions given by:

$$Eu'(W)(p_C + p_W w'(c)) = 0 \tag{21}$$

$$Eu'(W)p_W w''(c) + Eu''(W)(p_C + p_W w'(c))^2 \leq 0 \tag{22}$$

Just as before the second condition has two terms. Even if economies of
specialization are present (so that w''(c)>0) the risk averse behavior
indicated by the second term may lead to an interior optimum. The farmer is
led to diversify in order to hedge against fluctuations in income even
though this leads to technological inefficiency (Figure 5).

This tendency to diversify is quite strong, even in the face of the adverse
technological repercussions. In the appendix we extend Samulson's (1967)
argument that shows diversification generally pays for an individual expected utility maximizer.

At the social level, of course, things may be rather different. If the risk
to the farmers can be eliminated or shifted to other agents, an improved
pattern of production can be brought about. In the case described above,
future markets can be used to eliminate the uncertainty about price
fluctuations and thereby induce the technologically advantageous specialization.

Figure 5. Interior solution with nonconvexity

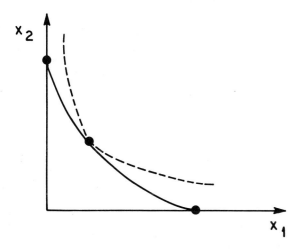

4. THE DESIRABILITY OF DIVERSIFICATION

The previous example has indicated that specialization may be desirable at the social level even though private interests indicate diversification. This phenomena arises because of nonconvexities in production.

Presumably a convex production set and a nonconcave objective function would give the same result. Consider for example the case in which the production possibilities set is linear as in Figure 6 - i.e., constant returns to scale prevails. Suppose, however, that the social objective function is not of the proper shape: for example, suppose it is max $\{x_1, x_2\}$. In such a case the optimal policy involves specialization in x_1 or x_2.

When might such an objective function arise? One common circumstance is that of a <u>race</u>: coming in first is all that matters. Suppose for example that a firm is allocating resources to several research projects in an attempt to develop a new product before its competitors. Then, of course, only the project that develops the product first is relevant; only the winner matters.

Let us formalize this statement in the following way. Suppose a firm is allocating funds to various projects; let x_i be the funds allocated to project i and write the budget constraint of the firm as $\Sigma x_i = B$. Each project produces output $f_i(x_i)$ and the objective function of the firm is given by $W(f_1(x_1), \ldots, f_n(x_n))$. The resource allocation problem is then:

$$\max W(f_1(x_1), \ldots, f_n(x_n)) \qquad (23)$$

$$\text{s.t.} \quad \Sigma x_i = B \qquad (24)$$

When will the optimal solution involve specialization?

Figure 6. Boundary solution with convex objective

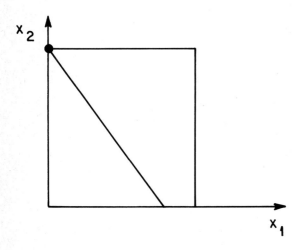

THEOREM 1. Suppose that $W(y_1,\ldots,y_n)$ is increasing and convex as a function of $(y_1,\ldots,y_n)$ and that each $f_i(x_i)$ is a convex function of x_i. Then there is an optimal solution that involves specialization: for some i, $x_i^* = B$, $x_j^* = 0$ for $j \neq i$.

<u>Proof</u> Clearly all that we need show is that

$$V(x_1,\ldots,x_n) = W(f_1(x_1),\ldots,f_n(x_n))$$

is a convex function of $x = (x_1,\ldots,x_n)$. But this follows directly from the hypotheses:

$$V(tx + (1 - t)x^-) = W(f_1(tx_1 + (1 - t)x_1^-),\ldots,f_n(tx_n + (1 - t)x_n^-))$$

$$\leq W(tf_1(x_1) + (1 - t)f_1(x_1^-),\ldots,tf_n(x_n) + (1 - t)f_n(x_n^-))$$

$$\leq tW(f_1(x_1),\ldots,f_n(x_n)) + (1 - t)W(f_1(x_1^-),\ldots,f_n(x_n^-))$$

$$= tV(x) + (1 - t)V(x^-). \quad \square$$

The above (trivial) argument establishes the desired result: when the objective function is convex and the production functions are convex, specialization is optimal. Note that only weak convexity is needed: a linear welfare function and linear production functions are perfectly compatible with the above result.

Now let us ask how this result might be modified in the presence of uncertainty. There is an intuition that suggests that if uncertainty is present, it might pay to diversify: to hedge one's bets so that complete specialization is not desirable.

Let us model this in a rather general way by writing production functions as dependent on n random variables $(\varepsilon_1,...,\varepsilon_n)$ with joint probability density $g(\varepsilon_1,...,\varepsilon_n)$. The social objective now becomes:

$$EW(f_1(x_1,\varepsilon_1),...,f_n(x_n,\varepsilon_n)) =$$

$$\int W(f_1(x_1,\varepsilon_1),...,f_n(x_n,\varepsilon_n))g(\varepsilon_1,...,\varepsilon_n)d\varepsilon_1.....d\varepsilon_n \qquad (25)$$

We now have the main result of this section:

THEOREM 2. Supoose that the hypotheses of Theorem 1 hold for each realization of $(\varepsilon_1,...,\varepsilon_n)$; then there is an optimal solution x* that involves specialization.

Proof. Simply note that for each realization of $(\varepsilon_1,...,\varepsilon_n)$, $V(x_1,...,x_n)$ is a convex function by Theorem 1. But a weighted average of convex functions is still convex. Hence, there is a boundary optimum.$\square$

The proof of Theorems 1 and 2 are mathematically trivial but surprisingly nonintuitive. Let us illustrate this result in one simple case.

Suppose that output of project i is given by $y_i = a^i x_i + b^i$, where a^i and b^i are random variables. Suppose that only the winner matters so that the social objective function is $W(y_1,...,y_n) = \max\{y_1,...,y_n\}$. Then the hypotheses of Theorem 2 are satisfied and the optimal policy involves specialization. In fact, in this case, the policy is especially simple: we just compute the overall unconditional expected values of output resulting from specialization:

$$\bar{y}_i = \bar{a}_i B + \bar{b}_i \qquad i = 1,...,n \qquad (26)$$

and then choose to specialize in that activity with the highest expected output. In general we will <u>not</u> want to "hedge our bets" and diversify.[2]

It seems nonintuitive that we will never want to diversify but on reflection it becomes clear: diversification is implied by the convexity of the constraints or the concavity of the objective function. If these conditions are not met, diversification is not necessarily optimal.

This simple point can have some interesting consequences for resource allocation. In the absence of a social planner who omnisciently chooses optimal behavior, decisions must be made by individuals - who may or may not have the same objective function as society. It seems that there can be errors of two sorts: society has a convex objective while the individual's objective function is concave, or vice versa.

As an example of the first case, consider research. Society does not really care whether there is a <u>second</u> firm to discover a new piece of technology: only the winner matters. Yet individual rewards to research directors may be such as to encourage diversification. The opposite kind of distortion may occur with political decisions: since winning is much more highly rewarded than coming in second, overly extreme social policies may be promulgated. Even though social welfare may be concave in the relevant variables the convex nature of the individual rewards could lead to inappropriate decisions.

APPENDIX

The farmer's maximization problem is given by:

$$\max \; Eu(p_c c + p_w w)$$

$$\text{s.t.} \quad w = f(c)$$

We want to find conditions under which the optimal solution has $c^* > 0$, $w^* > 0$, that is under which some diversification is deemed desirable. Let us suppose then that we are currently operating at the boundary $c = 1$, $w = f(c) = 0$ and that we contemplate a feasible change $\Delta c < 0$, $\Delta w > 0$. The change in utility will be

$$\Delta u = Eu'(p_c c)p_c \Delta c + Eu'(p_c c)p_w \Delta w$$

Define:

$$\bar{m} = Eu'(p_c c)$$

$$\bar{p}_c = Ep_c$$

$$\bar{p}_w = Ep_w$$

$$\sigma_{mc} = cov\,(u'(p_c c),p_c)$$

$$\sigma_{mw} = cov\,(u'(p_c c),p_w)$$

Then using the standard covariance identity that $EXY = cov\,(X,Y) + (EX)(EY)$ we can rewrite the expression for Δu as:

$$\Delta U = (\sigma_{mc} + \bar{m}\bar{p}_c)\Delta c + (\sigma_{mw} + \bar{m}\bar{p}_w)\Delta w = \sigma_{mc}\Delta c + \sigma_{mw}\Delta w + \bar{m}(\bar{p}_c \Delta c + \bar{p}_w \Delta w)$$

Consider the sign of each of these three terms. First σ_{mc} is certainly negative since p_c and the marginal utility of income move in opposite directions; since $\Delta c < 0$, $\sigma_{mc}\Delta c$ is positive. The sign of the second term depends on the covariance between p_w and p_c. If they are nonpositively correlated, we will have $\sigma_{mw} \geq 0$. Thus, $\sigma_{mw} w$ will also be positive.

The sign of the last term depends on the expected profitability of the change. As long as $\bar{p}_c/\bar{p}_w$ exceeds the marginal rate of substitution - $\Delta w/\Delta c$ the last term will also be positive.

Hence, the sign of ΔU is sure to be positive when p_w and p_c are nonpositively correlated and the expected profitability is positive, but even if the expected profits are negative the gain from the reduction in risk may induce some amount of diversification.

FOOTNOTES

*) Harvard University and The University of Michigan, respectively. We are indebted to Ingemar Hansson for his careful discussion and criticism of this paper. Marie Auersberg and James Poterba helped us to develop this topic. Our research was in part supported by grants from the Guggenheim Foundation and the National Science Foundation.

1)   This result is, of course, closely related to Diamond's result that a competitive stock market is pareto efficient under multiplicative uncertainty.

2)   Although it may be technologically efficient to support only one research project, it is then difficult to provide proper incentives to ensure that the project managers minimize costs. These issues are discussed in Nalebuff (1982).

REFERENCES

Diamond, P. (1967), The Role of a Stock Market in a General Equilibrium Model with Technological Uncertainty, American Economic Review 5, 759-773.

Nalebuff, B. (1982), Prizes and Incentives, D. Phil Thesis, Oxford University.

Samuelson, P. (1967), General Proof that Diversification Pays, Journal of Financial and Quantitative Analysis, March.

ARNE RYDE SYMPOSIUM ON SOCIAL INSURANCE
L. Söderström (editor)
© Elsevier Science Publishers B.V. (North-Holland), 1983

INCOME REDISTRIBUTION AND THE DEMAND FOR SOCIAL INSURANCE

Bengt-Arne Wickström*

1. INTRODUCTION

We want to study the relationship between the marginal tax rate, the degree of redistribution and the demand for social insurance in an economy. Building on the general framework developed in Wickström (1979), we construct a model with a continuum of agents who demand two goods: leisure and consumption. Each agent is endowed with a certain ability to work, i.e. transfer of leisure into consumption. His work is taxed and the proceeds from the tax are used to redistribute income in two ways. Part of the proceeds goes as a subsidy to those who can work and part of them goes as social-insurance benefits to those who are unable to work. Whether a person is able to work or not is stochastically determined.

The taxation changes the incentives to work, and total production in the economy will depend on the tax rate and on how the tax proceeds are distributed. We find an equilibrium in the economy, and the equilibrium values of each agent's demand for leisure and consumption. This gives us the indirect expected utility of each agent as a function of the tax rate and the way the revenues are disposed of. We find conditions for optimal provision of social insurance for each individual and make some comparative static analysis.

2. THE INDIVIDUAL AGENTS

We assume that we have a continuum of agents defined on the unit interval and indexed $i \in [0,1]$. The total (Lebesgue) measure of the agents is one. Further, we have two goods, leisure, which can take on values between zero and one, and consumption, which can take on any positive value. Each agent has an initial endowment of one unit of leisure. We make the following definitions:

Definition 1: The utility function of agent i is a twice differentiable real-valued function of leisure, $\theta \in [0,1]$, and consumption, $q \in R_+$, written

$$U^i: [0,1] \cdot R_+ \to R_+ .$$

We also write $x = (\theta,q)$.

<u>Definition 2</u>: The <u>potential work endowment</u> of an agent i is a positive real number, written $\bar{\omega}i$ giving the rate at which the agent can convert leisure into consumption.

In general we will use the bar over a variable name to denote that it is a potential variable that is independent of the states of nature. Its realization, the actual variable, will occur in one or the other state of nature.

<u>Definition 3</u>: The <u>actual work endowment</u> of agent i, written ω^i, is defined by

$$\omega^i = \bar{\omega}^i \xi^i$$

where $\xi^i \in \{0,1\}$ is a stochastic variable such that $P(\xi^i=0) = p$ and $P(\xi^i=1) = 1-p$, P being a probability measure. Further, if $i \neq j$, ξ^i and ξ^j are stochastically independent.

For short we write this condition as

$$\omega^i = \begin{cases} \bar{\omega}^i \text{ with probability } 1-p, \text{ and} \\ 0 \text{ with probability } p. \end{cases}$$

The value of p is thus the, exogenously given, probability that an agent will find his work endowment to be equal to zero and hence receive social-insurance benefits, which he will do only if he is unable to work. We note that the probability of being unable to work is independent of the potential work endowment. We also note that the measure of agents receiving social insurance will be p.

For the rest of this section we omit the superscript i. Denoting partial derivatives by subscripts we make the following assumptions.

<u>Assumption 1</u>: The marginal utilities satisfy the following properties:

$U_1(x) > 0 \quad \forall x \in (0,1) \cdot R_{++}$,

$U_2(x) > 0 \quad \forall x \in (0,1) \cdot R_{++}$,

$U_1(x) = 0 \quad$ if $\theta = 1$ and

$U_2(x) = 0 \quad$ if $\theta = 0$.

<u>Assumption 2</u>: The utility function is strictly concave and an expected-utility function formed from it satisfies the expected utility-hypothesis.

The first two conditions of assumption 1 state that, for both goods, "more is better"; the last two conditions are merely technical and insure us that we will get an interior solution to our maximization problem. Assumption 2 is an assumption of risk aversion and gives meaning to the expected-utility function we will use in the analysis.

We move on to the study of the constraint facing the agent. The following notation is introduced:

y, the amount of the consumption good that the agent produces,

t, the amount of the consumption good that the agent pays in taxes,

q, the amount of the consumption good that the agent consumes if he does not receive social-insurance benefits,

κ, the amount of the consumption good that the agent consumes if he receives social-insurance benefits,

μ, the total production of the consumption good in the economy and,

θ, the amount of leisure of the agent.

We also make the following definition.

Definition 4: A linear tax function is a function of the form $t = s(y-b)$ where s is the marginal tax rate and b a standard deduction.

If the agent is able to work we find from definition 2 that his production will be

$$y = \bar{y} := (1-\theta)\bar{\omega}, \tag{1}$$

where := is to be read as "is defined to be".

The tax payment will then be

$$t = \bar{t} = s(\bar{y}-\bar{b}), \tag{2}$$

where each agent takes $\bar{b}$ as given. We readily find the following expression:

$$q + (1-s)\bar{\omega}\theta = (1-s)\bar{\omega} + s\bar{b}. \tag{3}$$

The reader is reminded of the convention that the bar denotes potential (state independent) variables and that the actual realized variables are written without bars.

If the agent is unable to work, y and t will both be zero and he will consume $\kappa = \bar{\kappa}$, the same for all agents. Each agent takes $\bar{\kappa}$ as given. The values of $\bar{b}$ and $\bar{\kappa}$ will have to be related in the equilibrium of the economy as will be shown below. Thus expression (3) gives us the agent´s "budget" constraint if he does not receive benefits. If he does receive social insurance benefits the size of those benefits is $\bar{\kappa}$. In other words, he faces (3) with probability (1-p) and consumes $\bar{\kappa}$ with probability p.

The agent acting as an atomist wants to maximize his expected utility subject to the constraint (3) and κ being a constant. Since his only decision variables are q and θ this problem reduces to a non-stochastic one:

$$\max_{\theta,q} U(\theta,q), \text{ such that (3) holds}, \tag{4}$$

The solution to (4) will give us the demand functions, where the tilde denotes functions of $\bar{\omega}$, $\bar{b}$ and s:

$\tilde{q}(\bar{\omega},\bar{b},s)$ and

$\tilde{\theta}(\bar{\omega},\bar{b},s)$,   (5)

which hence are the agent´s demand functions if he is able to work. The definition of the utility function, assumption 2 and the implicit-function theorem give us the following lemma.

Lemma 1: The demand functions $\tilde{q}$ and $\tilde{\theta}$ are continuous on their ranges and differentiable on the interior of their ranges.

We also have the following lemma

Lemma 2: $\tilde{\theta}$ = 1 if s = 1 and

$\tilde{\theta}$ < 1 if s < 1 and ω > 0.

Proof: Follows from assumption 1 and expression (3).

3. EQUILIBRIUM

Noting that the index i of the previous section in this section becomes a variable on the unit interval we introduce the following notation.

Ex is the (Lebesgue) integral of x as a function of i over the unit interval.

We also make the following assumptions:

Assumption 3: The potential work endowment $\bar{\omega}$ is a Lebesgue-measurable function of i. It is also bounded.

Assumption 4: The demand functions $\tilde{q}$ and $\tilde{\theta}$ and the utility functions U are Lebesgue-measurable functions of i.

We make the following definition:

Definition 5: If $\bar{x}$ is Lebesgue measurable as a function of i, and if x^i for any value of $i\in[0,1]$ is defined by the following

$$x^i = \begin{cases} \bar{x}^i & \text{with probability } 1-p, \text{ and} \\ 0 & \text{with probability } p, \end{cases}$$

then the integral of x

$Ex := (1-p)\overline{Ex}.$

We are now ready to define an equilibrium of the economy. Before doing so it is convenient to introduce a new variable, δ, instead of $\bar{b}$ by the transformation $\bar{b} = \mu(1-\delta)/(1-p)$, where μ is the total production in the economy. Denoting the demand functions as functions of the new variables by a circumflex we define

$$\hat{q}^i(\omega^i,\mu,p,\delta,s) := \tilde{q}^i\left(\omega^i,\mu\frac{1-\delta}{1-p},s\right)$$

$$\hat{\theta}^i(\omega^i,\mu,p,\delta,s) := \tilde{\theta}^i\left(\omega^i,\mu\frac{1-\delta}{1-p},s\right)$$

(6)

We also make the following definition:

Definition 6: An equilibrium, given s and δ, is a collection $\{\overline{q},\overline{\theta},\overline{\kappa},\mu\}$ such that $\mu = (1-p)E\overline{q} + p\overline{\kappa}$, $E t = p\overline{\kappa}$, $\overline{q} = \hat{q}$ and $\overline{\theta} = \hat{\theta}$.

Using the fact that $\mu \equiv Ey = E(1-\overline{\theta})\omega$ we at once see from definition 6 that in equilibrium $\overline{\kappa} = s\mu\delta/p$. That is, δ is the fraction of the total tax revenues that goes to the provision of the social-security program; $(1-\delta)$ is thus the fraction that is payed back to the able agents in an attempt to redistribute income. We can now prove the following theorem.

Theorem 1: Under assumptions 3 and 4 there exists an equilibrium in the economy.

Proof: Taking $\overline{\kappa} = s\delta\mu/p$, we need to show that there exists a μ which satisfies $E\omega - E\omega\hat{\theta}(\omega,\mu,p,\delta,s) \equiv \mu$. We write the left-hand side as $g(\mu)$. We know from lemma 1 that $\hat{\theta}^i$ is continuous in μ (and in the other, suppressed, arguments). From the Lebesgue convergence theorem (see for instance Royden, 1968) we thus find, since $\hat{\theta}^i$ is bounded, that g is continuous in μ (as well as in the other arguments).

The range of g is the interval $[0,E\omega]$ and the domain is $[0,\infty)$. The intermediate value theorem can be applied giving us at least one $\mu^* = g(\mu^*)$, q.e.d..

Corollary: If leisure is a normal good for almost all agents (except a set of agents of measure zero) then μ^* is unique and furthermore a continuous function of p, δ and s. We write it $\mu^*(\delta,s)$, suppressing the argument p.

Proof: One only needs to observe that normality makes $\hat{\theta}^i$ a non-increasing function of μ.

4. THE OPTIMAL AMOUNT OF SOCIAL INSURANCE

In order to study the optimal amount of social insurance we form the indirect expected utility of an agent:

$$V^i(\omega^i,\mu,p,\delta,s) := (1-p)U^i(\hat{\theta}^i,\hat{q}^i) + pU^i(1,\overline{\kappa}).$$

(7)

We have here assumed that if the agent receives social insurance benefits he will also have one unit of leisure.

We have seen that in equilibrium, if leisure is a normal good, μ^* is continuous in its arguments. Thus, under the assumption that leisure is a normal good, we can write the demand functions, the social-insurance benefits and the indirect expected-utility functions as continuous functions of δ and s (suppressing the arguments ω^i and p). These functions we denote by an asterisk:

$q^{i*}(\delta,s)$

$\theta^{i*}(\delta,s)$

$\kappa^{i*}(\delta,s)$

$v^{i*}(\delta,s)$

We make the following assumptions:

<u>Assumption 5</u>: Leisure is a normal good for almost all agents.

<u>Assumption 6</u>: The functions μ^*, q^{i*}, θ^{i*}, κ^{i*} and v^{i*} are differentiable.

If we have continuity as assumption 5 guarantees, then differentiability is merely a technical assumption. In the following we will again suppress the superscript i.

We are interested in finding the optimal amount of social insurance for a given tax rate, s, and for a given individual. In order to do this we maximize the indirect expected utility function with respect to δ, the fraction of the tax revenues which provide the insurance coverage. We find from (3) that

$$\frac{1}{U_q} \frac{\partial V}{\partial \delta} = s\mu^*Q + \frac{\partial \mu^*}{\partial \delta} s(1+\delta Q) \tag{8}$$

where

$$Q := \frac{U_\kappa}{U_q} - 1,$$

$$U_q := U_2(\theta^*,q^*) \text{ and}$$

$$U_\kappa := U_2(1,\kappa^*).$$

Similarly we also find that

$$\frac{1}{U_q} \frac{\partial V^*}{\partial s} = \mu^* - (1-\theta^*)\omega(1-p) + \mu^*\delta Q + \frac{\partial \mu^*}{\partial s} s(1+\delta Q). \tag{9}$$

We note that Q is the difference between the marginal rate of substitution and the marginal rate of transformation of consumption when receiving social-insurance benefits and when not receiving them.

In order to study expression (8) we have to find an expression for $\partial \mu^*/\partial \delta$. To do that we introduce the following notation:

$$m_{abc} := \frac{\partial \frac{U_a}{U_b}}{\partial c} \text{ and}$$

$$d := \frac{d^2 q}{d\theta^2}\Bigg|$$
$$U(\theta,q) \text{ is constant,}$$

We can now state the following lemma and proposition:

Lemma 3: The derivative $\partial\mu^*/\partial\delta$ is of the following form:

$$\frac{\partial\mu^*}{\partial\delta} = \frac{s\mu^*}{1-p} \frac{A^*(\delta,s)}{1 + \frac{s(1-\delta)}{1-p} A^*(\delta,s)}$$

where

$$A^*(\delta,s) = E \frac{\omega \, m_{\theta qq}}{d}.$$

Proof: Differentiate the first-order conditions of the program (5).

Proposition 1: The derivative $\partial\mu^*/\partial\delta$ is positive.

Proof: Normality of leisure, θ, is the same as saying that $m_{\theta qq}$ is positive.

The result in proposition 1 is interesting in itself. It says that the total production in society will increase if the fraction of tax revenues going to a social insurance program increases given the marginal tax rate. The result depends on the condition that leisure is a normal good. The normality of leisure insures that μ^* is continuous and that the derivative is positive. The intuitive reason is of course that the first-order effect of a change in δ is an income effect, reducing income if the agent is not receiving social-insurance benefits causing the agents to take out less leisure thus producing more thereby increasing the total production and the gross taxes. This will unambiguously insure that the social-insurance benefits also increase.

Writing Q explicitly as a function of δ and s, $Q^*(\delta,s)$, we find the following results:

Lemma 4: If consumption is a normal good then

$$Q^*(\delta,0) > 0,$$

$$Q^*(0,s) > 0 \text{ and}$$

$$\lim_{s \to 1} \frac{Q^*(1,s)}{\mu^*(1,s)} = \frac{1}{p} \frac{U_{22}(1,0)}{U_2(1,0)} < 0$$

Proof: Consider figure 1. We need to compare the value of U_2 in points A, B and C. Because of the strict convexity of the utility function we find that

$$U_2\big|_C > U_2\big|_B.$$

Figure 1. Construction for proof of lemma 4.

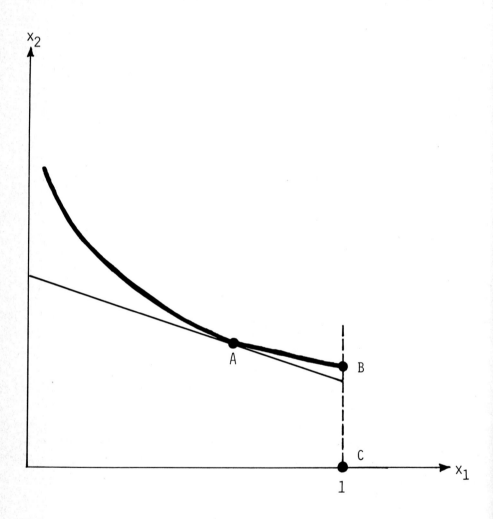

The change in U_2 along an indifference curve can be found:

$$\left. \frac{\partial U_2}{\partial x_1} \right|_{U \text{ is constant}} = U_{12} - U_{22} \frac{U_1}{U_2} = m_{122} U_2 .$$

Normality of x_1, leisure, implies that m_{122} is positive. Hence U_2 is increasing as x_1 increases along an indifference curve. We thus find that $U_2|_A < U_2|_B < U_2|_C$.

This proves the first two inequalities. To prove the third one we return to expression (3) setting $\delta = 1$ and $s = 1 - \epsilon$:

$$q + \epsilon \omega \theta = \epsilon \omega$$

This gives us

$$(1-\theta)\omega = \frac{q}{\epsilon}.$$

Thus

$$\mu^* = E(1-\theta^*)\;\omega = E\frac{q^*}{\epsilon} \quad \text{or}$$

$$\epsilon \mu^* = Eq^*\;.$$

Expression (4) gives us

$$\kappa^* = \frac{(1-\epsilon)\mu^*}{p}$$

Thus,

$$\frac{\kappa^*}{Eq^*} = \frac{(1-\epsilon)}{p\epsilon} \quad \text{and}$$

$$\lim_{\epsilon \to 0} \frac{\kappa^*}{Eq^*} \to \infty.$$

By lemma 2 $\theta^{i*} \to 1$ as $\epsilon \to 0$.

We expand Q^* at $\mu^* = 0$ only including the leading terms:

$$Q^* \doteq \frac{U_2(1,\kappa)}{U_2(1,0)} - 1$$

$$\doteq \frac{U_2(1,0) + U_{22}(1,0)\kappa}{U_2(1,0)} - 1$$

$$= \frac{U_{22}(1,0)}{U_2(1,0)} (1-\epsilon)\frac{\mu^*}{p}$$

Hence

$$\lim_{\epsilon \to 0} \frac{Q^*}{\mu^*} = \frac{U_{22}(1,0)}{pU_2(1,0)}$$

Thus concavity of the utility function insures us that Q^*/μ^* is negative in the limit, q.e.d.

Lemma 5: $\lim\limits_{s \to 1} \dfrac{A^*(1,s)}{\mu^*(1,s)} = \eta > 0,$

where η is a constant only dependent on the form of the utility functions and the work endowments.

Proof: From assumptions 1 and 2 and definition 1 it follows that A^* is zero in the limit. Using L´Hôpital´s rule we can write

$$\lim_{s \to 1} \frac{\dfrac{\partial A^*}{\partial s}}{\dfrac{\partial \mu^*}{\partial s}} = \lim_{s \to 1} \frac{E \dfrac{\omega \dfrac{\partial m_{\theta qq}}{\partial s} d - \omega\, m_{\theta qq} \dfrac{\partial d}{\partial s}}{d^2}}{-E \dfrac{\omega^2}{d}}$$

where the denominator is found by differentiating the first-order conditions of (4). The strict convexity of the utility function ensures us that d^i is positive making the denominator negative in the limit. Let

$$\lim_{s \to 1} d^i = \zeta^i.$$

Looking at the numerator we find that in the limit it can be written as

$$E \lim_{s \to 1} \frac{\omega}{d} \frac{\partial m_{\theta qq}}{\partial s} \quad,$$

where we again have made use of the fact that $m^i_{\theta qq}$ vanishes in the limit. We write

$$\frac{\partial m^i_{\theta qq}}{\partial s} = \frac{\partial m^i_{\theta qq}}{\partial q} \frac{\partial q^{i*}}{\partial s} + \frac{\partial m^i_{\theta qq}}{\partial \theta} \frac{\partial \theta^{i*}}{\partial s}.$$

But

$$\lim_{s \to 1} \frac{\partial q^{i*}}{\partial s} = 0,$$

$$\lim_{s \to 1} \frac{\partial m^i_{\theta qq}}{\partial \theta} = \lim_{s \to 1} \frac{\partial m^i_{\theta q\theta}}{\partial q} = \beta^i < 0 \text{ and}$$

$$E\omega \frac{\partial \theta}{\partial s} = - \frac{\partial \mu^*}{\partial s} < \infty .$$

Thus

$$\lim_{s \to 1} \frac{\partial \theta^{i*}}{\partial s} = \gamma^i > 0.$$

The numbers, γ^i and ζ^i only depend on the form of the utility function U^i in a neighborhood of the point $(1,0)$ and β^i in addition on the work endowment. We can thus write

$$\lim_{s \to 1} \frac{A^*}{\mu^*} = - \frac{E\beta \ \gamma \frac{\omega}{\zeta}}{E \ \frac{\omega}{\zeta}^2} := \eta > 0, \text{ q.e.d.}$$

We are now ready to study expression (8). Writing

$$J^{i*}(\delta,s) := \frac{1}{U^i_q} \frac{\partial V^{ix*}(\delta,s)}{\partial \delta} ,$$

we find the following results:

<u>Lemma 6</u>: If consumption is a normal good for agent i, then for agent i,

$$\lim_{s \to 0} \frac{1}{s} J^*(\delta,s) > 0 \quad \text{and}$$

$$\frac{1}{s} J^*(0,s) > 0$$

and, if p is sufficiently small, then

$$\lim_{s \to 1} \left(\frac{1}{\mu^*}\right)^2 J^*(1,s) < 0.$$

<u>Proof</u>: Follows directly from lemmata 4 and 5.

The economic content of lemma 6 can be written as

<u>Theorem 2</u>: If both consumption and leisure are normal goods, then an agent will demand that all tax revenues go to the provision of social insurance if the marginal tax rate is sufficiently small, and he will demand that less than all tax revenues go to the provision of social insurance when the tax rate is sufficiently high if the probability of needing social insur-

ance is sufficiently small. Also, the agent will demand that some of the tax revenues go to the provision of social insurance independent of the marginal tax rate.

We can thus, somewhat losely, say that each agent´s demand for social insurance, in the sense of the fraction of total tax revenues going to social-insurance benefits, will decrease as the marginal tax rate increases.

We stress that what we are looking at is the optimal value of δ for each individual. Generally the optimal δ will vary from individual to individual dependent on the values of Q. Q varies over the agents depending on the form of the utility functions, which can be different for different agents, and on the value of ω, the endowment, which influences q* and therefore U_q.

It is thus impossible to determine the socially optimal value of δ, given the marginal tax rate, without specifying a welfare function or some rule about how to aggregate the optimal δ´s for each individual into one value for the society. However, if one assumes that the aggregation rule is monotonically non-decreasing in the individual optimal δ´s then the above-mentioned result carries over to the aggregated δ.

5. CONCLUDING REMARKS

The main result of this study is that the optimal fraction of tax revenues that should go to social insurance will be a decreasing function of the marginal tax rate. The reason for taxation in this model is twofold. There is a desire to redistribute incomes in a more equitable fashion and one wishes to provide social insurance. An interesting question is what will happen to the redistributional effect as one decreases δ. Taking the work endowments ω as a proxy for income and assuming that everyone has the same utility function, we can look at the values of J* for different values of ω keeping s and δ constant. Only Q varies with ω and J* is monoton in Q. Using the same argument as in the proof of lemma 4 we find that Q increases with an increase in ω. Thus, J* increases as ω increases. That is for a given value of δ the "high-income" agents wish δ to increase and the "low-income" agents wish δ to decrease. A decrease in δ will thus have an equitable effect on the income distribution if we keep the marginal tax rate constant.

Decreasing δ gives rise to two effects. The decrease in the social-insurance benefits, which are the same for all, will tend to make the "income distribution" more unequal. However, the added amount of direct transfers more than compensates for this. This is in agreement with the findings in Aaron and McGuire (1970).

We should note, however, that our analysis the whole time is done ex-ante in terms of expected utility. A discussion of the relationship between an ex-ante expected-utility optimum and ex-post justice can be found in Harsanyi (1955) and Wickström (1979). With this qualification we thus find that the desire to equalize "income" through increasing the marginal tax rate is reinforced by the effect of decreasing δ to the new optimal value. For a similar discussion of the distributional effects of changes in the supply of collective goods see Maital (1973).

Finally we note that the results of this paper are normative in the sense that we are interested in the "best" value of δ given individual preferences. We do not discuss any institutional framework that would lead us to the optimal values of δ. Further, the study is partial in the sense that we take s, the marginal tax rate, as given. A normative extension of the model would be to introduce a "veil of ignorance" with respect to the potential work endowments, thus randomizing the initial "income distribution" and letting the agents optimize expected utility in an original position, e.g. see Harsanyi (1955) or Wickström (1979). This would give us an optimal value of both s and δ. A positive extension would be to introduce an institutional structure within which the agents choose s.

FOOTNOTES

* Noregs handelshøgskole. (The Norwegian School of Economics and Business Administration), Bergen.

I received many interesting comments on the first draft of this paper from Bo Larsson and other participants at the Fifth Biennial Arne Ryde Symposium in August 1981. Lars Thorlund-Petersen has read the manuscript and constructively commented upon it. I thank them all. All remaining shortcomings are my own.

The last revisions of this paper were done when I as a research fellow of the Alexander von Humboldt Foundation was a guest at the Fakultät für Volkswirtschaftslehre und Statistik an der Universität Mannheim. I thank the Alexander von Humboldt Foundation, the Fakultät and the Sonderforschungsbereich 5, Universität Mannheim, for their assistance.

REFERENCES

Aaron, H. and McGuire, M. (1970), Public Goods and Income Distribution, Econometrica 38.

Harsanyi, J.-C. (1955), Cardinal welfare, individualistic ethics, and intertemporal comparisons of utility, Journal of Political Economy 63.

Maital, S. (1973), Public Goods and Income Distribution: Some Further Results, Econometrica 41.

Royden, H.L. (1968), Real Analysis (2nd ed.), Macmillan, New York.

Wickström, B.-A. (1979), Economic Justice and Economic Power, forthcoming in Public Choice.

ARNE RYDE SYMPOSIUM ON SOCIAL INSURANCE
L. Söderström (editor)
© Elsevier Science Publishers B.V. (North-Holland), 1983

INSURING AGAINST RISK IN PRIMITIVE ECONOMIES:
THE ROLE OF PRESTIGE GOODS

Mats Lundahl*

> ˋ...the central policy issues of ends
> and means for the governments of all
> countries, rich and poor, cannot be
> thought of wholly in economic terms.
> "Social policy" must therefore be
> analysed in a broad political and
> geographical framework. The perspective
> gained from comparative studies helps in
> the understanding of the social policies
> of one˴s own country˝ (Titmuss, 1974,
> pp. 21-22).

1. THE NEED FOR SOCIAL INSURANCE

In the present paper we will deal with primitive social insurance arrangements in a wide sense, i.e. we will include both arrangements which work to
prevent risks of various kinds from materializing and arrangements that
dampen the effects of adverse outcomes ex post, with some emphasis on the
latter. The arrangements are not formal in the Western sense of being administered by specialized agencies basing their work on a set of written,
codified rules. On the contrary, as we will see, they may even be unintentional. The lack of written codes does not, however, mean that the arrangements are improvised as the need arises. They are institutionalized in that
there are recurrent patterns with a very definite structure.

The need for social insurance arrangements arises in two, frequently overlapping, situations (Ståhl, 1973). The first one is connected with the individual's life-cycle pattern of incomes and expenditures. Basically, the
expenditure stream is evenly distributed in time, while the income stream
exhibits a marked peak during the middle, working years of life. Thus, to
make the necessary income available for meeting expenditures at each point
in time across the life cycle, some type of system allowing for intertemporal redistribution of incomes is called for. In principle, this problem can
be solved by a system which allows the individual to borrow against future
income during the early stages of life, then repay and accumulate reserves

for the retirement age. Since the length of the retirement period cannot be foreseen, however, even a perfect capital market must be complemented by a system of intergenerational income transfers or an insurance system.

The second situation differs from the first in the important respect that the timing of the events calling for insurance is not always known. The in-dividual may find either that his expenditure rises sharply and suddenly, as when he becomes seriously ill, or that his income falls drastically, as when he loses his job.[1] Obviously, this type of situation calls for some kind of insurance arrangement as well, especially since not even a perfect capital market will solve the problem.

In the present paper, which deals exclusively with primitive economies, only the second type of problem will be considered. The situation where ex-pected incomes suddenly fail to materialize is connected with some basic production problems of these economies. One salient characteristic of such societies is that the risk of an unfavorable outcome in the process of pro-duction for subsistence is always high. Natural uncertainties loom large. Liebig´s law of the minimum assumes a special significance here. This law (cf. e.g. Odum, 1963, pp. 65-66) states that in a set of factors con-trolling the production of crops (or animals) it is the permissible minimum value, and not the average, of each factor that is limiting. Take the case of drought. A human population living under primitive conditions in a par-ticular ecological setting survives within a fairly wide range of precipi-tation conditions, because the plants and animals on which it is dependent do, but if a severe drought occurs, the population may be drastically reduced in a short time. The harvest fails. The domestic animals that can be eaten die. Hunting and gathering activities bring a yield which is too low to allow avoidance of hunger or outright starvation.[2] In societies where essential inputs and outputs in the production process are bought and sold in a market there is in addition the risk of unfavorable price movements that will serve to reduce incomes to untolerably low levels.

The existence of various types of risks naturally affects the behavior of those who live and work in economies where formally organized modern social insurance systems are either lacking altogether or are at best extremely undeveloped. When production decisions are made, care is taken to avoid undesirable outcomes, if possible. If the prevailing standard of living is low and the high perishability of consumption goods does not permit any savings to be made for leaner years,[3] production ex post cannot be allowed to differ too much from production calculated ex ante. The extent of trade is often limited in these economies. This means that local fluctuations in the supply of food may create very serious problems for the individuals, since then the level and intertemporal distribution of consumption becomes intimately connected with the level of local output and its distribution in time. By the same token, the premium on dampening the impact of lean years, once they occur, will be high. A number of social insurance systems which Western observers often tend to regard as primitive in a somewhat derogato-ry sense, but which often display a high degree of sophistication, exist in primitive economies (Lundahl (1974), Posner (1980)).

2. PRESTIGE GOODS AND THEIR FUNCTIONS

In anthropological literature, great stress is often laid on ceremonial and other non-economic aspects of social life, while economic reasoning is kept in the background. However, as Melville Herskovits has noted, ´Many societies ... afford striking instances of the manner in which economic and non-economic factors may combine to produce economic results˜ (Herskovits, 1952, p. 156). One such instance is the use of prestige goods. Prestige is a non-economic factor which most of the time is not sought as a means of obtaining economic rewards. On the contrary, obtaining prestige very often entails heavy pecuniary outlays. Sometimes these are of an order which is sufficient to bring the person almost to the point of ruin. (Cf. Codere, 1950, Ch. 3, for an example of the high costs that may be involved.)

Prestige goods may (in their pure form) be defined as ˜products which are not needed for actual material support of life, but [are] definitely needed for social and political position within the society˜ (Ekholm, 1972, p. 100). It is often the control of prestige goods on which the entire social ladder of primitive societies is built. By monopolizing or otherwise controlling the supply of these goods in society, a family or larger kinship unit possesses an instrument with which to prove excellence and superiority (cf. Ekholm (1972), Persson (forthcoming) for examples).[4]

An institution may, however, serve many purposes simultaneously. It may have been designed with a single explicit purpose in mind and yet at the same time perform a number of other, unintentional or latent, functions.[5] This is true of the creation of prestige and the employment of prestige goods as well (Pearson, 1957, pp. 337-38):

> ˜In primitive or archaic societies the function of prestige seems rather the reverse of that found in our own economy. For there it appears as a culture pattern sui generis with a rationale and institutional fittings of its own, and capable, vis-à-vis the economy, of stimulating feverish goods and person movements...
>
> Prestige is the prize of all this activity which may itself involve the accumulation of symbolic wealth, but it also functions indirectly as a mobilizer of relatively large quantities of material means as well as human services to be employed in a variety of ways, utilitarian and not, as they otherwise would not be. It is here that we see the surplus creating function of the prestige factor in early society. For with the prestige gained in the prestige economy go honorific duties and public trustee functions which result in making available to the community services and material means which would not otherwise be put to use.˜

It is the thesis of the present paper that sometimes the use of prestige goods in primitive societies contains an element of social insurance, in the wide sense referred to above. The very way in which these goods are handled gives rise to a number of mechanisms which may vary greatly from society to society but which have the common feature that they provide a means of coping with some of the risks that permanently or periodically threaten the material existence of primitive communities. We will in the following give some examples of how such primitive insurance systems, based on prestige goods, work. Before doing that, however, we must discuss the concept of reciprocity which is central to the understanding of some of the insurance functions of prestige objects.

3. GIFTS AND RECIPROCITY

Prestige goods are used, among other things, as gifts. A ˜classic˜ problem of sociology and anthropology is why people make gifts. The ˜classic˜

answer to this question was provided by Marcel Mauss in 1925 (Mauss, 1970). Drawing on a variety of ethnographic material, Mauss noted that in all transactions involving a gift, there is an obligation to receive the gift and, more importantly, an obligation to reciprocate with a counter-gift at some later point in time. All gifts in primitive societies imply a social relationship between the giver and the receiver.[6] This relationship is created or expressed by the gift, and the gift goes beyond the material wealth of the goods changing hands in the act. The gift establishes a continual relationship between the giving and receiving parties, one which creates prolonged (in principle, life-long) social interdependence. This interdependence is, however, according to Mauss, not a mere interdependence between the individuals directly involved in the transactions, but in prim-itive societies ˜it is groups, and not individuals, which carry on exchange, make contracts, and are bound by obligations; the persons repre-sented in the contracts are moral persons - clans, tribes, and families...˜ (Mauss, 1970, p. 3).[7]

Mauss˜ notion of reciprocity and his stress on large social aggregates rather than on individuals was picked up and developed by Karl Polanyi (1957), who, however, reversed the order of causality between gifts and so-cial relations. As Raymond Firth has noted, Mauss dealt mainly with ˜cases of gift and return where the general social status concerned was broadly equivalent˜ (Firth, 1967, p. 13). Polanyi, proceeding along the same lines, defined reciprocity as ˜movements between correlative points of symmetrical groupings˜ (Polanyi, 1957, p. 250). Reciprocity, according to this view, should not be taken to imply mere personal interrelations or aggregates thereof. ˜Reciprocity behavior between individuals integrates the economy only if symmetrically organized structures, such as a symmetrical system of kinship groups, are given. But a kinship system never arises as the result of mere reciprocating behavior on the personal level˜ (Polanyi, 1957, p. 251).

Polanyi considered that he was able to identify ˜a tendency in larger com-munities to develop a multiple symmetry in regard to which reciprocative behavior may develop in the subordinate communities. The closer the members of the encompassing communities feel drawn to one another, the more general will be the tendency among them to develop reciprocative attitudes in regard to specific relationships limited in space, time or otherwise˜ (Polanyi, 1957, p. 153).

The Mauss-Polanyi line of reasoning was further developed and generalized by Marshall Sahlins who pointed out that reciprocity does not have to be a neatly balanced, unconditional one-for-one exchange (Sahlins, 1972). Three types of reciprocity exist: generalized, balanced and negative. Generalized and negative reciprocity constitute the endpoints on a scale where balanced reciprocity is found somewhere in between. Generalized reciprocity ˜refers to transactions that are putatively altruistic, transactions on the line of assistance given and, if possible and necessary, assistance returned.˜ Balanced reciprocity means ˜direct exchange˜, and if the balance is ˜per-fect˜, ˜the reciprocity is the customary equivalent of the thing received and is without delay.˜ Negative reciprocity, finally, is ˜the attempt to get something for nothing˜ (Sahlins, 1972, pp. 194, 195).

Sahlins suggested that the mode of exchange which prevails between two parties is to a large extent conditioned by the social distance between them. Close relations lead to generalized reciprocity and distant relations make for a move towards the negative end of the reciprocity scale. He, however, acknowledged that causality may run in both directions: "If friends make gifts, gifts make friends. A great proportion of primitive exchange, much more than our own traffic, has as its decisive function this latter: the material flow underwrites or initiates social relations" (Sahlins, 1972, p. 186).

In the remainder of the present paper we will, in so far as we are dealing with reciprocity,[8] be concerned mainly with the latter type of causality, i.e. the one indicated by Mauss rather than the one pointed to by Polanyi, although the latter will at times come into the picture as well, since it is obvious that here, to some extent, we are dealing with a chicken-and-egg chain of causation. Now, let us proceed to the presentation of three concrete instances of the employment of prestige goods for insurance purposes.

4. CASE 1: POMO TRADE FEASTS

Our first example shows how prestige goods can be directly traded for food and how, conversely, a temporary food surplus in one community can be "banked" with another to be recovered at a future date when a surplus arises in the latter community. This example comes from the Pomo Indians, a people living in central California (Loeb (1926, pp. 192-194), Barrett (1952, pp. 352-53, 416), Vayda (1966)). One of the devices employed by these tribes before the first contacts with the whites was an institutionalized system of invitations to so-called trade feasts when one community found itself with an unusually large surplus of a particular type of food.

These surpluses, of fish, acorns and, occasionally, seed, could not usually be stored in the conventional sense of this word. By redistributing the surpluses to other tribes, however, by means of a trading ceremony which built on generalized reciprocity, against receipt of prestige goods, the tribe in question could make certain that whenever the tribe to which the surplus was redistributed produced a surplus, it would let the redistributing tribe share it in the same way.

The prestige goods involved in these transactions were wampum, strings of magnesite and shell beads, which were used for gift-giving, for settlements of feuds among villages, for funerary and other offerings, for discharging blood-revenge debts etc.[9] The trade of food surpluses for these prestige goods took place in the following manner. Suppose that a particular tribe had a surplus of fish. Then, a messenger would be sent off to some other tribe which, after accepting the invitation, would pool resources to amass as much wampum as possible in a common fund. Upon arrival, the guests would present their offer of beads. After several days of festivities, the chiefs of the inviting tribe would decide how much fish they would trade for the wampum. The fish would then be redistributed in equal amounts to his followers by the chief of the guests who would keep for himself whatever could not be redistributed in an egalitarian fashion.[10]

This case, which pretty exactly follows the pattern envisaged by Mauss, where chiefs act on behalf of their tribes in carrying out the transactions, illustrates how by trading food for prestige items, successive redistributions of foodstuffs in time and space fulfil an insurance function in that they prevent surpluses from accumulating at one point in time or space and deficits prevailing at others.

5. CASE 2: STOCK ASSOCIATES IN EAST AFRICA

The prestige good <u>par excellence</u> in East Africa is cattle, which is used in all important ceremonies of the herding peoples of that part of the continent. Cattle are everywhere used in connection with ceremonies related to birth, death, marriage etc., and cattle constitute the most important source of power and prestige (Herskovits (1926), Evans-Pritchard (1940, Ch. 1), Colson (1951), Peristiany (1951), Evans-Pritchard (1953), Gulliver (1955), Hedlund (1980)). Naturally, cattle are not a pure prestige good as their main function lies in the extremely important subsistence role they fulfil (Evans-Pritchard (1940, Ch. 1), Gulliver (1955), Schneider (1957)).

The two roles of cattle combine in certain practices which may be interpreted in terms of insurance. In East Africa there are two (formerly three) main risks against which cattle herding peoples must guard themselves. The first is drought. In many areas the ecological setting is such as to make longer or shorter dry spells recurring events (Evans-Pritchard (1940, Ch. 2), Gulliver (1955, Ch. 2)). The second is cattle diseases of various kinds, notably rinderpest, which when they strike easily eradicate a herd. The third, which, however, is now largely a thing of the past, is that of being raided for cattle by other tribes or clans. In all three cases, the result for those hit may easily be fatal. Therefore, a number of practices have developed which minimize these risks.

One such device is the custom of making stock associates by means of gifts and counter-gifts of cattle. P.H. Gulliver (1955, p. 196), describes how among the Jie and Turkana on the border between Uganda and Kenya an individual by exchanging animals with other people

> ...with each of these people maintains well-recognized, reciprocal rights to claim gifts of domestic animals in certain socially defined circumstances. Thus a particular kind of inter-personal relationship is consciously translated into the right to seek stock in times of need and the roughly corresponding obligation to give stock in times of others' needs.

These stock associates may be both kin and non-kin (bond-friends).[11] The association builds on a constant giving and taking of cattle.[12] Gifts create or maintain the bonds which can be drawn upon in times of need. "Rights with reference to all stock-associates are maintained essentially by the factor of reciprocity. A right is balanced by an obligation such that the social relationship consists in mutual assistance and mutual support", writes Gulliver (1955, p. 203). This is a quite conscious policy. Elisabeth Colson (1955, p. 70) notes that

> "Probably it is safe to say that over much of Africa, even today, life is conditioned by certain attitudes toward property and persons which are characteristic of a non-industrial stable society, in which opportunities and power depend on status within social groups rather than upon control of investments; where, indeed, the safest form of investment, and often the only one, is still to be found in the building up of claims against persons.

The more stock a man has, the greater his wealth, power and prestige. The relation, however, is a double-sided one, since the prestige associated with large cattle herds "is not a pure function of possession" but "it is derived basically from the willingness of the owner to help meet the needs of the community˘ (Schneider, 1957, p. 293). To make many stock associates, i.e. to obtain much prestige, one must fulfil the reciprocity obligations scrupulously.

The insurance arrangement established by the stock associate system is a very flexible one which can be used for a number of purposes. The first one is when the calamity is already a fact, after the outbreak of a stock disease or after the failure of pastures, and the owner who has lost animals attempts to rebuild his herd. Stock association is, however, functional also before the herd has been reduced. During the dry season a herd owner can fall back on his stock associates to use their waterholes when his own has dried out. He may also have to move the herd out of his customary grazing area to find food for his cattle. In foreign territory, support is always needed. Gulliver (1955, pp. 211, 212) describes the situation among the Turkana:

> ˘...normally a man must go to an area where someone will stand surety for him in local, informal discussion...Through his bond-friendships a man endeavours to ensure that he has a potential supporter in most or all of the areas to which, in any year he may wish to shift. This is a quite conscious policy, and each Turkana accepts the corresponding liability to help his bond-friends similarly.˘

Finally, the stock associates also tend each others˘ cattle. Thus, by spreading one˘s cattle on many hands, the risk that drought or disease will strike major portions of the herd at the same time is lessened.

6. CASE 3: YAMS GIFTS IN THE TROBRIANDS[13]

In the Trobriand Islands northeast of New Guinea, a <u>locus classicus</u> of anthropology, the threat to subsistence is insufficient precipitation. The rainfall varies from year to year, both in volume and in timing. Prolonged drought makes the yields of all normally consumed crops fall drastically (Malinowski, 1935a, pp. 160-61):

> ˘When there has been a drought, the natives begin to feel the pinch about the fourth moon of their year... Then women would be seen scouring the grove and jungle for leaves, roots and wild fruits with which to supply their households. If any of the desirable fruits... of the grove and jungle... have survived the drought, they would gather these; if not, they would have to fall back on the despised fruit of the <u>noku</u> tree, which is hardly edible but hardly ever fails. But if drought lasts for two years, then the natives may find themselves face to face with real famine... then with empty storehouses and fruit-trees barren, with the jungle parched and dry, the swamps... "hard as rock, broken with crevices", with the... grass on them brown and dead and even the <u>noku</u> fruit insufficient - the dreaded calamity comes upon the natives.˘

Before the contact with the whites had taught the Trobrianders to cultivate hardier crops than the traditional ones and outside supplies helped to avert famine, the consequences of the latter were serious. Rivalry over the remaining scarce resources immediately ensued. The inhabitants of the agricultural districts in the interior would be driven to the coast to attempt fishing but would clash there with the coastal communities with bloody battles and deaths from starvation as the ultimate consequences (Malinowski, 1935a, pp. 161-64). One does, however, not have to go to these extremes. According to Malinowski (1935a, p. 164),

> ˊEven the ordinary <u>molu</u>, insufficiency of food, is bad enough. Before it
> strikes a native directly in his organic needs, it affects his pride and
> makes him feel disappointed and dissatisfied with his work. On such oc-
> casions the Trobrianders fall back on the unripe crops, they start their
> thinning out ... very early, they eat "black and white" tubers alike,
> and incidentally they expose themselves to epidemics of dysentery, for
> unripe yams are apparently bad for the digestion. In such years they
> make bigger taro gardens on the swampy soil, they plant more of the big
> yams... and they systematically exploit the village groves and the
> jungle - all of which entails much harder work and work which they do
> not like. After all, they are gardeners and not wild-fruit-gatherers.ˊ

Thus, the Trobrianders had good reasons for wanting to protect themselves
against the consequences of one or more consecutive bad harvests. In this
protection, the employment of yams as a prestige good played a central
role. In any normal year, about twice as many yams as could be eaten were
produced (Malinowski, 1961, p. 58). In the more distant past, any excess
was simply allowed to rot, but only after the surplus had been employed for
certain ceremonial and social purposes. About fifty percent of the yams
produced by any household were handed over to the household of the hus-
bandˊs sister as a ceremonial gift and to the community leader (leader of
the sub-clan) (Malinowski, 1935a, pp. 208, 209):

> ˊAccording to native law, custom and morals, [a manˊs] ... real duty
> lies with his sisterˊs household. It is consequently for this household
> he has to raise and harvest the ... [yams]. It is on the size and quali-
> ty of this part of the result of his labours that his reputation as a
> gardener depends... The <u>urigubu</u> gift therefore lends itself to that
> boasting, display, comparison... which is so dear to the Melanesianˊs
> heart...The display, the measurement in public, the taking and recording
> of tally, provide both a psychological spur to the giver and a handle to
> the community, whether it be for praise or for blame. When his work has
> been successful as well as efficient, the generous gift is appreciated,
> the glory of the giver and his lineage extolled, and the normal moral
> approbation of the community bestowed, and this to a Trobriander is a
> great satisfaction and a real reward.ˊ

Later, these yam gifts were put into special storehouses where they were
displayed as symbols of prestige and power before they rotted.

Since that part of the yams harvest which we are discussing was not used
for food at all, this giving of yams may appear an odd practice from an
economic point of view. They did, however, serve an important economic
function in that they provided an incentive for cultivation in excess of
the daily needs. During the lean, dry years yields fall drastically, but if
much more is planted than is necessary from the food point of view, the
chances are that even with heavily decreasing yields the harvest is large
enough to allow the population to subsist without starvation (Harris (1959,
pp. 191-92), Keesing (1976, pp. 314-17)). Hence, the strong connection between the prestige aspect of the yams and their ability to satisfy basic
human needs stressed by Malinowski (1961, pp. 171, 172; cf. 1935b, p. 47):

> ˊ... what is socially enjoyed is the common admiration of fine and
> plentiful food, and the knowledge of its abundance...It is this indirect
> sentiment, rooted of course in reality in the pleasures of eating, which

makes for the value of food in the eyes of the natives. This value again makes accumulated food a symbol, and a vehicle of power. Hence the need for storing and displaying it. Value is not the result of utility and rarity, intellectually compounded, but is the result of a sentiment grown around things, which through satisfaying human needs, are capable of evoking emotions.´

7. CONCLUSIONS: VULGAR MATERIALISM?

In the foregoing we have given three examples of insurance practices connected with the exchange of prestige goods. In two of our cases the insurance was against harvest failure. In the third the problem was to preserve an animal herd. These cases have something in common. The risks which the prestige goods were employed to reduce are no ´ordinary´ risks but risks threatening the entire existence of the populations in question. In two of the cases (trade feasts, cattle) the insurance element is directly founded on reciprocity. It is via the very establishment of reciprocal bonds that insurance is obtained.

Thus, no doubt, prestige goods can and do serve as an instrument of insurance. The establishment of interpersonal contacts in different ways increases the likelihood of survival in a risky environment. An important question which we have only mentioned in passing, however, is whether the insurance mechanisms created with the aid of prestige goods arise as a result of deliberate action. We have noted that the cause-effect relationship between gifts and social relations may run both ways, but, provided that gifts actually make friends, are they intentionally used for insurance purposes?

For economists, this is an appealing thought (Posner, 1980, p. 14):

> ´The obligation of sharing with kinsmen is not the only device by which primitive society, lacking formal insurance contracts or public substitutes therefore, provides hunger insurance for its members. Generosity - toward other members of one´s village or band as well as toward kinsmen - is a more highly valued trait in primitive than in modern society and the reason appears to be that it is a substitute for formal insurance. The fact that a man obtains prestige in primitive societies by giving away what he has rather than by keeping it (the potlatch of the Northwest Indians is only the most dramatic example of "buying" prestige by giving away one´s goods on a seemingly extravagant scale) has been thought evidence of the inapplicability of the economic model to primitive society. But since, in a society where consumption goods are limited in variety and durability, giving away one´s surplus may be the most useful thing to do with it, at least from society´s standpoint, one is not surprised that it should earn the prestige that in a different kind of society is bestowed on a great inventor, scientist, captain of industry, or entertainer.´[14]

On the other hand, Marshall Sahlins (1969) and Jonathan Friedman (1974) have both strongly argued that the ´new functionalism´ as applied by authors like Marvin Harris (1966) actually does not explain anything at all. (See Harris (1980, pp. 242 ff.) for a rejoinder. Cf. also Rappaport (1979), and Friedman (1979) for a continuation of the debate.) Thus, Sahlins (1969, pp. 29-30) points out that ´proof that a certain trait or cultural arrangement has a positive economic value is not an adequate ex-

planation of its existence or even of its presence¯ and that ¯to say that a
certain cultural trait is "adaptive" in the light of its economic virtues
is only a weak kind of functionalism, accounting not for its existence but
merely for its feasibility.¯ Friedman, (1974, p. 457) referring to the new
functionalism as ¯vulgar materialism¯ points to the meaninglessness of the
statement that ¯the function of x is to do what it does.¯ This is ¯pure
description¯. On the other hand, when the new materialism intends to go
beyond description, by extending the sense of the word ¯function¯ to the
teleological meaning ¯the function is assumed rather than demonstrated.¯

Friedman goes on to argue that ¯formally, what is going on in these functional analyses is the description of negative feedback systems, that is,
systems in which certain variables are kept within certain crucial limits
by the operation of other variables which are dependent functions of those
limits¯ (Friedman, 1974, p. 459), but that often the regulatory mechanisms
are triggered way before these limits are reached. Thus, to label systems
of the kind referred to presently ¯functional¯ or ¯homeostatic¯ is not appropriate, because the very mechanism that is supposed to govern self-regulation in the system will never come into play.

It is, however, quite possible that the mechanism triggering regulation is
such that the system does not have to hit the limit before regulation sets
in. It may be enough to experience deviations in the wrong direction from a
reference value for corrective action to be taken (Rappaport, 1979, pp. 69-
70). Alternatively, the logic of regulation may be altogether different.
The system in question could be viewed in terms of a sequence of periods.
At the beginning of each period a decision has to be made which has implications for the whole period and no corrective action is possible once the
decision has been made. Maximization of some expected value, for example,
may then perhaps not be feasible unless some specified constraints can be
met, e.g. that the probability of falling short of a certain lower limit
must not exceed a predetermined figure. If that is not the case, the decision maker may instead proceed to minimize this probability (Roumasset,
1976, Ch. 2). We are then no longer dealing with a feedback system.

All three types of regulation can be illustrated with our present cases.
Thus, the Pomo trade feasts illustrate how a limit value regulates operations. When the food surplus exceeds a maximum value, an invitation for a
feast is sent out and redistribution takes place. The Trobriand yams case,
on the other hand, is an example of sequential decision making without
feedback. Once the yams have been planted there is not very much one can
do. Nature takes over. By planting enough to obtain a harvest which during
normal years is excessive from the consumption point of view, the probability that hunger or starvation will occur during a bad year is minimized.
The case of stock association, finally, is slightly more complex. On the
one hand, the practice of spreading cattle reduces the risk that the herd
shrinks if a drought occurs or a disease breaks out, but the previous
establishment of stock association relationships also makes corrective
action (moving the herd to other grazing areas) possible once a deviation
from a reference value (or precipitation) takes place.[15]

Thus, it is possible to argue that primitive social insurance systems of
the type dealt with presently, do behave like negative feedback systems as
described by Friedman, where corrective action sets in when the target variable reaches a limit for what is considered permissible.[16] This is, however, not the only possible mechanism. As we have pointed out, other types of
regulation are equally plausible.

The above does, however, not invalidate the first point of criticism against the ´new functionalism´. Sahlins and Friedman are certainly right in their insistence that causality should be demonstrated rather than assumed. Here, we may be dealing both with intentional and unintentional systems. From one point of view, however, this is of minor importance, since even if the system has been created with a completely different purpose in mind, the fact that as a by-product it generates social insurance as well means that the development of <u>intentional</u> insurance systems becomes less necessary.[17] Thus, we do not have to attempt any teleological interpretation. It is sufficient for our purpose to discover how the system <u>actually</u> works, and this is hardly ´vulgar´ materialism.

Primitive insurance generated with the aid of exchange of prestige goods is often insufficient (cf. Lundahl, 1974, pp. 366-67). As a rule, these systems are not capable of providing more than limited assistance. In particular, they are insufficient when it comes to dealing with persistent trends in unfavorable directions (e.g. prolonged drought). The primitive economy in general is characterized by a low technological level, which in turn means that the output obtained with given inputs is low. The same holds true for intentional insurance systems, and if the systems are unintentional it is of course also possible that inefficiencies of various kinds arise. The existence of unintentional systems of limited efficiency, which nevertheless are sufficient when it comes to handling minor calamities but which cannot cope with more difficult situations, may even preclude the development of the type of intentional institutions that would have been necessary for dealing with the latter.[18]

This, however, inevitably raises another important question which we have not attempted to answer in the present paper. If insurance systems such as those we have analyzed above provide only insufficient protection and sometimes are not even intentional, why do they survive? Should they not be superseded by other, more appropriate mechanisms? To this question, different answers can be given. In the first place, there is always the possibility that they do <u>not</u> survive. It is often impossible to know whether we are observing a long-run equilibrium or not. Real economies do not behave as smoothly as some of our models would perhaps lead us to suspect. The world is full of frictions and obstacles to change of various kinds (cf. e.g. Lundahl, 1979, Ch. 12, for examples). It is thus in some instances quite possible that we are dealing with transitory phenomena which sooner or later will give way to systems providing better protection.

Secondly, it may be the case that the economies we have looked at are not characterized mainly by maximization processes of the kind usually postulated in economics. The real world to a varying degree is characterized by procedures that build on satisficing behavior rather than maximization or minimization. In economics, this has been persistently pointed out by Herbert Simon (notably Simon, 1961), and in anthropology a yet older tradition exists in this field. Sahlins, in particular, has stressed that primitive economies often (´the main run of them´, according to Sahlins) fail to realize their productive capacities. Labor, capital and land are all constantly underutilized (Sahlins, 1972, Ch. 2-3). If this is the case, neither should we expect efficiency in the technological sense to prevail as far as social insurance systems are concerned. Thus, (Sahlins, 1969, p. 29)):

    ´...maximization, economizing admits only one solution to any problem of resource allocation: "the one best way". But survival is any way that

works. Success is ecologically established from a minimum point - the
minimum required of a cultural system to meet the selective pressures
that would decompose it. And between this threshold of what the system
must do (in the environment as presented) and what it could do (with the
techniques available), any number of intermediate selections differing
in cultural quality and productive quantity are positively adaptive...
Various degrees of resource exploitation falling short of the optimum,
thus not predictable from the formal praxeology, are nonetheless functional for the cultural praxis.¯

What is more, the systems may be optimal or rational from another point of
view. One of the cornerstones of modern anthropological thinking is that of
cultural relativism, and this concept, in turn, ¯raises the question, rational according to what scale of values¯ (LeClair & Schneider, 1967, p.
457). Therefore, even when from the efficiency point of view it is possible
to point to better solutions of the insurance problem, such solutions may
simply not be forthcoming in the given cultural context (Rappaport, 1979,
p. 74):

> ¯Although "items" other than those present could conceivably fulfill
> indispensable functions at a particular time and place, given the lim-
> ited cultural materials (structural, ideological, technological, social,
> political, or whatever) usually available, only the item or form
> present, or a limited range of them, could have emerged.¯

Thus, the existence of primitive insurance devices that provide only limited protection and which may in addition be inefficient in the sense that
better protection could be obtained with the same resources does not have
to be considered an anomaly. In societies where the norms governing human
behavior differ from what Western economists are used to postulate in their
analyses, they may well (but of course do not have to) be optimal in the
overall cultural setting.

To conclude, the present paper is an exploratory venture. It is founded on
the simple observation that the use of prestige goods can serve as a means
of primitive social insurance and does not purport anything beyond raising
the possibility that this could be a pattern found elsewhere as well among
primitive societies. Essentially, two hypotheses emerge for further research. The first is that prestige may be directly traded for insurance and
the second one states that prestige may be granted indirectly to the person
or group who organizes the activities that make social insurance possible.
Finally, the extent to which such patterns have been deliberately created
should be found out.

FOOTNOTES

* University of Lund. Thanks are due to Jonathan Friedman, Hans Hedlund,
Stefan Hedlund, Marianne Lundahl, Gunnar Persson, Johnny Persson, Lars
Söderström and an unknown referee for comments on an earlier version.

1) Illness, of course, is an example of this too.

2) See Vayda, Leeds & Smith (1961, note 5, p. 72) for numerous references
to such occurrences in Melanesia.

3) The very limitations on the capacity to postpone consumption because

of the high perishability of consumption goods is one of the hallmarks of a
primitive economy (Forde & Douglas, 1956, p. 15). For a discussion of other
characteristics of such economies, see e.g. Posner (1980, pp. 9-10).

4)   The reader who doubts the existence of status validation on the basis
of prestige goods in Western society is referred to the chapter on conspic-
uous consumption in Veblen (1953).

5)   ´We...owe to... [Adam Smith] our still imperfect understanding of the
degree to which man accomplishes many of his ends as an epiphenomenon, a
by-product of activities pursued for other purposes. Income distribution,
resource allocation, and economic growth are accomplished as by-products of
petty self-serving individual decisions to buy and sell. Sociologists subsequently picked up the idea of epiphenomenal effects in their concept of
latent functions of social institutions. But the inquiry into epiphenomena
begun by Smith remains to be completed´ (Lindblom, 1977, p. 8).

6)   This is of course true for more advanced societies as well. Alvin
Gouldner points to the gift exchange as a ´starting mechanism for social
relationships´ (Gouldner (1960, pp. 176-77); cf. also Schwartz (1967)). In
modern societies of the Western type, however, gift transactions typically
have a much less important place in the economy than in primitive societies. In The Elementary Structures of Kinship, Claude Lévi-Strauss (1969,
p. 61) argues that ´Reciprocal gifts are diverting survivals which engage
the curiosity of the antiquarian...´ (For a different view, see Titmuss
(1970). A criticism of Titmuss is offered e.g. in Arrow (1974).) The very
complexity of modern society and the concomitant stress on impersonal relations in many instances, at the expense of the closer, more personal, face-
to-face relationships, preclude direct reciprocity principles from coming
into play.

7)   The statement needs some qualification. Individuals who do not represent the social unit may very well engage in single gift transactions with
other individuals which do not involve the entire elaborate set of
prestations referred to by Mauss (cf. Firth 1967, p. 9). the borderline between the two types of transactions is, naturally, a floating one.

8)   A discussion of different notions of reciprocity is carried out in
Pryor (1977, Ch. 2 and 7).

9)   In all these transactions, ´the greater the liberality of payment, the
greater was the resultant prestige´ (Vayda, 1966, p. 496).

10) Instead of directly providing the fish, the inviting tribe could allow
its guests to use its fishing waters in return for wampum, redistributing
the latter in proportion to the catches made in each man´s section of the
waters.

11) There are many varieties here. A particular form of association is
that of tilia which is established among the Pakot (Suk) of Kenya during
the sapana ceremony when young men are initiated into adulthood. The father
of the initiate obtains an ox from a wealthy friend and relative. The ox is
speared by the initiate and fed to his guests. As a counter-gift, the ox
giver receives a heifer. This exchange creates a partnership which ´assumes
many of the characteristics of clan ties´ (Schneider, 1957, p. 284) and ´as
long as the heifer´s female offspring survive, a special relationship
(tilya) will bind... [the] agnatic descendants of the ox giver who keep

these cattle in their kraals to the initiate and his descendants´
(Peristiany, 1951, p. 191).

The brideprice or bridewealth is another case in point. One of the functions of the payment of bridewealth (with cattle) is to establish ´the
joint participation of the new affines with a gradually increasing co-oper-
ation and friendliness formally expressed. At this period relations are
established which are to persist for a lifetime with an acknowledged and
tremendous potentiality for mutual assistance in all manner of social and
individual matters´ (Gulliver, 1955, p. 205).

12) Cf. Colson (1951, p. 19), for an account of this practice among the
Plateau Tonga of Zambia, Hedlund (1980) for a discussion of Maasai customs
and Colson (1955, note. p. 77) for evidence from other East African
peoples.

13) A parallel to this case is found in the operations of the big men of
Guadalcanal as described by Hogbin (1938; 1964, Ch. 6).

14) The potlatch is a somewhat unfortunate example, however. The available
evidence hardly supports the view that holds this practice to be an insurance device (Drucker & Heizer (1967, pp. 136-54), Friedman (1974, pp. 457-
58)).

15) Alternatively, this may be interpreted as corrective action which is
taken once precipitation drops to a certain lower limit.

16) To do Friedman justice, it must be pointed out that his argument is
primarily directed against the reasoning in one particular book, that of
Rappaport (1968). It may, however, also be the case that this is an observation which has general validity for the types of societies we are
presently dealing with. (Cf. also Friedman, 1979.) Hence, the present discussion.

17) An obvious parallel here is when the existence of built-in stabilizers
in the economy automatically prevents fluctuations in export earnings from
affecting per capita incomes, investments etc. in less developed countries.
In this situation it is not necessary to develop devices to stabilize
export proceeds or to compensate for downward movements in the latter
(MacBean, 1966, Ch. 3).

18) This should not be interpreted as a call for institutions that make
insurance against catastrophes a reality. That is of course not possible.

REFERENCES

Arrow, K.J. (1974), Gifts and Exchanges, Philosophy and Public Affairs 1,
343-62.

Barrett, S.A. (1952), Material Aspects of Pomo Culture, Part Two, Bulletin
of the Public Museum of the City of Milwaukee 20, 261-508.

Codere, H. (1950), Fighting with Property. A Study of Kwakiutl Potlatching
and Warfare 1792-1930, University of Washington Press, Seattle and London.

Colson, E. (1951), The Role of Cattle among the Plateau Tonga of Mazabuka

District, Rhodes-Livingstone Journal 11, 10-46.

Colson, E. (1955), Native Cultural and Social Patterns in Contemporary Africa, in Haines, C.G. (ed.), Africa Today, Johns Hopkins Press, Baltimore, 69-84.

Drucker, P. and Heizer, R.F. (1967), To Make my Name Good. A Reexamination of the Southern Kwakiutl Potlatch, University of California Press, Berkeley and Los Angeles.

Ekholm, K. (1972), Power and Prestige. The Rise and Fall of the Kongo Kingdom, Ph D Thesis, Uppsala University.

Evans-Pritchard, E.E. (1940), The Nuer, Clarendon Press, Oxford.

Evans-Pritchard, E.E. (1953), The Sacrificial Role of Cattle among the Nuer, Africa 23, 181-98.

Firth, R. (1967), Themes in Economic Anthropology: A General Comment, in Firth, R. (ed.), Themes in Economic Anthropology, Tavistock, London, 1-28.

Forde, D. and Douglas, M. (1956), Primitive Economics, in Shapiro, H.L. (ed.), Man, Culture and Society, Oxford University Press, Oxford, reprinted in Dalton, G. (ed.), Tribal and Peasant Economies, The Natural History Press, Garden City, 1968, 13-28.

Friedman, J. (1974), Marxism, Structuralism and Vulgar Materialism. Man, n.s. 9, 444-69.

Friedman, J. (1979), Hegelian Ecology: Between Rousseau and the World Spririt, in Burnham, P.C. and Allen, R.F. (eds.), Social and Ecological Systems, Academic Press, London, 253-70.

Gouldner, A. (1960), The Norm of Reciprocity: A Preliminary Statement. American Sociological Review 25, 161-78.

Gulliver, P.H. (1955), The Family Herds, Routledge & Kegan Paul, London.

Harris, M. (1959), The Economy Has No Surplus? American Anthropologist 61, 185-99.

Harris, M. (1966), The Cultural Ecology of India´s Sacred Cattle, Current Anthropology 7, 51-59.

Harris, M. (1980), Cultural Materialism. The Struggle For a Science of Culture, Vintage Books, New York.

Hedlund, H. (1980), Contradictions in the Peripheralization of a Pastoral Society: The Maasai, Review of African Political Economy No 15/16, 15-34.

Herskovits, M.J. (1926), The Cattle Complex in East Africa, American Anthropologist 28, 230-72, 361-88, 494-528, 633-64.

Herskovits, M.J. (1952), Economic Anthropology, Norton, New York.

Hogbin, H.I. (1938), Social Advancement in Guadalcanal, Solomon Islands, Oceania 8, 289-305.

Hogbin, I. (1964), A Guadalcanal Society. The Kaoka Speakers, Holt, Rinehart & Winston, New York.

Keesing, R.M. (1976), Cultural Anthropology. A Contemporary Perspective, Holt, Rinehart & Winston, New York.

LeClair, E.E. and Schneider, H.K. (eds.) (1968), Economic Anthropology. Readings in Theory and Analysis, Holt, Rinehart & Winston, New York.

Lévi-Strauss, C. (1969), The Elementary Structures of Kinship, Revised edition, Eyre and Spottiswoode, London.

Lindblom, C.E. (1977), Politics and Markets. The World´s Political-Economic Systems, Basic Books, New York.

Loeb, E.M. (1926), Pomo Folkways, University of California Publications in American Archaeology and Ethnology 19, 149-404.

Lundahl, M. (1974), Riskgardering i den traditionella ekonomin, Ekonomisk Debatt 6, 358-68.

Lundahl, M. (1979), Peasants and Poverty: A Study of Haiti, Croom Helm, London.

MacBean, A.I. (1966), Export Instability and Economic Development, George Allen & Unwin, London.

Malinowski, B. (1935a), Coral Gardens and Their Magic. Volume One. The Description of Gardening, American Book Company, New York.

Malinowski, B (1935b), Coral Gardens and Their Magic. Volume Two. The Language of Magic and Gardening, American Book Company, New York

Malinowski, B. (1961), Argonauts of the Western Pacific, Dutton, New York.

Mauss, M. (1970), The Gift, Cohen & West, London.

Odum, E.P. (1963), Ecology, Holt, Rinehart & Winston, New York.

Pearson, H.W. (1957), The Economy Has No Surplus: Critique of a Theory of Development, in Polanyi, K., Arensberg, C.M. and Pearson, H.W. (eds.), Trade and Market in the Early Empires, The Free Press, New York, 320-41.

Peristiany, J.G. (1951), The Age-Set System of the Pastoral Pokot, Africa 21, 188-206, 279-302.

Persson, J. (forthcoming), Cyclical Change and Circular Exchange: A Reexamination of the Kula Ring, Oceania.

Polanyi, K. (1957), The Economy as Instituted Process, in Polanyi, K., Arensberg, C.M. and Pearson, H.W. (eds.), Trade and Market in the Early Empires, The Free Press, New York, 243-70.

Posner, R.A. (1980), A Theory of Primitive Society, with Special Reference to Law, Journal of Law and Economics 23, 1-53.

Pryor, F.L. (1977), The Origins of the Economy. A Comparative Study of Distribution in Primitive and Peasant Economies, Academic Press, New York.

Rappaport, R.A. (1968), Pigs for the Ancestors, Yale University Press, New Haven.

Rappaport, R.A. (1979), Ecology, Meaning, and Religion, North Atlantic Books, Richmond, California.

Roumasset, J.A. (1976), Rice and Risk. Decision Making among Low-Income Farmers, North Holland, Amsterdam.

Sahlins, M. (1969), Economic Anthropology and Anthropological Economics, Social Science Information 8, 13-33.

Sahlins, M. (1972), Stone Age Economics, Aldine-Atherton, Chicago and New York.

Schneider, H.K. (1957), The Subsistence Role of Cattle among the Pakot and in East Africa, American Anthropologist 59, 278-300.

Schwartz, B. (1967), The Social Psychology of the Gift, American Journal of Sociology 73, 1-11.

Simon, H.A. (1961), Administrative Behavior, Second editon, Macmillan, New York.

Ståhl, I. (1973), Socialförsäkringarna - en avslutad reformepok? Ekonomisk Debatt 1, 43-52.

Titmuss, R.M. (1970), The Gift Relationship. From Human Blood to Social Policy, George Allen & Unwin, London.

Titmuss, R.M. (1974), Social Policy, An Introduction, George Allen & Unwin, London.

Vayda, A.P. (1966), Pomo Trade Feasts. Humanités. Cahiers de l´Institut de Science Economique Appliquée, reprinted in Dalton, G. (ed.), Tribal and Peasant Economies, Natural History Press, Garden City, 1968, 494-500.

Vayda, A.P., Leeds, A. and Smith, D.B. (1961), The Place of Pigs in Melanesian Subsistence, in Garfield, V.E. (ed.), Symposium: Pattern of Land Utilization and Other Papers, Proceedings of the 1961 Annual Spring Meeting of the American Ethnological Society, University of Washington Press, Seattle, 69-77.

Veblen, T. (1953), The Theory of the Leisure Class, Mentor Books, New York and Toronto.

ARNE RYDE SYMPOSIUM ON SOCIAL INSURANCE
L. Söderström (editor)
© Elsevier Science Publishers B.V. (North-Holland), 1983

SOCIAL INSURANCE IN SWEDEN

Per Gunnar Edebalk
and
Åke Elmér*

1. INTRODUCTION

This paper describes the main features of the Swedish system of social insurance. To give an unambiguous definition of a concept like social insurance is however not easy. Social insurance usually means social security arrangements based on insurance principles. There is, so to say, a mixture between welfare and insurance components. In a genuine social insurance system the balance must be weighed in favour of the insurance component.

According to the conventional Swedish conception of social insurance the balance however might be weighed in favour of the welfare component. This means that income maintenance programmes which are sponsored by the government are labelled insurances as soon as there is no means test. The philosophy then being that the insurance contributions which match the benefits are paid as a part of the general taxes in so far as they are not paid by special taxes on labour or as traditional fees by the insured or their employers. Only the means tested social assistance then fall outside the system of social insurance.

In this paper the conventional Swedish definition will be used. Part 2 gives a short historical background and part 3 a description of the present system of social insurance. A discussion of some main principles in the Swedish system will also be given in part 3.

The meaning of the term social insurance is however evolving towards a wider definition. According to some welfare politicians and theorists, social insurance should include not only income maintenance programmes but all governmental benefits that are paid out without a means test. This means that, for instance, general family allowances, housing allowances and labour market training allowances are to be included in the term social insurance. A newly published official report made a proposal of this kind and recommended the introduction of a general (and simplified) social insurance system. This proposal will be dealt with in part 4.

During the last two decades new schemes of social insurance have been introduced via agreements between the Swedish Confederation of Trade Unions
and other labour unions on one side and the Swedish Employers´ Federation
and the central and local authorities on the other side. These schemes are
complements to the governmental social insurance in Sweden. Insurances provided through collective agreements are described in part 5.

2. GROWTH OF THE SOCIAL INSURANCE PROGRAMMES

The present Swedish social insurance system has its roots partly in "provi-
dence societies" which have existed in Sweden since the time of medieval
guilds. After the abolition of the guild system many of the programmes grew
into the voluntary benevolent societies that began to flourish in the
1870´s. The first trade unions, temperance organizations and other societies included sickness benefits as part of their operations and in the
1890´s trade unions also began to establish unemployment relief funds.

In the Swedish Parliament the question of social insurance was taken up for
the first time in 1884. The source of inspiration was of course the newly
introduced social insurance system in Germany. Hereafter liberals and many
conservatives often regarded social insurance as a means of lessening the
antagonism between labour and capital. The idea of social insurance as such
was thus early accepted by the emerging labour movement and established
politicians.

As early as 1891 formal regulations were approved concerning sickness benefits societies. Societies which conformed to the legislation were given
official approval and were accorded small government subsidies. Over the
years to come these subsidies were increased quite substantially. The voluntary sickness benefits societies arranged for medical care for their members at modest cost and paid them cash benefits in case of sickness.

A modest form of work injury insurance was established in 1901. Initially
it was a form of voluntary insurance for employers. It was made compulsory
in 1916. At the beginning this insurance covered only accidents in the
place of work but later, in the 1920´s, it was extended to cover occupational diseases.

Social insurance was in the beginning called "workers´ insurance." An important historical milestone was Sweden´s first national pensions act of
1913 according to which old age and disability insurance for all citizens
was provided. This was the first social insurance scheme in the world for
the entire population. The scheme was dual in nature. One part was financed
by individual contributions and utilized the premium reserve system. This
part guaranteed every citizen a pension related to his previous income. The
other part was financed by taxation and provided a supplementary pension
for those in need.

Even before the First World War unemployment insurance and a compulsory
health insurance was debated. The World War and the economic strains during
the 1920´s delayed positive decisions in both cases and generally hampered
the development of social insurance. At the beginning of the 1930´s, during
the Great Depression, special recovery measures were initiated in Sweden.
The new economic policy had as one part the strengthening and broadening of
the social security system. Unemployment insurance, for instance, was introduced in 1934. The system chosen was the so called Ghent-system which

means that the State subsidizes the unemployment relief funds of the unions. That system functions comparatively well in Sweden, as most employed persons are organized in unions.

The Second World War brought the expansion to a halt. The pensions had been increased before the war by supplements paid out of general taxes and these supplements took the greater part of the total. After the war a new era of expansion began. According to the national pension act of 1946, which went into effect in 1948, all citizens of age 67 (nowadays 65) would receive the same pension regardless of income. This basic pension was criticized as insufficient to meet the needs of many pensioners.

There was therefore a pressure for the establishment of an income-related, compulsory and contributory programme which would provide more substantial benefits. After a long debate, and political struggle, such a general supplementary pension (in Swedish called ATP) was introduced in 1959. The first ATP-pensions were paid out in 1963.

Proposals for compulsory health insurance had been made since the beginning of the century. The voluntary sickness benefits societies had thrived under government sponsorship but there were too great differences in benefits between various societies and the benefits were in most cases insufficient. Besides, the coverage was, by far, not universal in the voluntary system. Consequently the parliament passed an act in 1947 providing for compulsory health insurance. After some delay the national health insurance programme went into effect in 1955.

By 1960 the cornerstones of Sweden´s social insurance system had been laid. The reforms to come were characterized as extensions and improvements: better coordination of programmes, more generous benefits and so on. New important parts of the social insurance system were introduced in the mid 1970´s. Cash labour market assistance was introduced in 1974 as a complement to the voluntary unemployment insurance. Its benefits are available for uninsured workers and are based on attachment to the labour market. As such they can be claimed as a right.

One important aspect of sick pay had been maternity coverage. Up to 1974 there was a lump sum benefit plus a cash benefit for a total of 6 months. In 1974 maternity benefit was replaced by a broader programme of parent benefits (available for both parents). A general dental insurance was also introduced in 1974 as a part of the health insurance programme. Finally, in 1976, a bill on partial pension was passed. According to that law working people between the ages of 60 and 65 can be compensated for loss of income due to voluntary partial retirement.

3. THE SOCIAL INSURANCE PROGRAMMES

3.1 Health Insurance

The health insurance programme is divided into two major parts namely medical care and sickness cash benefits. Health care is available to the whole population while cash sickness payments is available to working people as a compensation for income loss during periods of sickness. The third part of health insurance consists of parental benefits.

As regards medical care the health insurance programme pays for some of the cost of medical treatment. The rules for how much a patient will have to pay depend on the doctor consulted. The rules distinguish between doctors employed by the county councils, private practitioners affiliated to the health insurance system and private practitioners not taking part in the health insurance scheme. For the first two groups the patient is charged a very low fee while he for a treatment by a doctor of the third group has to pay full cost. This third group is however small.

Dental insurance covers everybody from the year of their 20th birthday. (Persons under the age of twenty receive free dental care through the public dental health service.) The patient never pays more than half the cost of a visit to the dentist if the charge for the full course of treatment comes to less than 2 500 SEK and not more than one quarter of the amount in excess of this figure.

Swedish hospitals are run by the county councils. The health insurance pays part of the cost direct to the county council for every day treatment is given. The patient himself pays nothing for this service although the cash sickness payments, if any, will be reduced by a small amount.

There is a diversity of services within medical care. Besides the above mentioned, the health insurance programme also pays for at least some of the costs of, for instance, nursing, physiotherapy and related treatment, testing and fitting of aids for the handicapped, travel fares, and all costs for contraception and abortion. Prescribed medicines can also be obtained through the insurance scheme, either at a reduced price or free of charge.

Before describing sickness cash benefits the concept "basic amount" will be introduced. The basic amount, which is frequently used in Sweden´s social insurance system, is an artificially designated amount of money, which is indexed to the cost of living. The basic amount is determined for each month and is seen as some kind of minimum of subsistence per annum. In June 1981 the basic amount was 17 300 SEK. (From 1982 the basic amount is changed only once a year, for 1983 it is 19 700 SEK.)

A person is entitled to "sickness cash benefits" if his capacity for work is reduced by at least half as a result of illness. Those who are unable or are not allowed to work receive the full amount of sickness benefits. For half normal working hours or less, half the benefit is received.

There is no time limit for sickness benefits unless the sick person is granted a pension instead. One of the duties of the insurance offices is to inquire whether the person who is reported sick needs special assistance in order to be able to start working again. This special inquiry is made after 90 days´ continued illness.

As a rule sickness cash benefits are paid out from the day following that on which the illness was reported. If the time of illness lasts more than a week a medical certificate is required in order to qualify.

The amount of sickness benefits depends on income loss. The lowest income which gives entitlement to benefits is 6 000 SEK per annum while the highest which will affect their size is 7.5 times the basic amount in January each year (1981: 120 000 SEK). The maximum sickness benefit per day is 90% of the income on which the benefit is based divided by 365 (the number of days per year). The benefits are taxable and qualify for pension payments under the ATP supplementary pensions scheme.

Parental benefits following the birth of a child are payable for a maximum of 180 days to the parent who abstains from work for taking care of the child. The parents themselves make the decision as to how they are to divide this time. The benefits are payable to the mother up to 60 days before the birth. Parents' benefits normally amount to the same rates as sickness cash benefits.

Special parental benefits are payable for days above 180 days following the birth of a child when a parent abstains from work for taking care of the child. The special benefits are in principle given half to the father and half to the mother. For the first 90 days the benefits are at the same rate as the sickness cash benefits and for a further 90 days the benefits are 37 SEK for each full day. Special parental benefits can be claimed up to the child's eighth birthday.

Parental benefits for temporary care of a child are paid out if a parent has to stay away from work in order to look after a sick child. Parents are entitled to this benefit for up to 60 days per year for every child under the age of twelve.

The health insurance programme is administered by 27 semi-autonomous regional social insurance funds at the county level. These funds, which have their roots in the voluntary sickness benefits societies, are supervised by the National Insurance Board which establishes and enforces regulations and policies in accordance with the law. The social insurance funds and their offices also administer other social insurance programmes with the exception of the unemployment insurance scheme. The decisions of the funds and of the National board can be appealed against to special social insurance courts.

3.2 The Basic Pension

There are three major kinds of benefits included in the basic pension. The three types are old-age, disability and family pensions. The basic pension, which is universal in coverage, provides flat-rate benefits regardless of previous work.

The age of retirement in Sweden is 65. Old-age pension may be drawn as early as age 60 but then the benefit will be reduced by a 0.5 per cent for every month under 65. At the age of 60 the pension will consequently be 70 per cent of a normal pension. This lower amount will be paid out during the remaining life-time. Retirement may also be postponed to the age of 70 and the benefit then increases by 0.6 per cent for every month over age 65. The pension in this case will be 136 per cent of a normal pension.

All pensions in Sweden are calculated from the basic amount. A full old-age pension is 95 per cent of the basic amount for single persons and 155 per cent for pensioned couples.

Disability pensions are payable when a person's work capacity is reduced by at least one half. It is payable between the age of 16 and 65. At the latter age it is replaced by old-age pensions. The full benefit is 95 per cent of the basic amount. Lesser benefits are proportionate to the degree of disability. The work capacity is decided by the officers of the regional

social insurance funds. Their decisions are based on doctor´s certificates.
They can be appealed against to the social insurance courts.

Family pensions include provision for widows and orphans. A widow´s pension
is payable to a widow over 36 years old who has been married at least five
years prior to the husband´s death. If she was at least 50 at the time of
the husband´s death she will receive full benefit, 95 per cent of the basic
amount. This is reduced for every year under 50, except that if she has a
child under 16 there is no deduction. A child under 18 whose father or
mother is dead receives at least 25 per cent of the basic amount. More can
be paid out if the benefits from the general supplementary pension are
small.

Beside the basic pension, there is in Sweden a separate benefit payable to
those who voluntarily reduce their working time between the ages of 60 and
65. The partial pension compensates 50 per cent of the difference between
the former income (maximum is 7.5 times the basic amount) and the income
after partial retirement. To qualify for partial pension one has to have
earned a pension-bearing income for at least 10 years since the age of 45.

3.3 The General Supplementary Pension (ATP)

The general supplementary pension, known in Sweden as ATP, is work-based
and compulsory. It is payable in addition to the basic pension and includes
survivor´s and disability benefits as well as retirement payments.

For the old age pension the normal age of retirement is, as for the basic
pension, 65 with the same possibility of early or postponed retirement. One
qualifying condition for the supplementary pension is that one must have
earned a pension-bearing income for three years. The pension-bearing income
is that part of the income from gainful occupation which lies between the
basic amount and 7.5 times this amount.

For each year that a person receives a pension-bearing income he is cred-
ited with a certain number of pension points. The pension points are
obtained by dividing the pension-bearing income by the basic amount at the
beginning of the year. The amount of pension is determined by the average
of the pension points accumulated or, if points should have been accumulated for more than 15 years, the average for the 15 best years. To calculate the pension one multiplies the average number of pension points by the
basic amount for the month for which the pension is paid out. Thus, the
average pension-bearing income has been brought up to current value. A full
pension, according to the main rule, requires 30 years´ contribution and
represents 60 % of the average pension-bearing income. The pension is
reduced by one-thirtieth for every year less than thirty. For persons born
before 1924 transitory rules are in use.

The prerequisites for disability pension are the same as for the basic pension. For the amounts, the rules are, in principle, the same as for the
supplementary old age pension. Pension points in this case, however, can be
gained not only by points actually earned but also by the computation of
what are called "assumed points". It is, so to say, assumed that a disabled
person would have gained a certain amount of points up to the age of 65.
The level of pay is based upon the degree of reduction of working capacity.
Those who have lost all or nearly all of their working capacity receive the
full pension.

If on his decease a man was in receipt of a supplementary pension or would have qualified for such a pension by the pension points he had earned, his widow and children are entitled to a family pension. The qualifying conditions for a widow's pension (there is no widower's pension) are that the marriage has lasted for at least 5 years and was contracted before the deceased attained the age of 60 or that the deceased left children who are also children of the widow. Children's pensions are payable to dependent children under the age of 19. The family pension is calculated on the basis of the pension which the deceased was entitled to receive. A widow without children or a single child without parents receives 40 per cent of the deceased's pension. In addition to this 10 per cent of the deceased's pension is payable for each child.

3.4 Supplementary pension programmes

Beside the basic pension and the general supplementary pension there are other benefits for retired and disabled persons within the social insurance system.

The Pension supplement is paid to those pensioners who receive nothing or only a small amount under the general supplementary pension scheme. A pensioner is always guaranteed an income equivalent to 140 % of the basic amount which means that the pension supplement is 45 % of the basic amount when general supplementary pension is not payable. If the supplementary pension is payable the pension supplement is reduced correspondingly. The corresponding guaranteed income for a pensioned couple is 245 % of the basic amount and, for a person who receives disability pension, 185 %.

To low-income pensioners there are also means tested supplements available such as family supplement for children, wife's supplement and housing supplements. The housing supplements are the most important. They cover most of the rent for almost half the retired population.

The Handicap allowance is a benefit available to disabled persons regardless of income. It is payable to a person who before the age of 65 requires much assistance from another person or has heavy expenses due to this handicap. The amount of the allowance depends on need and extra expenses (the upper limit is 60 % of the basic amount).

A child care allowance equal to full disability pension is payable to the parent mainly responsible for care of a child under 16 who because of handicap needs special supervision and care of an extensive nature. This benefit is available regardless of income. In normal cases the care allowance is turned into disability pension for the child when it reaches the age of 16.

3.5 Work Injury Insurance

The work injury insurance is compulsory and universal in coverage. It is administered by the regional social insurance funds.

Work injuries comprise accidents occurring in connection with a person's employment and occupational diseases. Accidents occurring on the way to or from work are also included in this category. There are in the work injury insurance programme four forms of compensation, namely sickness cash benefits, medical care, life-annuities and funeral allowance.

Work injury insurance is co-ordinated with health insurance during the so called co-ordination period. This covers the first 90 days after the work injury. During this period sickness cash benefits are paid through the health insurance. After the co-ordination time sickness cash benefits are raised to the same level as the former income (up to a maximum of 7.5 times the basic amount) and are paid by the work injury insurance.

During the co-ordination period medical care is also paid through health insurance. After that all essential expenses for medical and hospital treatment are paid by the work injury insurance. The cost of spectacles, artificial limbs, etc. is reimbursed through work injury insurance even during the co-ordination period.

A person is entitled to life-annuity if his capacity to earn an income is reduced due to work injury. The important thing here is the income loss, not the degree of disablement in itself. The basic principle is that 100% compensation is granted which means that the life-annuity covers the gap between the former income (up to a maximum of 7.5 times the basic amount) and the actual income after the work injury (which for instance can be the disability pension described under headings 3.2 and 3.3).

In case of death resulting from work injury life-annuities to survivors are in broad outline paid out according to the same principles as for the basic pension. A funeral allowance is also paid out in this case. This is the only kind of funeral allowance in Sweden's social insurance system.

3.6 Unemployment Insurance

Unemployment insurance in Sweden has traditionally been managed by unemployment relief funds connected with trade unions (there are some 45 funds) under the supervision of the National Labour Market Board. Unemployment insurance is thus quite separate from other social insurance programmes. Contributions to the funds are shared by employees, employers and the state. The government subsidy varies considerably between funds, especially according to rate of unemployment.

A claimant must have been a member of the fund for 12 months and must have been in work for at least 5 of the 12 months prior to the period of assistance. The claimant must also have applied to the Employment Exchange and must not refuse suitable work. Another qualifying condition is that unemployment is involuntary.

The members of a fund are placed in daily benefit categories between 80 SEK and 210 SEK (1983:90-280). The maximum benefit payable amounts to 91.7 per cent of the individual's normal wage in his occupation. Unemployment benefits, like most social insurance benefits such as sickness cash benefits and pensions, are taxable.

In recent years the daily benefits have not been raised as much as the average wages which means that there is an increasing degree of undercompensation.

Daily benefits are payable for 5 days a week and for a maximum of 300 days (60 weeks), for persons aged 55-65 450 days. The first five days of unemployment constitute the qualifying period. Such a qualifying period does not exist in other parts of the social insurance system.

3.7 Cash Labour Market Assistance

Cash labour market assistance is payable to persons who are not insured against unemployment or who are insured but have not yet qualified for benefits or have lost entitlement to benefits on reaching the age of 60 (in some cases 55).

The assistance is a flat grant of 75 SEK a day (1983:100). The duration of benefit varies with age: 150 days up to age 55, 300 days from age 55 to 60 and an indefinite period between ages 60 and 65. Like unemployment insurance the benefits are payable 5 days a week and are taxable. The qualifying period is also in this case 5 days.

The qualifying conditions are in many respects the same as in unemployment insurance. In cases of unemployment after education or training, the employment condition (at least 5 months´ work during the 12 months´ immediately preceding unemployment) is replaced by a condition that the claimant has been registered as seeking employment for 3 months.

3.8 Sources of Finance

One salient feature in Sweden´s social insurance system is the importance of employers´ contributions as a source of finance. This can be seen in table 1.

Contributions paid by insured persons play a minor part as a source of finance in all schemes but unemployment insurance. In other schemes contributions paid by insured refer to some kind of voluntary supplements or to contributions from self-employed persons.

Central government grants cover administration expenses and, together with local government grants, special benefits like housing supplements to pensioners. Only in unemployment insurance do government grants finance a considerable portion of the benefits.

Employers´ contributions to the different schemes are proportional, and uniformly so, to wages paid out. They are calculated on the total sum of wages and salaries, paid out by the same employer and not attributed to the individuals. As these contributions are compulsory and not variable according to any type of risk, they might be regarded as taxes rather than insurance premiums. This is definitely the case for the "basic pension fees" which are not connected with the benefits at all. All social insurance fees are paid together in a lump sum every second month (1982: abt. 33 % of wages and salaries).

Historically, funds have been accumulated in all the schemes. For the basic pension, accumulation of reserves has, however, terminated. In health insurance, work injury insurance and unemployment insurance the purpose of the funds is to meet any unforeseen and exceptional excess of payments over income. The ATP-fund is meant to be consumed in the decades round the year 2000 when the older groups will be comparatively numerous, whereafter the programme can become a downright pay-as-you-go-system. The reason for

Table 1. Sources of finance 1978. Per cent distribution

	Central government grants	Local government grants	Employers´ contributions	Contributions paid by insured	Interest, funds etc	Total
Health insurance	14.4	-	83.7	0.1	1.8	100
Basic pensions (incl supplements)	25.0	8.6	63.0[1]	3.1[1]	0.3	100
General supplementary pensions (ATP)	-	-	63.1	2.2	34.7	100
Work injury insurance	4.4	-	95.4	-	0.2	100
Unemployment insurance incl labour market cash assistance	51.4	-	32.4	12.6	3.6	100

Source: Statistical Abstract of Sweden 1980

[1] The benefits are paid by the state out of general revenue. The contributions are not earmarked for the benefits but are in reality a pay-roll tax.

establishing the fund (1960) was, however, mainly to ensure that the total savings would not decrease when earlier pension plans were replaced by the ATP-programme. The fund now plays an important role in the Swedish capital market. The size of the reserve amounts to more than 200 billion SEK. Most of the assets are housing credits and loans to industrial companies. Government bonds are of course also important. A minor part is placed as shares in industrial companies.

3.9 Some Basic Characteristics of the Swedish System

The description of the Swedish system of social insurance has demonstrated some basic characteristics in the system:

1) With the exception of unemployment insurance, the programmes are compulsory and universal in coverage. Unemployment insurance administered by special funds connected with trade unions has a long, and strong, tradition in Sweden. In principle at least, unemployment insurance is voluntary. In practice, however, it is compulsory since almost all workers and officials are members of unions and unions have as a rule made membership in the unemployment insurance funds compulsory for their members. Together with

its complement, the labour market cash assistance, unemployment insurance has a universal coverage (this does of course not mean that all persons in the labour market are eligible to unemployment benefits).

2) The goal of the Swedish programmes is to provide basic security for the whole population and an almost full compensation for income losses within the average wage range. In this case, too, unemployment insurance differs from the rest of the programmes because of the waiting period and the maximum duration of unemployment benefits (in normal cases 60 weeks).

3) Means-tested benefits are rare nowadays. They only exist for certain pension supplements.

4) The widely use of the "basic amount" means that the majority of cash benefits are guarded against inflation.

5) Cash benefits are, in normal cases, taxable. This fact is intimately bound up with high marginal taxes prevailing in Sweden. If for instance net sickness cash benefits amounted to 90% of net wages it would, in certain cases, mean an effective compensation of more than 100 % as a person would get not only sickness cash benefits but a lower income tax as well.

6) The dominant source of finance is employers´ contributions. In an early stage of development of social insurance, contributions paid by in-sured played an important role. Today, they are of no importance except in unemployment insurance. Even there they only finance a small percentage of the benefits.

7) Contributions according to risk exist only for members´ contributions to unemployment insurance funds. Employers´ contributions are paid as a percentage of total payroll. Today the total is about 33%. No form of merit rating exists in the Swedish system.

8) Contributions (even though they in fact are taxes) and objectivity in payment give the Swedish system its insurance character. Welfare aspects like equalization have played an important part in the construction of the system. This is most evidently seen in the (almost complete) absence of risk differentiated contributions and in programmes like medical care, basic pensions and survivors´ benefits. The welfare goals of the system have sometimes been so predominant that events that hardly can be connected with risk or insurance, like parental benefits, are included in the system.

4. TOWARDS A GENERAL SOCIAL INSURANCE SYSTEM

For some years it has been customary in Sweden to regard as social insur-ance benefits all (or nearly all) social cash benefits not being condi-tional on need. Undoubtedly social insurance is widely held to be a concept of honour in Sweden.

The total system of social cash benefits consists of (1) benefits to famil-lies and children (in addition to all general family allowance and parental benefits), (2) study assistance, (3) pay and other benefits to national servicemen, (4) housing allowances, (5) benefits in case of sickness and disability, (6) benefits in case of unemployment (including training allow-ance and relocation assistance), (7) benefits to retired persons and to adult survivors and (8) means tested social assistance. The social insur-

ance system, as defined in part 3 ((5) to (7) above + parental benefits)
accounts for about 80 per cent of the total expenditure on social benefits.

The social benefit system in Sweden may not be very complicated when
compared with many other countries, but for the ordinary Swedish citizen it
is complicated enough and difficult to survey. The differences between the
different programmes are not always rational. Some examples may serve as
illustrations.

There are different concepts of "income" used: sometimes the last taxable
income, sometimes current income, sometimes calculated future income.
Eligibility rules are badly harmonized: some children´s allowances go on to
the age of 16, others to 18, others to 19; the rules for widow´s pension
are different in different programmes. There are different rates of compensation for events where the need for cash benefit is the same, for instance
in sickness and unemployment. For sickness cash benefits the week has seven
days, for unemployment benefits only five. In the light of this an official
report has proposed the introduction of a uniform and simplified system of
general social insurance.

According to the report the proposed social insurance system would consist
of four main programmes: (1) Income insurance for income losses due to
sickness and pregnancy, care of children, unemployment, adult education,
military service, disability, old age and loss of breadwinner; (2) Child
allowances; (3) Housing allowances; (4) Handicap allowances.

This is not the place for a detailed description of the proposed social insurance system. Suffice it to say that the proposal clearly indicates the
need for co-ordination and simplification of the Swedish system of social
benefits and the evolution of the concept of social insurance.

5. LABOUR MARKET INSURANCES

Long before the social insurances were introduced the civil servants, some
categories of workers in public service, and many salaried employees in the
private sector were covered by programmes which gave them security in old
age and in case of illness. The social insurances can be seen as a way of
spreading those privileges to the rest of the population. But the social
insurances did not give the receivers quite as much as the former privileged groups got (and still get). That is one of the reasons why the trade
union movement in Sweden since the beginning of the 1960´s has submitted
claims for insurance benefits to be included under the terms of collective
agreements.

These claims have resulted in the introduction of a group life insurance
scheme in 1963 (in Sweden called TGL), a severance pay in 1965 (AGB), a
sick pay and disability pension insurance in 1972 (AGS), a complementary
pension insurance in 1973 (STP) and a Labour Market no-fault liability insurance in 1974 (TFA). These five insurances are seen as important complements to the national social insurance system and might as well, under
other circumstances, have been incorporated in that system. They, so to
say, represent a new way of handling the protection against certain risks
which traditionally belong to the sphere of social insurance.

The five insurances are based on the fact that agreements are in existence.
If agreements exist, these constitute a guarantee quite apart from the pay-

ment of premiums. The wide coverage of collective agreement in Sweden means that practically all workers are covered by the schemes. The schemes are administered by two companies in which the parties of the labour market have equal holdings.

The group life insurance scheme, TGL, provides for lump sum payments to surviving members of the family in the event of death. The size of benefits depends upon hours of work, length of employment, age and dependents. Benefits are adjusted to ensure a stable value and are calculated on the basis of the basic amount. The maximum level of pay during a year is 6 times the basic amount of November the year before. There are also special children´s benefits which are payable for each child under the age of 20.

The severance pay, AGB, is designed to protect workers when a firm has to make cuts in its labour force or closes down. A worker is entitled to AGB if he is over 40, has worked for five consecutive years for the same employer and has worked 4 full AGB-years (one AGB-year is at least 832 working hours during a calendar year). There are two levels of pay. The A-benefit amounts to 2 000 SEK for 4 full AGB-years and a further 200 SEK for every additional AGB-year in the labour market. The B-benefit is payable to those who remain unemployed over a long period. The maximum level here is 18 000 SEK.

AGS, the sick pay and disability pension insurance, offers supplementary benefits if a worker is sick for 31 days or more. The supplement is paid for the entire period of sickness up to the age of 65. During the sickness benefits period a small uniform amount is paid per day regardless of income lost. To a worker who is receiving a disability pension from national social insurance the AGS supplement depends upon the income lost.

The complementary pension insurance, STP, complements the national basic pension and the supplementary pensions benefits under the ATP scheme. The basic rule requires that a person has worked for at least 30 years for full STP-benefits. If he has not, the pension will be reduced. The STP-benefits are 10 per cent of the pensionable income which is calculated on the basis of the three best years between the ages 55 and 59. It applies to pensioners born 1911 or later.

TFA, the Labour Market no-fault liability insurance, covers injuries caused by accidents at work, injuries suffered while travelling to or from work and industrial disease lasting longer than 90 days. The TFA scheme compensates for net losses, i.e. for expenses and loss of income remaining after subtraction of national insurance benefits. Compensation can also be obtained for pain and suffering and, if a worker becomes an invalid, for disablement and other inconveniences suffered.

The premium for the above mentioned schemes are paid by the employers as a percentage of wages paid out. All social benefits arrived at through legislation and agreements represent approximately 39 % of a workers wage. The proportions are 33.4 % for benefits via legislation and 5.4 % for benefits via agreements.

As a supplement to the national unemployment insurance there has been in Sweden since 1964, besides the severance pay, an agreement between the Swedish Employers´ Federation and the unions that wages shall be paid out during periods of temporary lay-offs. These periods are often not covered by unemployment insurance benefits because of the waiting period (5 days).

Wages during temporary lay-offs are not paid out when a worker is qualified for unemployment insurance benefits. This means that, in normal cases, the wage is paid out for a maximum time of five days a year.

If a temporary lay-off lasts more than two consecutive weeks (or in total 30 days during a calendar year) a worker is entitled to his normal wage according to a law of 1973. The purpose of the law is obviously to reduce the amount of temporary lay-offs.

In cases of temporary lay-offs the benefit situation is quite complicated. Let us, to make it simple, assume a three weeks´ period of unemployment due to a temporary lay-off. During the first week the unemployed worker gets his wage through agreement, during the second week he receives unemployment insurance benefits and during the third week he gets his wage through legislation. The trade unions are working for agreement or legislation that would ensure the workers full wage paid by the employer during all temporary lay-offs. This would give the workers the same position as the salaried employees have. The present situation must be seen as half-way to that aim.

The earlier privileged groups also have adjusted their benefits to the social insurances by collective agreements. (In Sweden almost all salaries are settled by agreement, even for civil servants of higher ranks, military officers, clergymen and others.) The extra benefits for sickness are not very important but the pension rules give substantial supplements.

For public employees the supplement is constructed as a "gross pension" which means that the pensioner is guaranteed 65 % of his/her income on retirement. The government pays the whole pension and gets from the National Insurance Board the basic pension (Fp) and the ATP-pension to which the receiver is entitled (for the central government this is of course a matter of book-keeping). No fees are calculated. There are two systems, one for the state employees (SPV) and another for people employed by local authorities (KPA). They do not differ very much from each other.

Private employees get their public pension from the National Insurance Board and the private pension from a special institution. There are some minor systems but the majority get their benefits (ITP) from a mutual insurance company which is owned by the employers insured. The ITP-pensions are financed through a premium-reserve-system like commercial insurance policies. The fees are calculated individually. No deduction is made from the salaries but the existence of the ITP-pensions is obviously taken into consideration when the salaries are settled. The ITP-pensions, like the SPV- and KPA-pensions, give the difference between the public pensions and 65 % of the previous income.

All the supplementary pensions (also STP) are in one way or another tied to the "basic amount" and thus have their purchasing power secured.

The outcome of the different pension programmes is shown in Figure 1. It will give an approximative picture of the pensions in different income brackets and also some idea of the effect of the tax rules. See Figure 1.

6. CONCLUDING REMARKS

The social insurance expenditures in 1980 were about 83 billion SEK. The

Figure 1. Public and Private Pensions in Sweden

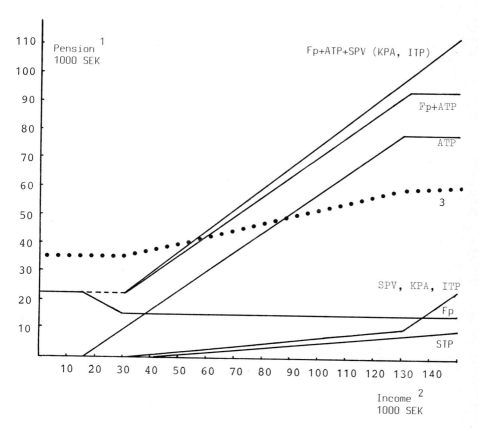

¹ Pension for single person.

² For ATP, mean value of "15 best years" in relation to the basic amount for that year. For STP, mean value of 3 best years between 55 and 59. For the other pensions, last year before retiring. Figures in "1981 money".

³ Fp + ATP + housing supplement after tax. Housing supplement is locally decided. It is usually equal to the actual rent up to a certain limit. 12 000 SEK a year is a common amount (most pensioners have lower rent).

N.B. A common income for an industrial worker is 70 000 SEK/year. Some have less, many have more. A university professor gets about 150 000. (After tax, 46 000 and 69 000 respectively, if no other income and no special tax deductions). Most married couples have two incomes, all have two pensions (a housewife always getting the basic pension).

The figure does not give exact values. It is meant to give a fair approximation.

amounts for the different programmes are shown in table 2.

Table 2. Social insurance payments 1980 (million SEK)

Health insurance	26 134
Basic pensions (incl supplements)	34 473
General supplementary pensions	19 028
Work injury insurance	1 219
Unemployment insurance (incl labour market cash assistance)	2 051
Total	82 905

The total expenditure corresponds to about 16 per cent of the Swedish GNP. A substantial part is, however, paid back in taxes.

Since the Second World War there has been a substantial expansion of social insurance payments, not only in absolute amounts but also as a percentage of GNP. The 1970´s seem, for the moment, to be the last expansionary decade. New reforms were launched and improvements in existing benefits were made. The national economic situation in the years ahead will definitely hamper growth. There will probably be no major reforms (such as a compulsory unemployment insurance which has been proposed), benefits will not be raised as in the past and the rate of compensation will consequently probably be lower (for instance due to an income maximum of 7.5 times the basic amount in some programmes). In some cases eligibility rules will perhaps be tightened up (for instance through the introduction of a waiting period for sickness cash benefits).

In the light of the current financial situation it is probable that a further expansion of benefits, if any, will take place for labour market insurances. As more and more wage-earners reach maximum compensation limits in the social insurance system, labour market insurances will compensate a bigger portion of income losses. Consequently, labour market insurances will in the future probably play a more important role in the total benefit system.

FOOTNOTES

*   University of Lund.

REFERENCES

Andersson, K.-O. (1979), Arbetsmarknadshandboken (Labour Market Handbook), Stockholm.

Bruzelius, A., Danielsson,G. and Åström, L.Å. (1981), Sociallagarna - Socialförsäkring (Social Law - Social Insurance), Lund.

Edebalk, P.G. (1975), Arbetslöshetsförsäkringsdebatten (The Debate around Unemployment Insurance), Lund.

Edebalk, P.G. (1973), Socialförsäkring - några principer (Social Insurance - Some Principles), Lund.

Elmér, Å. (1960), Folkpensioneringen i Sverige (The National Old-age Pensions Scheme in Sweden), Malmö.

Elmér, Å. (1981), Svensk socialpolitik (Swedish Welfare Policy), Lund.

Månadsstatistik för allmän försäkring och arbetsskadeförsäkring mm (Monthly Statistical data concerning the Swedish National Insurance Scheme, Work Injury Insurance etc.) 1981:4, Stockholm.

SOU 1979:94. En allmän socialförsäkring (A General Social Insurance), Stockholm.

Statistisk årsbok (Statistical Abstract of Sweden) 1980, Stockholm.

ARNE RYDE SYMPOSIUM ON SOCIAL INSURANCE
L. Söderström (editor)
© Elsevier Science Publishers B.V. (North-Holland), 1983

THE WELFARE ECONOMICS OF PUBLIC HEALTH INSURANCE: THEORY AND CANADIAN PRACTICE

R.G. Evans*

1. INTRODUCTION: PUBLIC HEALTH INSURANCE IN CANADA

Two pieces of federal legislation, the Hospital Insurance and Diagnostic Services Act of 1957 and the Medical Care Act of 1966, form the cornerstones of the Canadian public health insurance system.[1] These Acts set out the terms and conditions which public hospital and medical insurance programs established by the ten provincial governments must meet in order to be eligible for financial contributions (of roughly 50% of costs) by the federal government.[2] In the Medical Care Act these conditions were summarized in four principles, which had previously been enunciated by Prime Minister Pearson in 1965. A conforming provincial medical insurance plan is required to be:

Comprehensive in scope of benefits,

Universal in its coverage of all provincial residents on equal terms and conditions,

Publicly Administered by a government agency or commission rather than by private firms, for profit or otherwise, and

Portable across provincial boundaries when beneficiaries are temporarily away from home or move between provinces.

The public health insurance programs themselves are established by the provincial governments, because constitutional authority over health matters is allocated to them rather than the federal government. But the leverage of 50% federal cost-sharing was sufficiently strong that all provinces which did not previously have a conforming program established one at or shortly after the date on which federal legislation became effective. Hospital insurance coverage was thus complete across Canada by 1961, and medical care coverage by 1971.[3]

Under the Medicare program, medical services in or out of hospitals, GP or specialist, are reimbursed by direct payments from the provincial agency to the individual physician according to a schedule of fees negotiated period-

ically between each provincial medical association and the insuring agency.
The patient is not in general billed for services used, although some provinces permit physicians to charge amounts additional to the provincial payment ("double-billing") while others permit physicians to bill their patients directly at rates of their own choosing, and then reimburse the patients at the negotiated rate ("opting-out"). Still others permit neither.
In total dollars such direct charges are quite small,[4] although they remain
a very contentious political issue as both their advocates (primarily
medical associations) and their opponents (virtually everyone else) view
them as a way of undermining the present form of insurance and moving
toward multiple-source funding.[5]

Hospitals, on the other hand, are reimbursed for their operating costs
through global budgets negotiated annually on a prospective basis and subject to end-of-year settlement. Individual hospitals work out with the provincial insurance agency a projected patient load and approved service
pattern, and an associated requirement for staff and supplies. Matched with
wage and price forecasts, this forms the basis for the annual budget. Each
individual province has developed over the years techniques of greater or
lesser sophistication for this budget projection process; nowhere is it
considered wholly satisfactory but better alternatives are not obvious.[6] Of
particular importance, however, is the fact that such budgets not only
avoid reimbursement by service unit (whether cost or charge based), with
its obvious incentives for multiplication of procedures subject to economies of scale (diagnostic tests), but also reimburse only operating expense. Capital funding, - buildings, beds, and major equipment - is provided separately, shared between provincial and regional governments, so
that control over system capacity and technological evolution is much more
effective than when an external regulator confronts an independent hospital
with its own (or privately borrowed) money to spend.[7]

The conditions of eligibility for cost sharing under the Hospital Insurance
and Diagnostic Services Act were essentially similar to the four principles
of the Medical Care Act, and were in fact embodied in a much more detailed
contractual agreement. But the "Four Points" in the Medicare program were
accorded much more prominence in the debate over the extension of public
insurance from hospital to medical care. A number of alternative approaches
to medical insurance had been suggested, and indeed strongly advocated in
various interested quarters, many of the arguments being the same as have
surfaced in the periodic fruitless U.S. debates over "National Health Insurance".[8] The final choice of program design was based on a massive report
by the Royal Commission on Health Services (Hall Commission) (Canada, 1964)
which from 1961 to 1964 conducted hearings across Canada and commissioned
an extensive series of background studies on specific aspects of medical
insurance and medical care delivery.

The "Four Points" thus represent the result of an extended process of analysis and advocacy, of canvassing and comparing alternatives, and of reflecting on the experience of existing insurance programs. Judging by the
public response to a special review of the system in 1980, conducted by
Justice Hall at the request of the Canadian Minister of National Health and
Welfare (Hall, 1980), these principles have stood the test of time rather
well. Health care is a turbulent political field in every country, but Canadians who make cross-national comparisons find themselves relatively very
well served.

While the principles expressed in the "Four Points" are viewed as fundamental by those who deliver, administer, or study health care in Canada, it is striking that they find no reflection in the conventional economic analyses of health insurance. In theoretical treatments, insurance is insurance is insurance, despite the conviction of practitioners that how you do it matters enormously in determining its effects. Attempts to provide a theoretical basis for discussions of universal public insurance in the U.S., for example, have proceeded with models which impose as assumptions program characteristics derived from private, for profit insurance models. Public insurance is treated as if it were merely an extension of private coverage, perhaps in a more comprehensive form, to the entire population; and studies of its impact on resource allocation and wealth distribution are made on this basis. The analytic "results" are usually unfavourable to universal public insurance, as well as strikingly different from actual Canadian experience.

It might, of course, be possible to design a public health insurance system as a generalization or scaling-up of private, for-profit models, but it is hard to see why anyone in his right mind (other than an insurance salesman) would wish to do so. Public health insurance in Canada is qualitatively different from the programs envisioned in theoretical analyses of health insurance, in ways which were consciously and deliberately chosen. In consequence it has had a social impact, including resource allocation and wealth distribution but going well beyond these, which is much more favourable than that predicted by such analyses. This performance is believed by most Canadians to be much superior to that generated by the very different forms of health care organization and payment which have evolved (from rather similar starting points) in the past quarter century in the U.S., and available data appear to bear out this view (Evans, 1980b, 1982).

In this paper we shall interpret the "Four Points" from an economic perspective, in terms of their impact on resource allocation and wealth distribution. Their socio-political significance is perhaps even greater, as they determine the characteristics of the largest single public program in each province, touching directly the greatest number of citizens, often at critical and sensitive points in their lives. The importance of Canada's health insurance system as an expression of a fundamental equality of all citizens in confronting illness and death, and the general hostility to "multi-class medicine", are not just political rhetoric. But the economic dimension has a number of interesting characteristics of its own.

The requirements of universality and comprehensiveness of coverage on "equal terms and conditions" means that provincial programs must be compulsory, de facto if not de jure. Combined with the requirement of public, not-for-profit administration, this establishes in each province a public monopoly over the insurance function. In some provinces this is achieved by funding the whole program from general tax revenue; in others there remains a system of public "premiums" partially related to income class. But private insurers are not permitted to sell insurance in competition with the public plans.

In those provinces still using a premium system for part of program finance, most premiums are either paid by the employer (as a taxable benefit) or deducted from wages along with income taxes and other compulsory social levies. Most of the population therefore follows the national income accountants in regarding premiums, where they exist, as part of the tax system. Consistent with this view, premiums are partly or fully subsidized

for elderly or low income people. Indeed (although it is not widely pub-
licized) people whose coverage has lapsed remain de facto eligible for
care. Later efforts may or may not be made to recover from them. In any
case, costs of coverage cannot be related to expectation of use ("equal
terms and conditions") except in the rather different sense that family
premiums are larger than individual ones.

Portability is merely an aspect of universality, although it is politically
significant as a way of preventing provincial governments from discrimi-
nating against non-residents or recent arrivals. Public administration does
not necessarily follow from universality and "equal terms and conditions";
one might imagine a private monopoly (presumably regulated) or even a group
of private carriers, all required to provide open enrollment and identical
comprehensive coverage. This was in fact a transitional stage in several
provinces. But the private carriers had no real function in such an
environment - nothing to market, no rates to set, no one to screen.
Moreover, they stood in the way of more active public management, in particular by blocking the assembly of delivery system information, and had a
continuing vested interest, of their own and on behalf of providers, in the
deterioration and "reprivatization" of the insurance system.

Universality and comprehensiveness can be interpreted as excluding any form
of direct charges to patients, although this is an area of active debate.
Some advocates of such charges argue for their "deterrent" effect, presumably implying that care is overutilized at the margin, but deterrence is
generally viewed as conflicting with universality and comprehensivity and
is politically suspect. Accordingly other advocates have argued that such
charges do not deter, at least not those in need; they therefore try
to make the case for direct charges on equity or quality enhancement
grounds.[9] The whole area is characterized by more rhetoric than either evidence or analysis (although what there is of the latter does not seem to
support any of the pro-charges arguments). It is, however, safe to say that
universality and comprehensiveness are agreed to mean either no direct
charges, or not very large ones. And of course the public programs place no
upper limits on coverage in general, though specific services such as ambulatory fee-for-service psychiatric visits or preventive check-ups are
restricted as to (reimbursable) frequency. Comprehensiveness is interpreted
to include all necessary hospital and medical care, as judged by a licensed
practitioner, although the concept becomes rather strained as provincial
agencies try to determine the boundaries of coverage and the different
types of health practitioners who qualify for reimbursement.

In summary, however, and subject to certain minor exceptions, everyone is
insured, qualifying either by residence or (in some provinces) on payment
of a uniform premium. Contributions are related neither to expected risk
nor to utilization experience; and the hospital and medical insurance system in each province is a public monopoly, a sort of public utility. The
structure is one which theoretical economic analyses routinely demonstrate
to be unsatisfactory, yet it works, and (in relative terms) works very well
indeed. Why?

2. RISK AVERSION VS. MORAL HAZARD: THE CONVENTIONAL MODEL

Theoretical analyses of health insurance tend to focus on the tradeoff between its positive impact in reducing the level of risk faced by potential
illness sufferers, and its negative effects in increasing the overall ex-

pected loss associated with unpredictable illness events. If each transactor has a concave utility function defined over income or wealth, and if
an exogenous illness event can be expressed as a well-defined money-equivalent loss, it then follows that a transactor´s welfare is increased if she
can purchase actuarially fair insurance contracts which reimburse the totality of such unpredictable losses in return for a premium equal to their
mathematical expectation. Abstracting from transactions costs or costs of
the insurance activity itself, all such risks should be fully insured
(Arrow, 1963). But the money-equivalent loss associated with illness is
always larger, and in many cases very much larger, than the costs of treatment. It includes both lost earnings and, most importantly, the direct u-
tility loss associated with being ill. Optimal health insurance in a world
of perfect information would thus go well beyond reimbursing costs of
health care used, if any, and would extend to the payment of direct compensation to the ill whether or not they used care. Of course the difficulty
of determining that an illness event has occurred and of measuring its
impact on transactor utility in the real world of seriously incomplete information makes such an indemnity approach impossible. But it is important
to remember that even full, first dollar coverage of all health care expenditures, on the Canadian model, falls far short of full reimbursement of
the money-equivalent loss associated with illness.[10]

The negative effects of health insurance, the "moral hazard" problem, also
arise from the impossibility of direct monitoring of illness states and
their welfare effects. The reimbursement of health care expenditures is
based on the assumption that such expenditures are a signal for the occurrence of exogenous illness events (Spence and Zeckhauser, 1971). But the
linkage between illness and its associated "necessary" expenditures is far
from perfect; and the existence of insurance may create incentives to additional health care use for any given illness event. The loss resulting from
the illness event, whether measured in terms of care expenditures or in
terms of utility losses for the insured, would then be increased. If so,
the premium paid for what is in fact health care insurance, not health insurance, will exceed the expected cost of health care use in the uninsured
state, even abstracting from the administrative costs of the insurance
process itself.[11]

"Moral hazard" in its general form refers to any tendency for the presence
of insurance coverage to increase the expected value of losses insured
against, by raising either the probability of occurrence of loss, or its
amount. It can arise in the health care context in several ways, although
economic analyses have tended, incorrectly, to assume that it refers only
to the demand responses of consumer/patients to the effective reduction in
price of health care resulting from insurance coverage (Pauly, 1968). On
this interpretation, there is assumed to exist a well-defined demand curve
for "health care" as a commodity, such that insurance leads consumers to
demand more care for any given state of illness (including perfect health).
If one further assumes that the health care delivery system can be represented by some sort of well-defined price-dependent supply curve, then the
increase in demand for care leads to some combination of increases in price
of care and quantity used. This increase in the money expenditure component
of illness costs may have some off setting effect on the nonmonetary component; if we assume that the demand curve is that of a rational, utility-
maximizing, informed consumer then it must do so. More care consumption is
assumed to increase utility. But this offset is less than the expenditure
increase, or else the rational consumer would have expanded use in the
absence of insurance.

The rational transactor, and by extension the society collectively, should then on this argument design health insurance coverage so as to balance the additional costs of care induced by insurance against its associated bene- fits of risk reduction. If one further assumes that the health care deliv- ery system in the pre- or non-insurance state somehow generates prices for health care services which correspond to their marginal resource costs, then the response of consumer/patient demands to insurance-adjusted lower or zero prices will result (assuming some supply response) in excessive production/use of health care and a "welfare burden" on society corre- sponding to this resource misallocation (Pauly, 1969; Feldstein, 1973). Of course there is a "welfare benefit" as well, resulting from risk reduction, and the optimal level of insurance coverage would be that at which marginal benefit and burden are equated. If in addition we assume away the extensive lost productivity and direct utility costs of illness, and focus only on the cost of health care alone, then it can be shown that (assuming some elasticity of both demand and supply curves) the optimal insurance system will embody sharing of health care expenditures between consumer/patient and insurer. A structure of deductibles and coinsurance faced by the con- sumer/patient will increase her risk, but lower her premiums, relative to 100% coverage; and starting from 100% coverage marginal increases in con- sumer sharing will, over some range at least, raise her welfare (Mossin, 1968; Zeckhauser, 1970; Arrow, 1976).

All of this is of course well known, and in some quarters forms the conven- tional wisdom. It appears to provide the theoretical backdrop for most U.S. discussions of health insurance, in which patient cost-sharing plays an im- portant role. But even the cursory treatment above demonstrates the number of special assumptions about the nature of illness, the behaviour of pa- tients, and the structure of health care delivery, which are necessary to keep the story going. Even more interesting, of course, is what is <u>not</u> said. Health insurance, as a policy, is restricted to the reimbursement of <u>patients</u> for their expenditures on care; all relationships between patient and provider are worked out independently of the insurer in what is assumed to be a private (and sometimes even a perfectly competitive!) "market" for health care. Applying this model to the analysis of public health insurance programs amounts to assuming that all such programs are merely society-wide extensions of private health insurance.

3. FLAWS IN THE CONVENTIONAL MODEL

This simpleminded view of the impact of health insurance can be criticized on several levels. It has been noted that the existence of positive exter- nal effects from health care consumption may lead to underprovision by the private market, so that at least over a range, "moral hazard" effects on utilization may create benefits, not burdens (Lindsay, 1969; Culyer, 1971a, 1971b). But one person's health care use can also have negative effects on others - indiscriminate use of antibiotics, for example. In any case as outlined below the demand and supply framework applied to a uniform commod- ity and representative users is overly simplistic and misleading as a guide in this area.

The linkage from "moral hazard" to resource misallocation also depends critically on the assumed structure of the supply side of health care. If a monopolized supply side leads to under-allocation of resources to health care, then clearly the "moral hazard" effects of insurance may improve re- source allocation, again over a range (Crew, 1969). And while the appropriate theoretical characterization of the supply process, particularly of hospital care, is still an area of active debate, there must be few serious students indeed who would call it perfectly competitive and free from restrictions on entry or conduct!

Criticism at this level, however, does not touch the core of the model. If there are externalities, one can modify property rights distributions or introduce specific taxes/subsidies. If the supply side is imperfectly competitive, restructure it to improve competition. ("Deregulate" it, and prohibit or assume away collusive or predatory practices). In this context universal public insurance would be a peculiar and definitely "second best" policy response.

Such tinkering with the risk aversion/moral hazard trade-off framework misses its fundamental inadequacy, and serves to obscure the real issues in debate between public and private, universal and partial, health insurance systems. The heart of the problem is the formulation of the demand curve, as a positive and a normative construct. In the conventional tradeoff analysis the positive construct is inserted when the concept of "moral hazard" - expected loss dependent on insurance status - is restricted to and identified with only one of the possible sources of such dependency, consumer/patients´ responses to pre- and post-insurance prices. Normative significance is attached to the hypothesized consumer/patient response when it is assumed that the marginal contribution of health care to the social welfare function is adequately captured by the marginal willingness-to-pay of individual consumer/patients.

The assumption that a stable demand curve for health care exists independent of (non-price) supplier behaviour is very dubious. It has been unconvincing to students of health care generally, and presumably appeals to a sub-set of health economists because of its familiarity and analytical tractability.[12] And the assignment of normative significance to the utilization patterns assumed to result from such a demand curve is inconsistent with the entire regulatory structure which has evolved in every developed society to guide and direct, and in many cases mandate or prohibit, patients´ utilization patterns. To attach normative significance to "consumer choices" in this environment, one must presumably assume that this structure does not represent society´s "revealed preferences" for patterns of care consumption, and is all a terrible mistake, or one must reject those social preferences and substitute others (presumably the analyst´s?). Or one must simply assume the structure way.

But the "terrible mistake" approach has several disadvantages. Intellectual honesty would seem to obligate the analyst to argue for complete deregulatory policies in health care with as much vigour as s/he advocates particular insurance programs, since both follow from the same assumptions. Moreover, one must admit that existing utilization data reflect the distortions of consumer preferences imposed by the present regulatory system, which makes welfare analyses based on these data somewhat suspect. How do we know we are on the demand curve? And finally, if society´s revealed preferences are "wrong", the analyst really has some obligation to explain where his/her alternative social welfare function came from, and why s/he finds it compelling? It is not therefore surprising that analysts using the risk aversion/moral hazard tradeoff model have generally chosen to assume away the regulatory structure of health care as non-existent or without effect. The postulate of pre-insurance prices set by "long-run" horizontal marginal cost curves does this nicely and with minimal discussion.

4. HEALTH STATUS AND HEALTH CARE: UNDERSTANDING THE UTILIZATION PROCESS

A more satisfactory approach begins from the observation that the commodity
"health care" plays a rather peculiar role in the utility function. Its
primary impact is via its influence on health status. While of course all
commodities have some potential or actual impact on health, positive or
negative, what distinguishes a sub-set of commodities as "health care" is
that their (expected) health impact is the primary reason for their consumption. Health care services also enter the utility function directly,
but in general their partial effects, holding health status constant, are
negative. There is even a recognized form of mental illness, Münchausen´s
Syndrome, to describe a peculiar group of people who derive positive utility from health care when they are not ill! (Bardsley and Gibson, 1975).
This applies of course to palliative care as well; the various interventions to which the chronically or terminally ill patient may be subjected are intended to retard decline but are not themselves positive experiences.

Now the health status to which health care is expected to contribute is
clearly an argument in the utility function; improvements in health status
both increase well-being directly and modify the marginal rates of
substitution among other commodities. But health status does not enter lex-
icographically; people obviously do voluntarily pleasurable things which
threaten their health. From this perspective, it is clear that the WHO definition of health as complete physical, mental and social well-being, not
just absence of disease or injury, is too broad. Such a definition make
health equivalent to the economist´s concept of utility, not merely a
contributor to it. For our purposes, the narrower definition in terms of
absence of disease or injury is appropriate.

And in the formulation of marginal rates of substitution between health and
other sources of satisfaction we can quite reasonably postulate that the
individual consumer is the best judge, the most knowledgeable source of information, about the internal structure of her own utility function. Such
knowledge need not be perfect, but may still be the best available. Efforts
by suppliers to extend the professional prerogative beyond advising on the
relation between health care and health to include decisions as to what
level of health status the individual should choose and be prepared to pay
for, at whatever cost in money or direct disutility, (some cures really are
worse than the disease), are properly suspect.

Such suspicion may in some cases be mis-placed. The patient´s rationality
may well be impaired; or unrepresented others, as in the contagion case,
may be affected. But breaches of consumer sovereignty over choice of health
status require some further justification and defence (Williams, 1978).

The case of health care is very different. Health care is one argument in a
very complex production function, not a utility function, whose output is
(expected to be) improved health status. And there is no a priori ground
for assuming that consumers have superior, or any, knowledge about production functions. They may have such knowledge, but they have no such privileged access as is conferred by the location of the utility function in the
consumer/patient´s own mind. The connection between health care and health
is an external, technical relation, about which specialized providers
develop specialized knowledge, and this external relationship is described
by the concept of "need" in its positive sense. "Demand" for care reflects
willingness to pay; "need" describes an external expert´s judgement about

the marginal impact of a particular form of care on a particular patient's health status, and the two need not be connected.[13]

In some ideal world of fully informed patients, of course, one would expect a close, but not exact, correlation between needs and demands. Such consumer/patients would not use ineffective or harmful care, or at least not in the misapprehension that it would improve their health. And if the effects of care were uncertain, the calculation of expected benefits and adjustments for risk would be based on patients' weights and risk preferences, not those of providers. It is conceivable that certain ineffectual forms of health care might generate benefits of some more general sort, a sense of social integration or "belonging" resulting from participating in the health care system, for example. Or the patient might be attracted to the physician, or nurse. But it is not clear that we would want to describe their association as health care utilization.

In such a world, the socially optimal level of health care use might be described as that generated by the choices of fully informed patients faced with prices reflecting the true long-run marginal resource costs of their consumption, adjusted for any external effects, but with incomes adjusted independently of use by lump-sum transfers of wealth sufficient to compensate them for the utility losses resulting from illness itself and the associated expenditures.[14] Not all "needs", as viewed by technical experts, would be met; health would have a positive price at the margin and thus health care would have a positive marginal product in the health production function. As it should.

The interpretation of the innocent phrase, "adjusted for any external effects" is a bit tricky in this context. Purely "selfish" externalities, such as contagion, can be dealt with straight-forwardly by taxes and subsidies built into service prices. Abstracting from information and transaction costs, some prices might be negative. But much of public policy toward health care, and much literature on externalities, focusses on "the poor" and the problem of ensuring that people whose incomes are judged inadequate to buy the care they "need", or the insurance which could buy it for them, are nevertheless cared for. Thus the policy-relevant externalities appear to include income redistributional issues as well. Moreover there is also some ground for believing that the relevant interpersonal utility function interactions include direct influences of one person's health status or health care use on another's well-being, independent of contagion, income, or utility interactions. (Evans and Wolfson, 1980; Culyer and Simpson, 1980.)

Income distribution considerations do not appear to enter into our formulation of the "ideal" allocation, however, since the utility costs of illness and of care outlays are all compensated. (The necessary revenues are presumably raised through a lump-sum tax system.) Utility levels may still vary by income class, but not with illness experience. Similarly, since health care prices equal resource costs, input suppliers earn only competitive returns, and the issue of income redistribution between suppliers and the rest of society does not arise except as part of the overall income distribution question. Under these circumstances, but only under them, it is legitimate to evaluate a health care system strictly on its resource-allocative effects, and to ignore income distributional questions.

Of course in such a world poor people may well choose to consume less health care than the rich - if it is a normal good they will. Since they

are income-compensated for illness per se, this lower consumption is not
indicative of a more serious impact of illness on their welfare. But if
there exist, as there well may, interactions of a paternalistic type such
that A's welfare is affected by B's health status and thus B's consumption
of needed health care independently of B's welfare - A does not want the
ill B to spend his/her money on booze rather than drugs, even if B prefers
to - then these paternalistic externalities will have to be reflected in
the adjustments to market prices in our ideal case.

Returning to the real world, however, the focus on the distribution by income class of care use and financing burden may be justified by the absence
of both full lump-sum compensation for illness, and competitive service
pricing. (This is not to exclude the possibility of paternalistic externalities as well.) Since poverty and illness go together, the welfare burden
of illness tends to make the utility distribution even more unequal than
the income distribution; "free" care for the "poor" mitigates this
somewhat. But the utility distribution within income classes may also be
highly unequal due to illness, again "free" care at all income levels responds to this dispersion. Thus the inclusion of transfers from rich to
poor or well to ill among the welfare criteria for evaluating health insurance systems rests on the observation that all such systems in the real
world compensate imperfectly for illness cost, and the assumption that such
compensation would indeed (ceteris paribus) increase the value of the relevant social welfare function.

In the same way, inclusion of redistribution patterns between providers and
everyone else rests on the observation that no health system functions as a
perfectly competitive market, and that there are good reasons why the regulatory structures, which themselves have redistributional consequences, are
unlikely to be removed. Our ideal consumers were "fully informed", but in
reality the extreme asymmetry of information between consumer/patients and
providers leads to the possibility not merely of consumer "mistakes" but of
"unnecessary" mistakes (in the sense that better information was available
in the market) or outright exploitation. And consumption "mistakes" in this
field are potentially very costly and often irreversible; "learning by
doing" may be hazardous to one's health. To manage this asymmetry, institutions evolve in every society to create and support agency relationships
between providers and patients. This agency relation means not merely that
providers act for patients, but act in their interests, even when such interests conflict with those of the professional-agent. This seeking of the
principal's interest, sometimes at the expense of at least the agent's economic interest, is the essence of the professional relationship.[15]

The fundamental rationale for regulation in health care is the assumption
that if providers are "professionalized" and protected from market forces,
then they will act as patients' agents in the choice of health care utilization patterns. Since such providers respond to (their perception of)
needs, this in turn implies either a judgement that fully informed consumers' demands would be based primarily on technical need judgements, or
else an abandonment of any individual basis for the component of the social
welfare function defined over health care. The former seems more plausible.
The implicit view, then, is that the utilization generated by ill-informed
(and mis-informed) consumer/patients in unregulated competitive health care
markets will be farther from the full information ideal allocation than
that generated in heavily regulated "markets" dominated by professional ex-
pert/agents. If one rejects this view, of course, one is presumably
logically committed, as noted above, to the aboliton of professional self-

regulation and licensure. But if one accepts such institutions, it would seem that one must accept their implications, and the "demand curve", in both normative and positive senses, is undercut. Without it, the risk reduction/moral hazard tradeoff conceptualization of health insurance loses its cornerstone.

5. THE CANADIAN APPROACH: THEORETICAL UNDERPINNINGS

The Canadian approach to health insurance starts rather from the positive assumption that utilization of hospital and medical care is heavily influenced by suppliers, and the normative assumption that it ought to be. Part of the initial justification for such insurance was a desire to reduce "barriers to care" and increase consumption by those in <u>need</u>. This conversion of need from a positive, technical description of the marginal product of care in some individual´s health production function to a stimulus for social policy, from is to ought, reflects some form of external effect, from my use to your, or our collective, well-being. But it is important to note that this externality is rooted in the positive concept, it applies only to <u>needed</u> care. This is true at the very concrete level; your use of narrow spectrum antibiotics to resolve a diagnosed infection confers positive benefits on me in the form of reduced risk of contagion; your "prophylactic" use of broad spectrum antibiotics (in cough drops!) raises my risk of infection with a resistant strain. More generally, individuals, their political representatives, and their newspaper editors, speak and act as if the receipt of "needed" care by an individual labelled as "ill" by external experts is a source of satisfaction to the rest of the community, while unnecessary care consumption by those who are "malingering" or "frivolous" not only raises everyone else´s insurance costs but is itself offensive. The external effects of care cannot be separated from the issue of "need" and health status; there is no independent social desire for equality of use. The general external effects of A´s use of care on B´s well-being are positive or negative, depending on whether B perceives A as "needing" care in terms of expected gain in health status (Culyer and Simpson, 1980. A somewhat different approach with similar implications is Krashinsky, 1981).

The establishment of first dollar comprehensive coverage then follows logically, if one believes first that the influence of providers on utilization is sufficiently strong that user charges serve merely to redistribute income (from the sick to whoever collects the charges) rather than to reallocate resources, and secondly that any utilization response which does occur will not have any particular connection with need for care. In fact there are a number of studies now indicating that direct charges do affect patients´ decisions to contact the health care system, but not the total volume of utilization, and that they serve to reallocate access and use from lower to higher income groups. [16] One might hope to mitigate these effects if, as has been suggested, charges could be in some way income-related; but it should be recalled that illness affects utility levels <u>within</u> as well as across income classes. The ideal resource allocation scheme postulated above required that individuals be compensated, not for money income differences (as price or charge adjustment would do) but for the overall utility impact of differences in illness status - a very different thing.

But universal, first dollar coverage still poses problems. The volume and mix of care generated by professionals-as-agents advising consumer/patients

unconstrained by price may be superior to that generated in an unregulated
competitive market or in a self-regulated market with partial price constraints, but it does not follow that it represents the closest approximation possible to our ideal state. Professional agents are not themselves
perfect governors of resource allocation; their imperfections are of three
kinds.

First is the often-noted professional conflict of interest; the profession-
al-as-supplier benefits economically from the utilization which the profes-
sional-as-patient-agent directs. In its starkest form, deliberate recom-
mendation of profitable services known to be useless or harmful, this is
probably unusual among professionalized providers, although examples can
easily be found in those areas of health care dominated by for-profit providers.

But the bias imparted by economic interest enters into the second and
perhaps most important difficulty, which is that for a variety of reasons
providers tend to over-estimate both the technical efficacy of health care
services and the value of their effects (including underestimating costs of
side effects) to consumers.[17] Furthermore, the channels whereby they
acquire information on these matters are systematically biased both by personal, psychological considerations, and by external institutions with an
interest in "health industry sales". Hence the various forms of "Roemer's
Law"; health care suppliers respond to additional capacity by redefining
concepts of professional "need" so as to increase utilization.[18] "Need" is
endogenous - which does not mean vacuous.[19]

And finally, even if need were a well-defined, external standard, and the
professional were technically fully informed, his/her agency relation is
still with the individual patient. Utilization choices arising from that
relation cannot reflect society's interests in the external effects of
care. Insofar as these are related to the consumer's own needs, no problem
arises. But in an insured environment, full or partial, the patient's agent
will oversupply care relative to its social opportunity cost. Society's interest will go unrepresented.[20]

Such oversupply, insofar as it is traceable to the presence or absence of
insurance coverage rather than the professional imperatives and perceptual
biases of the provider, is included in the concept of "moral hazard". The
response of the provider to the existence of insurance tends to raise the
(apparent) incidence and treatment cost of illness, just as does the independent response of the patient. The care utilization process consists of
initiation of care episodes by patients followed by a joint determination
of the subsequent utilization pattern, in which the relative influence of
patient and provider will vary greatly by type of episode and personalities
involved (Stoddart and Barer, 1981). The process of episode initiation may
be subject to "moral hazard" of the conventional, demand curve sort, patients responding to prices, although as Cooper emphasizes, physicians
educate their patients as to when to initiate an episode. The physician-
patient relationship is a continuing one, not a spot market transaction.
But the intensity of utilization per episode is to a large extent con-
trolled by the provider, and these decisions too may respond to insurance
coverage. The equation of "moral hazard" with patient responses alone results from the assumption that stable demand curves can be drawn for utilization in total, not merely for episode initiation, which neglects the independent role of the provider.

Health care in a fully insured system may thus be oversupplied in either technical or economic terms - inefficacious (at the margin), or efficacious but not worth its cost. (Of course, the same is possible in a partially insured, or even an uninsured system). The available evidence suggests that the former is probably the more serious issue at this point. But such a system also embodies problems of price determination independent of care utilization/resource input use. If patients pay nothing, what limits physicians' fees and hospital charges or hospital workers' wages? This is of course an issue of income distribution, not resource allocation, but it is a very serious one in a world in which, unlike the "representative individual", not everyone is a physician or a nurse for part of the year (as is assumed, e.g., by Arrow, 1976).

The response to both of these problems is sole source funding through the public sector, at a level of government high enough to command sufficient political legitimacy and expertise to confront providers on more or less equal terms.[21] Rather than relying on the flimsy reed of patient cost sharing, with its peculiar supporting assumption of a price-competitive delivery system, to contain fee and charge setting, the Canadian insurance agencies/Ministries of Health in each province directly negotiate uniform fee levels with physicians and global budgets with hospitals. These negotiations are the principal, though not the only, factor influencing relative income levels in the hospital and medical care sectors. But equally important, they also serve as the channel through which the public agency can influence the mix and volume of health care services provided. The negotiated fee schedule for physicians, by determining who can be reimbursed and for what, limits the proliferation of medical technology outside the hospital. And the budget negotiation process, which separates operating from capital funding, enables the public sector to control, more or less, the availability of specific forms of service capacity. In the still longer run, of course, the public educational system and federal immigration policy can be used to influence the types and numbers of health care personnel available. Thus although no specific constraints are placed on the relationship between physician and patient, the range of discretion of the provider is restricted by the capacity made available. The process of allocation of this capacity among providers, within the hospital medical staff structure, is of course rather complex, but the expectation is that the final allocation to patients will be governed by professional judgements of relative need (Evans, 1980a).

6. "RATIONING" AND EXPENDITURE CONTROL: ALTERNATIVE MECHANISMS AND CRITERIA

This process is of course "rationing" - as is a price system, or indeed any system of resource allocation under constraint. Like a price system it is indirect, imposing general limitations on use rather than directives specific to individual cases. The fundamental difference is that while the price system responds to the willingness-to-pay of the individual patient, as determined by patient perceptions of "need" and constrained by wealth and/or insurance status, the capacity-rationing system responds to professional judgements of patient need subject to a global social resource constraint.

In evaluating the welfare implications of these alternatives, it would be naive to assume that either yields an optimal resource allocation as defined above or in the mind of God. It is arguable, however, on the basis of the considerations outlined above, that the Canadian approach comes closer to that welfare optimum than does a system of partial, private insurance coverage (Evans, 1980b). Comparing the cost, volume, and mix of health care services utilized in Canada with those in the U.S., for example, it is obvious that overall expenditure on health care is much lower in Canada as a direct result of the global constraint. This includes both price and quantity effects, although the measurement of aggregate quantity is somewhat ambiguous. But it appears in specific instances that the problem of marginally efficacious or inefficacious servicing is less severe in Canada than in the U.S., and certainly there is no evidence of the U.S. system yielding health advantages in return for its extra costs. Indeed U.S. analysts, particularly economists, have long argued that their system oversupplies health care, - this being the "welfare burden" imposed by excessive health insurance - implying that the mixture of public and private insurance with direct charges to patients has been inadequate as a rationing device. Their conclusion, that insurance coverage should be reduced, seems to owe more to the attraction of the conventional insurance model than to observation of real-life health care systems. The actual Canadian experience, that universal public coverage leads to a more effective rationing process, is easily understood if one abandons the demand-and-supply framework for a more sophisticated formulation of the utilization process in health care.

But there is a semantic problem. "Overutilization", has two different definitions. To most students of health care, and most policy makers, it means utilization of marginally efficacious, inefficacious, or harmful care. As defined relative to a demand curve, however, it means utilization of care for which the consumer would not have been willing/able to pay the pre-insurance price, or the resource cost. In this context, willingness of consumers to buy and use laetrile, e.g., is the measure of its value, and the issue of "necessity" in a technical sense does not arise.

If one adopts this position, and firmly rejects all issues of need or efficacy, then definitionally one cannot have an outcome superior to that generated in unregulated competitive private markets (except, of course, for external effects, which can be assumed either trivial or correctable by specific taxes). No evidence of outcomes in different systems is allowable; in such a neo-Panglossian world it is a particular process of resource allocation which is postulated as an objective.[22] The characteristics of the outcome are defined so as to be optimal under this process, and the analysis becomes completely circular. One cannot confirm or refute such a position, any more than one can refute Pangloss. One can only ask that in the name of intellectual honesty those who make policy recommendations on the basis of such analysis make clear all the implications of their assumptions.

Going back to the "Four Points", then, the establishment of a universal, comprehensive system under public administration creates both the framework, and the incentive, for governments to take an active role in influencing the mix and volume of health care utilization, and its price. The indirect exercise of this influence, through hospital system capacity and allowable billing patterns, depends on the ability of the reimbursement agency to separate operating from capital funding decisions, and to ensure that decisions over reimbursement impinge directly upon providers and cannot be "passed through" to someone else. Partial coverage, by contrast, means that what the insuring agency refuses to cover comes out of the patient's pocket, and fragmented multiple source reimbursement means that what one refuses to reimburse, another will. Further, if reimbursement comes from a mixture of public, private non-profit, and private for-profit sources, it is hard to see how one can avoid reimbursing capital costs through operating expenditures. And then, of course, one loses control of system capacity. It may be possible to regulate one dimension of capacity, e.g., beds, but not the totality of alternative inputs.[23]

But the incentive issue is equally important. Managing health care is politically difficult - and dangerous, A universal public system discourages "moral hazard" in the public sector, the shedding of public responsibility. If the public system is neither universal nor comprehensive, then government is under a standing temptation to resolve short-run budgetary pressures by cutting back eligibility or coverage. One can always find a small and politically ineffective sub-group as targets for restricted eligibility or reduced reimbursement. Under a universal system, the whole population is at risk and the pressures on government to maintain benefits and improve management are much greater.[24]

Similarly, if public and private insurance systems routinely reimburse only a portion of bills received by patients, then any discrepancy between provider price/income objectives and reimburser budget constraints can be resolved by a marginal adjustment in this sharing ratio. But if the principle is established that the insurer pays the provider, and patients are not economically involved, then insurer and provider must confront each other and negotiate the distributional questions directly.

These generalizations are confirmed by the different responses of health insurance systems in the U.S. and Canada to budgetary constraints and cost pressures. In Canada levels of expenditure are constrained, and such increases as occur are passed forward in general taxation. In the U.S. expenditure levels are not constrained, and the public component of the insurance system limits its losses by lowering its proportion of reimbursement and removing particular groups from eligibility. Efforts to control health care utilization and costs by regulation separated from reimbursement responsibility, or initiatives by individual insurers, are generally judged to have failed.[25] The analogy is made with a balloon; if one squeezes it at one point it pops out somewhere else. But it would be wrong to infer that gases cannot be compressed. The balloon must be fully enclosed first.

Yet another perspective on global versus partial cost control is provided by the current U.K. experience. Public, sole-source funding provides overall control of the NHS budget, but the residual private sector represents an area for the balloon to expand. As long as this sector appeared vestigial, and was under severe public pressure, the problem seemed insignificant. But a policy combination of severe NHS budget limits plus tax-expenditure subsidies to private health insurance (ironically, of the sort so universally condemned by students of the U.S. system) backed by ideological support from government, could lead to a rapid development of private insurance and payment. The result would almost certainly be substantial increases in expenditures and provider incomes, as well as a redistribution of access to care. Government may "benefit" from a transfer of costs to the private sector, at least in the short run. More general social benefits are harder to find (Evans, 1982).

7. RESOURCE ALLOCATION AND WEALTH REDISTRIBUTION

The discussion of expenditure control blends issues of resource allocation with those of wealth distribution, as the public system permits influence over not only patterns of care utilization but also relative incomes of providers. This can be thought of as providing a counterweight or corrective to the distributional "side-effects" of the other institutional characteristics of health care delivery.

Insurance of whatever type has redistributional effects in favour of suppliers (except in the rather implausible case of a horizontal supply curve at P = MC) insofar as it leads to an increase in prices of health care services. Thus an individual or a society "buys" risk reduction at a "cost" of wealth transfer across occupations, a "cost" which, being occupation-specific, is not addressed by general redistribution policy. Furthermore, as noted, the existence of the "cost" or side effect limits health insurance in a private or mixed insurance system to significantly less then full coverage even of health expenditures. In the absence of direct influence over fees and prices the redistributional "cost" rises sharply at 100% coverage (physicians' fees and hospital salaries are unbounded). Thus the global public system, by direct negotiations with suppliers, improves the risk reduction/wealth redistribution tradeoff to the extent that full expenditure coverage is possible at a lower redistributional "cost" than that of partial coverage in the mixed system. This yields benefits in the form of not only greater risk reduction, but also greater ex post redistribution from the well to the ill, which again appears to be a positive contribution to overall social welfare.

Professional licensure and self-regulation, and more generally the web of rules governing present or potential suppliers of health care, are, like insurance, a social mechanism to respond to a particular informational problem, in this case the asymmetry of information between provider and patient. But they too have redistributional side-effects, in that they limit the scope of competitive forces and permit monopoly gains for providers. And the "side-effects" of self-regulation and insurance coverage reinforce each other. Unless one is prepared to advocate complete deregulation of supply in health care, and perhaps even then, these side effects seem inevitable. But they can be limited by the counterpoise of public bargaining power. Unless one assumes that the social welfare function is neutral with respect to patterns of wealth distribution, the global insurance system leads to welfare gains through the restriction of unintended and presumably undesired redistributions from patients or society generally to providers. This fact, of course, goes far to explain the strong hostility of medical and dental associations to universal public insurance programs, and their satisfaction with multi-source private for-profit insurance.

8. EVALUATING THE RISK-BEARING SYSTEM

The establishment of a universal public program was motivated primarily by its expected impact on patterns of care use, initially to increase use by those "in need". The shift in emphasis to the restriction of "unnecessary" care is a more recent phenomenon. It was also intended quite explicitly as a redistributive program from well to ill, both ex post, as actual expenditures were shifted from patients to the public, and ex ante, as contributions to the system (premiums or taxes) were severed from expected use. But public insurance was also expected to improve significantly the efficiency of the risk-bearing process itself. The private, multi-agency insurance system was perceived to have two major problems, apart from its impact on utilization patterns and relative incomes. It was unnecessarily expensive, and it was incapable of extending coverage to the whole population. The former is the issue of loading charges, or the cost of the insurance process itself, and the latter combines issues of ex ante wealth distribution, ability to pay premiums, with the separate question of inability to buy fair contracts, or market failure due to adverse selection.

On the first question, the evidence seems quite conclusive. The resource costs of running the insurance system itself are much lower under the universal public system than in, for example, the U.S. mixed public and private system.[26] Counting only the recorded costs of "prepayment and administration" the mixed system costs about five or six times as much, per capita, as the public system. In addition of course there are extensive administrative costs built into the delivery system itself, as well as non-monetary disutility costs for the insured individual, which appear to be significantly greater when one must deal with a large number of insurers offering a multiplicity of forms of coverage. These major differences in resource costs are not captured in the risk aversion/moral hazard tradeoff model, which implicitly assumes that all insurers are equally efficient at doing whatever it is that they do. But the critical question is, what do they do? What services are received in return for the loading charge component of the premium?

The obvious answer, assumption of financial risk and administration of payments, points the issue sharply. Canadians are exposed, on average, to much less financial risk than Americans, and the claim payment process is at least as efficient. So where does the money go in a private system? Well, presumably to the development and marketing of a wide range of different contracts, which will both protect the insurance company against large losses, and (by a careful matching of premiums to risk) influence the ex ante wealth distribution between people with different probabilities of illness. But once it has already been decided, as a collective decision presumably rooted in some aspect of external effects, that everyone should be insured, then the extensive efforts of private companies to decide whom they will or will not insure, at what price, become merely a game of "hot potato" in which risk assessment is privately profitable but collectively irrelevant. The resources used up in assessment and marketing serve merely to identify and enroll the risks which are privately profitable to carry, leaving the remainder to public or publicly subsidized plans. If, as argued above, overall utilization and costs of health care are not particularly sensitive to individual patient decisions, then the primary function of private health insurance seems to be redistributive. It shifts the costs of health care to those who ex ante have a higher expected use of care (through premium variations) or ex post are higher users (through patient cost-sharing devices). Where this shifting breaks down, because such high (expected or actual) users are unable to pay for "needed" coverage or care, the public sector steps in. It is hard to understand the social justification for spending large amounts of real resources on an insurance system whose principal contribution is to redistribute health costs proportionately to illness burdens! But the private justification is obvious - insurance "costs" represent the multi-billion dollar sales of the insurance industry. Administering a game of "hot potato" is quite profitable. And the institutional framework provides no way in which individual or group buyers of insurance coverage can move away from this trap; individually rational buyer behaviour leads to a situation in which all buyers are worse off.[27]

This "prisoner´s dilemma" interpretation of private health insurance programs may not command universal assent. What seems undeniable, however, is
that these issues cannot even be addressed in the conventional risk aver-
sion/moral hazard tradeoff model of health insurance. That model thus
serves the interests of the private industry by making unaskable the principal questions about their raison d´être.

In addition to economizing significantly on the costs of running the insurance system, centralized public administration deals with the incom-
pleteness of risk-spreading which arises in private insurance markets from
the problem of adverse selection. It was observed in Canada that the private insurance market first expanded rapidly as not-for-profit agencies
wrote predominantly community-rated comprehensive group coverage on a large
scale. But its expansion halted well short of 100% of the population, and
at the time the public program was being developed, for-profit companies
were beginning to market less comprehensive policies on an experience-rated
basis. Extending this trend, it was anticipated that both the proportion of
the population covered, and the extent of coverage, would fall in response
to these market pressures. The issue of full versus partial coverage,
micro-rationality leading to macro-inefficiency, has already been considered above in the discussion of patient cost-sharing and the "hot potato"
problem. It is a fallacy of composition to assume that competition among
insurance companies to limit their own claims will lower overall costs. But
there is an additional problem of interest posed by those who are left
unable to buy any coverage, or coverage as comprehensive as they would
like, at a price reflecting expected loss plus administrative costs, in the
competitive market.

Those unable to buy fair coverage include two distinct groups of people. On
the one hand, there are those who for reasons of high risk status and/or
low income simply cannot afford to purchase comprehensive, or any, health
insurance even if it is competitively priced. For this group, the private
market has in no way "failed" - if there is felt to be a social obligation
to ensure that they receive "needed" care, a subsidy must be paid. It can
be paid through direct public service delivery, public insurance programs,
or subsidies to premiums in private plans, - the choice of form will presumably depend on other considerations of the sort described above. And the
fact that every society pays this subsidy, in some or other form, seems
compelling evidence that their various social welfare functions all attribute normative significance to "need" - indicating some form of extended effect of your consumption of health care, when needed, on my or our welfare.

But there is a second group, whose problem has recently become better
understood since the application of Akerlof´s "Lemons" analysis to insurance markets, who cannot purchase insurance at all, or as comprehensive as
they would like, because the market is unable to offer it to them at a
price reflecting its true cost. Imperfect information about buyer risk
status means that sellers of insurance have difficulty distinguishing good
from bad risks, and if in addition buyers have better information than
sellers - asymmetry again - purchasers of insurance will generally be worse
risks than the population generally. Depending on the system parameters
chosen, one can get a result in which no insurance is sold at all, even
though mutually advantageous contracts could be made if buyers could only
reveal their status to sellers.[28]

Of course the private market does exist; it deals with the adverse selection problem in two ways. First, insurers offer a range of contracts of

different degrees of comprehensiveness, such that buyers will sort themselves out by risk status, with low risk buyers finding partial coverage
more attractive, and high risk buyers choosing more expensive comprehensive
coverage. And secondly, the industry offers group contracts at favourable
rates where group membership is not chosen on the basis of risk status.

But while this "solution" to adverse selection means that people can buy
some insurance, it is far from optimal. Non-members of groups may find
themselves unable to buy coverage at all, or else only at rates which reflect maximum estimates of their risk status; and buyers of partial contracts may be in the position of wanting to buy more comprehensive coverage, but knowing that if they do, their premiums must rise to cover not
only their own greater benefits, but also the costs of the higher risk pool
which they will have to join - or which will join them. In this case it can
be shown that everyone´s welfare could be improved by compulsory, comprehensive coverage, although no low-risk individual, by himself, should buy
it (Wilson, 1976). Hence one may rationally buy group rated "major medical"
coverage in the private market rather than community rated comprehensive,
and yet vote for a comprehensive and compulsory public plan. Indeed that is
what Canadians appear to have done.

But it is necessary to maintain the public comprehensive coverage as de
facto compulsory, and to forbid private competition, otherwise there wiTT
always be privately micro-rational contracts which could be written between
identifiable low risk groups and private insurers which could lead to the
undermining of the collective system. The easiest way to ensure de facto
compulsion is to fund the whole system from taxes, but where provincial
governments have chosen, for various reasons, to maintain a premium system
and "voluntary" enrollment for at least part of the population, private insurers are forbidden to write competing coverage. Thus, the political
choice process remedies the myopia of the market.

9. CONCLUSION: MODELS AND MOTIVATIONS

Despite the heavy emphasis thus far on specific comparisons between the
health insurance and health care systems in Canada and the U.S., this paper
neither intends nor pretends to present a comprehensive evaluation of the
two. References to actual experience are intended rather to illustrate
inadequacies of the theoretical models of health insurance commonly used by
economists. Despite their apparent generality and abstraction, such models
are rooted in a very specific institutional context, specifically that of
private multi-source insurance in which there is no relationship between
health care providers and insurers. Patient/consumers enter into transactions with providers, and then insurers separately reimburse consumers for
all or part of the resulting expenditures. The drawing of welfare conclusions and policy recommendations from such models requires in addition a
specification of the utilization and price determining process in health
care delivery systems, and this specification too is institution and system
dependent.

Thus when a model of private third-party insurance imposed on hypothetical
fully informed transactors in a hypothetical competitive health care "market" is used to generate welfare conclusions about public universal health
insurance programs, the results are, not surprisingly, highly misleading.
The comparisons between U.S. and Canadian experience indicate that the conventional insurance model yields erroneous predictions, but more signifi-

cantly that its framework is inadequate even to raise some of the most important welfare issues. The specific characteristics of the Canadian public health insurance system can be interpreted as responses to these issues; efforts in the U.S. to analyse programs for universal public health insurance as merely extensions of the private system serve principally to obscure them.

In particular, we noted that one of the principal objectives of the public health insurance system is to improve the matching between service utilization and need. This can be interpreted as moving to a closer approximation to the service patterns which hypothetical fully informed consumers, fully compensated for exogenous welfare losses due to illness (not just insured against expenditure!) would choose. In addition it is a response to the obvious external effects or utility function interactions which link the members of a community. One person's care matters to another, as long as it is "needed" care.

Initially, the public system was based on the assumption of general "unmet need", and a rather naive view that reducing economic barriers to use would under professional guidance lead to both an optimal matching of use with need and a determinate size to the health care sector when all needs were met. It is now realized that since need is a continuum, the optimal scale of the health sector cannot be determined professionally, and the utilization decisions of professionals-as-agents, while considerably superior to those of uninformed patients, do not themselves make optimal use of the efficacy information available to society. Thus the perceived role of the public health care insurance system has shifted to that of determining the overall scale and specific capacities of the health care system, the "social cut-off" on the need continuum, and of generating, disseminating, and applying better information on the effectiveness of care so as to improve both professional and patient decision-making over utilization.

The potential for improving patterns of resource allocation to and within health care through the public insurance mechanism is suppressed in the conventional insurance model by the assumptions of a homogenous commodity, health care, and of a demand curve for such care by which welfare judgements can be derived from consumer/patients' willingness to pay. But a more sophisticated view of the health care utilization process, and of the range of policy instruments available to a universal public insurance program, enables one to set up the theoretical framework within which such improvements can occur. Canadian experience illustrates this framework in application.

Perhaps equally important, from a welfare perspective, are the wealth redistributive effects of insurance programs, as between the insured, the users, and the providers. Increasing insurance coverage of health expenditures increases ex post transfers from well to ill, and depending on the structure of the supply side it tends through higher prices to transfer wealth from users and/or the insured to providers. The financing structure of insurance contracts, which in a private system depends on the competitiveness of insurance markets, determines the ex ante transfer pattern from those with low to those with high probability of illness.

In the private model limitations on ex post transfers, (direct charges of various sorts to users), are the only instruments to limit transfers to providers. Moreover in a competitive insurance market with incomplete information such limitations are also used to reduce ex ante transfers among

different risk categories of insureds. But the limitation on ex post transfers seems per se to involve welfare losses, particularly since as
emphasized health expenditures represent only a small part of the welfare
cost of illness. Accordingly the fact that negotiation of provider fees and
incomes in a universal public insurance system limits the scale of these
transfers is a source not only of direct welfare gains (unless one is a
provider!) but also of indirect benefits from the increase which it permits
in ex post transfers from well to ill. There is of course no a priori reason why any particular social welfare function should respond positively to
transfers from well to ill, but the behaviour of all developed societies in
this regard suggests, by a revealed preference argument, that in practice
they do. Moreover the universal public insurance program permits direct administration of the ex ante redistribution pattern inherent in the relation
between premiums or other charges to those insured, and their expected risk
status. A public universal compulsory insurance system might, if desired,
embody a very sophisticated and detailed structure of premiums related to
risk status. The fact that the Canadian system does not obviously represents a social choice, and given the known characteristics of high risk
people it is not a surprising choice. We must presume, then, that Canadians
collectively view the resulting pattern of ex ante transfers as a welfare
gain, relative to a competitive market system.

Finally, as noted, the universal public insurance system appears to be more
efficient, by a very wide margin, when viewed simply as a mechanism for
risk-spreading. The insurance process itself uses far less real resources
than in the U.S., and yet succeeds in covering the entire population comprehensively. Viewing prepayment and administration costs as the price of
risk reduction, Americans pay far more than Canadians and get less. Individually, they may appear to receive additional benefits in the form of
choice among a much wider array of contract options. But in aggregate these
apparent benefits wash out because every dollar of expenditure has to come
from somewhere. And the mere fact that a wide variety of contracts is
bought, is not evidence that the availability of variety justifies its
cost. In the context of either adverse selection, or scale economies, a
competitive equilibrium with variety can persist despite the existence of a
Pareto-superior outcome with uniform contracts. In the health care field it
appears to do so.

Why then does the conventional risk aversion/moral hazard tradeoff model
persist as the theoretical vehicle used by so many economists to think
about, and evaluate, the welfare implications of public as well as private
health insurance? Probably because it is analytically tractable, familiar,
and enables one to build upon the extensive theoretical apparatus of private market analysis. These advantages may more than outweigh any weaknesses in terms of inappropriateness of assumptions and erroneousness (or
simply absence) of predictions. But there may well be, in addition, a more
disturbing explanation.

We have emphasized above that the choice of public versus private, universal versus partial, health insurance systems has very important redistributional implications. In particular, the establishment of full or partial
private health insurance (or a mixture of private and public coverage following private models), in a context of self-regulated or generally imperfectly competitive supply, yields substantial redistribution towards providers. But the necessity of negotiating prices with a public insurer
removes many of these gains. The private insurance industry also has a
powerful interest in the maintenance of private, fragmented health insur-

ance systems, because the very high overhead costs of such systems are the
sales revenues of the industry. In a universal public system, few of the
functions of the private system remain. Canadian experience with delegating
the remaining "post office" functions to private carriers on a regulated
basis showed that they were badly done and unnecessarily costly, hence the
consolidation of all insurance functions in the public agency. Thus, while
providers of health care see a threat to their rents, health care insurers
see a loss of their entire market.

In the debates over health insurance design, then, very large economic interests are at stake. And in this debate a supposedly general analytic
framework which "demonstrates" the welfare inferiority of universal public
health insurance by either assuming away or simply being unable to represent the issues on which it appears in practice to have the advantage, is
of obvious value to the advocates of the private system. It is no new
insight that rents can buy analysis, which in turn protects those rents by
obscuring their existence and supporting the institutional structures which
give rise to them, though the process seems to be increasingly open and institutionalized. The continuing popularity of the risk aversion/moral
hazard tradeoff model as a source of policy prescriptions in health insurance may be another example of this pattern.

FOOTNOTES

*)   University of British Columbia. Thanks, with the usual disclaimers,
are due to M. Barer, D. Donaldson, and two anonymous referees.

1)   The Canadian public insurance system covers the costs of care in general (and allied special) hospitals, and of physicians´ services in or out
of hospital. These costs amounted to over $10 billion, about 55% of total
health care costs ($19.1 b) in 1979. The remaining 45% includes drugs and
appliances supplied outside hospitals ($2.0 b) and dental care ($1.1 b)
which are still largely in the private sector although individual provinces
have programs which cover part of these costs for the whole population or
for sub-groups distinguished by age or income. Other expenditures (public
health, research, other institutional care) are predominantly public sector
programs. As of 1975, public sector funding covered 95% of hospital and
medical care, and 41% of other health expenditures, for a total public sector contribution of ´ just over 75% (Canada (1979) and unpublished data
supplied by the Department of National Health and Welfare). The expansion
of dental, pharmaceutical, and nursing home coverage by individual provinces since 1975 may have raised this proportion to 80%.

2)   The federal government contributed annually to each province a sum
equal to 25% of its expenditures on shareable hospital care, plus an additional sum equal to 25% of the national average per capita expenditure on
such care, multiplied by the provincial population. When the program was
extended to physicians´ services (Medicare), the additonal federal contribution to each province was equal to 50% of the national average expenditure on physicians´ services, multiplied by the provincial population. For
a variety of reasons, among them an alleged lack of incentives to provincial governments to control costs, as well as constraints on their ability
to do so imposed by the shareability rules, the reimbursement formula was
changed in 1977 to a complex mixture of direct payments and "tax points", -
increased shares in federal income tax collections, - whose critical feature is that a province´s receipts depend neither on its own, nor other

provinces´, expenditures.

3)   Saskatchewan established a universal public hospital insurance program in 1946, and medical insurance in 1962; these programs served as the models for the federal government´s definition of conforming plans. They were integrated into the national system when the federal legislation became effective. Most other provinces were able to establish similar programs on or shortly after the effective date, in many cases by taking over and extending existing not-for-profit community-rated service benefit plans, some originally physician-sponsored, in their provinces. Quebec, however, did not have as fully developed a private NFP system, and did not establish universal public coverage until 1961 (hospitals) and 1971 (medical care).

4)   Double billing (or as medical associations prefer, "balance billing") is prohibited in the three largest provinces, Ontario, Quebec and British Columbia, with about 70% of the Canadian population. Ontario and B.C. do permit opting out. In Quebec, if the physician bills the patient neither is reimbursed. The number of "opted out" physicians in Ontario is about 16%-18%; in Quebec and (more surprisingly) B.C. there are effectively none. The reasons for the difference are rather complex; the phenomenon of opting out in Ontario is examined in detail in Wolfson and Tuohy (1980). It appears that direct charges to patients for medical services are not significant overall, probably in the neighborhood of 5% at most of medical billings, but have important effects on patient access (and physician incomes) in specific small regions or specialties (Stoddart and Woodward, 1980).

5)   The political popularity of the universal plan is such that no serious political group can openly be against it. Proposals for its modification or, in the longer run, abandonment in favour of partial coverage by multiple insurers, are thus presented as "improvements".

6)   The most comprehensive descriptions of this process are those by external observers, e.g., Glaser (1980) and Lewin and Associates (1976).

7)   This process is discussed in more detail in Needleman (1980) and Evans (1980a).

8)   The private insurance industry position was clearly put by Anderson (1952) in calling for a public program consisting of a "catastrophic umbrella", covering costs above some income-based "bearable limit", with private voluntary plans up to that limit. It is unclear in what respect so-called "new approaches" to health insurance in the U.S. have advanced beyond this point. The counter-arguments were put by Willard and Taylor in their comments on that paper, and the Hall Commission (Canada, 1964) found the "catastrophic" case unconvincing. It is hard in retrospect to fault their judgement.

9)   An analysis of the issues involved, and of the logical and empirical foundations of the various pro- and anti-direct charges arguments is given by Barer et al. (1979). More recent work bearing on this issue includes Wolfson and Tuohy (1980), Stoddart and Woodward (1980), and Badgley and Smith (1979).

10)   One can define the transactor´s welfare as U(w,n) where w is wealth and n is some state of nature (Spence and Zeckhauser, 1971) which might be the individual´s health state. If "becoming ill" is represented by a shift from n to n´, clearly U(w,n) > U(w,n´), even abstracting from effects of

illness on earning capacity which would simultaneously lower w. The money loss equivalent to the change $n \to n^-$ would be a sum e such that $U(w-e,n) = U(w,n^-)$; the sum which would exactly compensate for the illness would be c such that $U(w,n) = U(w+c, n^-)$. It is, of course, a non-trivial restriction on the form of $U(\ )$ to assume that finite c and e exist.

If health care could produce instantaneous and perfectly effective "cures", of state n^-, at cost of v, then clearly the utility loss from illness is equivalent to (or no worse than) a money loss of v, since $U(w-v, n) \leq U(w,n^-)$ with equality if treatment is accepted. Only in this obviously unrealistic case is insurance against health care expenditures equivalent to insurance against illness events; and a policy paying a benefit of v will exactly compensate for occurrence of the illness event.

In the more general case, insurance coverage which fully compensated for the effects of illness would require a money payment p such that $U(w+p, n^-) = U(w,n)$ where p will be greater than v because the effects of care are neither instantaneous nor perfect - illness hurts - and indeed there may exist no finite p. In this case, however, optimal insurance (from the private buyer's perspective) does not necessarily imply full compensation. Private optimality requires equality of the marginal utility of wealth across health states: and the marginal utility of w will depend on n as well as w. Privately optimal coverage for illness will then exceed costs of care only if the marginal utility of wealth in the illness state exceeds that in the well state, after all relevant health care has had its best effects and been fully reimbursed. This need not be so even if the utility level in the illness state is unambiguously below that in the well state, as in general it will be (Dionne, 1982).

But this privately optimal level of insurance coverage will not be socially optimal; see note 14 below. The socially optimal level of coverage will, if some degree of egalitarianism is a social concern, respond to the differences in level of welfare associated with illness events, and thus involve further compensation.

11) Insurance against health care expenses rather than illness events does, however, provide some degree of coverage against the risks of inefficacious care - a sort of built-in product warranty. The efficacy of treatment cannot be certain, even if the competence of providers could be. Thus if initial treatment unexpectedly fails, and further or different treatment is necessary for a particular illness event, care reimbursement covers the risk of this eventuality (though not of the attendant further loss of utility) automatically. It does not require the definition of a reimbursable compound event, illness <u>and</u> failure of treatment, with its own specific reimbursement level.

12) Debate over this issue in the economic literature persists, because of the difficulty of developing tests which will unambiguously reject the conventional demand analysis at the level of aggregate price, quantity, and income data. A rich collection of unobserved variables and adjustment processes is always available to shift demand and supply curves so as to generate any particular empirical observation; see (but only as an example of a more extensive genre) Satterthwaite (1979). But in total the "Ptolemaic" approach to numerous anomalous results becomes unconvincing. And the medical literature contains large numbers of unambiguous examples of provider control over quantities of specific services, quite independent of price, which are consistent with the descriptive sociological literature

on health care. Some of the relevant Canadian evidence is assembled in Evans and Wolfson. (1978).

13) The problem of formulating an individual transactor's utility function with sufficient flexibility to reflect the direct and indirect influences of health care as well as the related interpersonal interactions is taken up in Evans and Wolfson (1980). Grossman (1970) introduced health status into a formal model of the health care utilization process, but by assuming that consumers had full knowledge of the production function linking health care to health he effectively assumed that all patients are at least as well-informed about medicine as their physicians! If true, this would have rather blunt implications for occupational licensure.

14) The tentative specification of this optimum is unavoidable. Quite apart from the acute unreality of the assumptions as to patient information and delivery system organization and product pricing, this "optimum" requires that the lump-sum redistribution process be determined by the effects of actual illness outcomes, combined with best-practice and least cost care as chosen by each consumer, on the (maximized) utility level of that consumer. Presumably one aspect of perfect information is no less, or more, plausible than another.

A different form of difficulty, however, is raised by the point referred to in note 10 above. If the individual's utility is a function of income/wealth and health status, there may be no finite payment which will compensate for illness; and even if such finite payment does exist, full compensation need not be privately optimal. The individual who can buy actuarially fair illness (not health care) insurance will maximize utility by doing so up to the point that the marginal utility of income/wealth, not the total utility level, is equal in each state.

It does not follow, however, that the optimal social insurance program would be one which merely redistributed wealth ex ante and then let individuals purchase their own insurance contracts so as to maximize their own expected utilities, and a fortiori it is erroneous to suggest that in practice redistributional concerns can all be addressed through the income or other tax systems while private markets handle the risk-bearing function.

In the first place, ex ante redistribution would have to be sensitive not only to relative money income or wealth positions, but also to ex ante expectation of loss due to illness - redistribution by risk as well as income class. Thus an additional major requirement of information and institutional flexibility is added to the requirement of complete, or at least symmetric, information between provider and consumer, and perfectly competitive markets for insurance and for health care.

But secondly, even if all these requirements were met, ex ante redistribution plus private expected utility maximization is not in general socially optimal. As Hammond (1980a,b) demonstrates, the ex ante social welfare function maximized over individual expected utilities is not equal to the expected value of the same social welfare function defined over ex post individual utilities, except under very restrictive, and dubious, restrictions on the functional form. The aggregation of the expected utilities does not equal the expectation of the aggregated utilities. We as a society will not like what comes out of the ex ante redistribution, private expected utility maximization process, and will quite rationally wish to do something about it ex post. Thus while the ex ante approach has the doctrinal advantage of preserving the efficiency of free markets, its ethical appeal is as Hammond notes, more limited than economists have been willing to admit. The ex ante and ex post approaches to welfare maximiza-tion are simply inconsistent, and neither has a privileged position a priori.

The full compensation approach taken here gives preference to ex post opti-mization, thereby taking no account of individuals´ risk preferences ex ante. This is I think rather more defensible in the real world of imperfect information and interpersonal externalities than it would be in the hypo-thetical world of perfect information and competition. The ex ante approach becomes rapidly less attractive as reality nears.

15) This is not to suggest that the agent always acts solely on the pa-tient´s behalf. The agency relationship is imperfect, and when there is a conflict of interest between principal and agent it is only the Hippocratic perfect agent, not the real-world professional, who always resolves it in the patient´s favour. The concept of the agency relationship as an institu-tional response to asymmetry of information between provider and consumer goes back to Arrow (1963); a detailed and very useful analysis of agency relations at the individual and collective levels is provided by Tuohy and Wolfson (1977). It must be stressed that it is the incomplete, or imperfect agency relationship which undermines the positive and normative signifi-cance of the demand curve, perfect agents (described as "generalized agents" or members of a "physician-patient pair") cease to be independent transactors and become merely informational adjuncts to the consumer. Some have used such assumptions to justify conventional demand analysis; apart from its surface implausibility and empirical problems perfect agency makes the supply side rather hard to specify!

16) This finding emerges from the pre- and post-Medicare surveys of utili-zation in Montreal (Enterline et al., 1973), as well as the studies by Beck and Horne summarized in Badgley and Smith (1979), Chapter 7. "Deterrence" of lower income groups by opting-out is also found by Stoddart and Woodward (1980) and is implicit in the findings of Wolfson and Tuohy (1980) on the importance of "practice streaming". Boulet and Henderson (1979) conclude from an analysis of utilization patterns that lower-income groups in Canada use more health care then the general population and that this is because they are in fact "sicker" - in contrast to Taylor´s (1957) demonstration that utilization was greater among upper income groups before public health insurance, despite the substantially greater burden of illness on lower-income people.

17) Thus a finding that physicians and their families use as much care as the general population, or more, does not necessarily indicate absence of professionally induced overutilization. Surgical procedures, in particular, provide illustrations of the rather peculiar processes governing physi-cians´ choices of interventions, and their tenuous connection with scien-tific evidence, Two decades ago, tonsillectomy was among the most common of procedures in North America, despite absence of any scientific justifica-tion in all but a small minority of cases. It has now largely fallen from favour. But a current favourite, coronary artery surgery, has been extensively and expensively provided across North America, despite absence of evidence that it prolongs life or prevents myocardial infarction (Preston, 1977). The claim that it provides relief of pain is anecdotal, not scientific, and must be viewed in light of earlier demonstrations that placebo surgery - making an incision in the chest and sewing it up - could

have the same effect.

Of course absence of evidence is not evidence of absence. But presumably physicians believe in the efficacy of what they do; and when these beliefs have no evidential foundation pro or con, their source becomes an interesting and economically significant question.

18) A nice recent example is given by Aday et al. (1980) in surveys 5 years apart of two groups of U.S. physicians which asked them to indicate "appropriate" utilization patterns for selected symptoms. The later survey leads to substantially higher "recommended" use for the same symptoms. Unfortunately the physician groups are not strictly comparable; the earlier group were "more expert" teaching hospital specialists.

19) Georgescu-Roegen (1966) labels as arithmomorphic the class of concepts which are susceptible of discrete distinction, such as the real line. But a concept such as "need" is nonarithmomorphic, in that it is not possible to make sharp cuts in the continuum and label one state as "need" and another not. Dialectical concepts may violate the Principle of Contradiction, and be both A and non-A (need and non-need) from different points of view. But it is a methodological error, common to the logical positivists, to assume that dialectical concepts are meaningless. The economist who regards the concept of need as meaningless might draw enlightenment from a hot abdomen.

20) This problem is frequently posed in terms of dramatic life-and-death situations, very expensive therapies which prolong (or offer a small chance of saving) an otherwise threatened life. But the stereotype appears erroneous. It is a consistent finding that a major source of health care cost escalation is low-technology conventional diagnostic and therapeutic interventions repeated many times (Martin et al. (1980) who reference a number of related studies). Zook and Moore (1980) and Schroeder et al. (1979) find a very high proportion of hospital care accounted for by a small number of heavy users with a wide variety of problems, but their patterns of use are not technologically dramatic. They merely have a large number of relatively ordinary-looking episodes.

21) Sole source public funding introduces a monopsonist element on the payment side of the utilization process, offsetting the market power of providers. As the U.S. and particularly the German case illustrate, it is the multiplicity of funding sources, not the presence or absence of large out-of-pocket payments by patients or the mode of organization of insurance carriers, that renders overall costs uncontrollable. But as Marmor et al. have pointed out (1976, 1980), "unbalanced political markets" can result in uncontrolled cost inflation even with full public funding. The U.S. experience with HSAs is an example of the impotence of low-level public planning agencies without fiscal control. But the Swedish example suggests that even public sole source funding can lead to uncontrolled cost escalation if the level of government responsible is relatively junior, has few or no competing spending responsibilities, and is able to blur the responsibility for the tax implications of its expenditures. The funding agency can be "captured" by providers if the "political marketplace" is not also balanced. The Canadian provinces, with full public responsibility for their taxing decisions, a wide variety of competing expenditure claims, and a constitutionally established sphere of sovereignty, appear to provide this balance.

22) Havighurst and Hackbarth (1979) openly assert (p. 1305): "The important factor is not so much the result itself - for example the share of the gross national product dedicated to health care - as the process by which that result is reached." In this argument, % of GNP is merely an example.

It is equally applied to patterns of utilization, and their associated health outcomes, and thus highlights the indifference to outcomes per se which is implicit in the normative use of willingness-to-pay. Their preference for the particular allocative processes of competitive markets over political systems is then justified by the assertion that such markets are more likely to reveal and adapt to consumers´ preferences, but this is of course untestable because no specific system outcome data (cost, effectiveness, use patterns) are admissable as evidence. The likelihood is a priori; and yet Schelling (1978) provides numerous examples of situations in which decentralized decision-making makes participants worse off than a collectively imposed decision. Havighurst and Hackbarth are unusual only to the extent that they make explicit the underpinnings of this analysis. If one is not prepared to join them in their "leap of faith", then one may still be interested in the concrete results of effectiveness, distribution, and resource use generated by a health care system.

23) The importance of the split between capital and operating cost funding is discussed in more detail in Evans (1980a).

24) This appears to be an example of a general phenomenon analysed by Hirschman (1970). Political "voice" and market "exit" are alternative ways of keeping organizational performance up to standard, each with strengths and weaknesses. But "exit" weakens "voice", and any public institution may deteriorate rapidly if the most politically potent and quality-conscious members of the society withdraw from it. The problem appears related to Akerlof´s (1970) "Lemons" model.

25) This statement might not command universal assent. Several authors, such as Havighurst and Hackbarth (1979), Goldberg and Greenberg (1977), and Enthoven (1978) have argued that initiatives by individual insurers could, in a more competitive, less regulated health care system, have beneficial effects on utilization patterns and costs. Goldberg and Greenberg, in particular, document attempts by private insurers to exercise some direct influence over the health care system. They emphasized that such efforts would be made, but gave less attention to the fact that they were total failures. To date the U.S. arguments for deregulation and private initiatives concern what might happen in hypothetical circumstances, not what has happened. Whether it would be possible to approximate these hypothetical circumstances by politically feasible modifications to the current U.S. system, and whether, even then, beneficial results would follow, no one knows. Developments during 1982 cast serious doubt on the political feasibility of change. But in fact (note 18 supra) the advocates of the unregulated marketplace do not really base their case on anticipated results.

26) In 1978, prepayment and administration costs in Canada were $243 million, (Canada, unpublished federal data) compared with $10.0 billion in the U.S. (Gibson, 1979) or $10.30 per capita compared with $44.94. But $1C ≈ 85 ¢ U.S. in 1978, so the Canadian cost would be $8.75 US per capita. Put another way, such costs in Canada are 1.5% of total health costs, and 2.6% of physician and hospital costs; in the U.S. they are 5.2% of the total and 9.0% of physician and hospital costs. Horne and Beck (1981) provide further

analysis of this difference.

27) It might be argued that the private, fragmented system produces "variety" as well as risk-spreading, that the multiplicity of different types of carriers and contracts offers purchasers a range of choice over risk/premium bundles which is itself valued. While one cannot absolutely refute this suggestion, since in general variety and choice are valuable ceteris paribus, nevertheless one can assert that the existence of such variety in a market is not a revealed preference for it. First, as noted above, what the private market sells is variety plus ex ante wealth redistribution, relative to a comprehensive system. The fact that there is a market for this combination does not indicate that variety per se in risk-spreading contracts is valued. Indeed Aday et al. (1980) report that most Americans would prefer more comprehensive coverage, ceteris paribus, but one cannot know whether these responses include a willingness to pay for any increase in their own claims. Secondly, Lancaster (1979) demonstrates that in markets characterized by variety and scale economies, there is no a priori presumption that competition will lead to an optimal balance of variety and efficiency. And finally, most private insurance is not bought individually, thus one cannot infer individual preferences for variety from market data without interposing a theory of employee group decision-making. If such purchases were individual, then in addition to the adverse selection problem, one should become much more suspicious of the zero transactions cost implicit in the assumption that variety is a "good".

28) Akerlof (1970) demonstrated that asymmetry of information between buyer and seller about the characteristics of specific products could lead to situations of sub-optimal, or no, equilibrium levels of prices and trades. The buyer of health insurance is assumed to have better information about his/her personal risk status than the seller, although the seller may have better information about the characteristics of buyers as a group. Wilson (1976), and Rothschild and Stiglitz (1976) have explored the question of whether such markets will reach equilibrium, and if so, what kind. Their model focusses only on the adverse selection problem, as the loss of each individual insured is exogenous and insurance contracts are made up of fixed pairs of premium and indemnity.

Pauly (1974) considered the sale of continuously variable levels of coverage to people who could, at some cost, influence their level of loss (moral hazard) and while reaching the conventional conclusion that full loss coverage is non-optimal, suggested that the private market led to "overinsurance" as high risk people would buy from several companies and then "underspend" on prevention. A public monopoly could determine each person´s total coverage, and make premiums rise with coverage. Here the principal focus is on moral hazard, but the conclusion is of interest because of course public plans in practice respond to perceived under-insurance, not overinsurance. Their justification includes, but goes beyond, the market failure issues addressed by the Rothschild/Stiglitz/Wilson analysis.

REFERENCES

Aday, L.A., Anderson, R. and Fleming, G.V., (1980), Health Care in the U.S.: Equitable for Whom?, Sage Publications, Beverly Hills, California.

Akerlof, G.A. (1970), The Market for "Lemons": Qualitative Uncertainty and the Market Mechanism, Quarterly Journal of Economics, Vol. 84, No. 3,

August.

Anderson, W.M. (1952), Voluntary Health and Pension Plans - Can They Meet the Major Needs?, and Discussion by J. Willard and M.G. Taylor, Institute of Public Administration of Canada, Proceedings.

Arrow, K.J. (1963), Uncertainty and the Welfare Economics of Medical Care, American Economic Review, Vol. 53, No. 5, December.

Arrow, K.J. (1976), Welfare Analysis of Changes in Health Coinsurance Rates, in Rosett, R. (ed), The Role of Health Insurance in the Health Services Sector, Universities - NBER Conference £27, Neale Watson, New York.

Badgley, R.F. and Smith, R.D. (1979), User Charges for Health Services. Ontario Council of Health, Toronto.

Bardsley, J.E. and Gibson, J.E. (1975), The Münchausen´s Syndrome, Modern Medicine of Canada, Vol. 30, No 11, November.

Barer, M.L., Evans, R.G. and Stoddart, G.L. (1979), Controlling Health Care Costs by Direct Charges to Patients: Snare or Delusion? Ontario Economic Council, Toronto.

Boulet, J.-A. and Henderson, D.W. (1979), Distributional and Redistributional Aspects of Government Health Programs in Canada, Discussion Paper £146, Economic Council of Canada, Ottawa, December.

Canada, Department of National Health and Welfare (1979), National Health Expenditures in Canada, 1960-1975, Ottawa: National Health and Welfare, Information Systems Branch, January.

Canada, Royal Commission on Health Services (Hall Commission) (1964), Report, Vol. 1, The Queen´s Printer, Ottawa.

Crew, M.A. (1969), Coinsurance and the Welfare Economics of Medical Care, American Economic Review, Vol. 59, No. 5, December.

Culyer, A.J. (1971a), The Commodity "Health Care" and its Efficient Allocation, Oxford Economic Papers, Vol. 23, No. 2, July.

Culyer, A.J. (1971b), Medical Care and the Economics of Giving, Economica, Vol. 38, No 151, August.

Culyer, A.J. and Simpson, H. (1980), Externality Models and Health: A Rückblick over the Last Twenty Years, Economic Record, Vol. 56, No. 154, September.

Dionne, G. (1982), Moral Hazard and State-Dependent Utility Function, Journal of Risk and Insurance, Vol. 49, No. 3, September.

Enterline, P.E. et al (1973), The Distribution of Medical Services Before and After "Free" Medical Care - The Quebec Experience, New England Journal of Medicine, Vol. 289, No. 22.

Enthoven, A. (1978), Consumer - Choice Health Plan (2 parts), New England Journal of Medicine, Vol. 298, Nos. 12, 13, March 23, 30.

Evans, R.G., (1980a), The Fiscal Management of Medical Technology, in Banta, H.D. (ed.), Resources for Health: Technology Assessment for Policy Making, Praeger, New York.

Evans, R.G. (1980b), Is Health Care Better in Canada than in the U.S.?, Paper presented at the Seminar on Canadian-United States Relations, University Consortium for Research on North America, November.

Evans, R.G. (1982), Health Care in Canada: Patterns of Funding and Regulation in McLachlan, G. and Maynard, A. (eds.), The Public-Private Mix for Health: The Relevance and Effects of Change, Nuffield Provincial Hospitals Trust, London.

Evans, R.G. and Wolfson, A.D. (1980), Faith, Hope, and Charity: Health Care in the Utility Function, Department of Economics Discussion Paper £80-46, University of British Columbia, Vancouver.

Evans, R.G. and Wolfson, A,D. (1978), Moving the Target to Hit the Bullet: Generation of Utilization by Physicians in Canada, (unpublished), Department of Health Administration, University of Toronto.

Feldstein, M. (1973), The Welfare Cost of Excess Health Insurance, Journal of Political Economy, Vol. 81, No. 2, Part 1, March/April.

Georgescu-Roegen, N. (1966), Analytical Economics: Issues and Problems, Harvard University Press, Cambridge, Mass.

Gibson, R.M. (1979), National Health Expenditures, 1978, Health Care Financing Review, Vol. 1, No. 1, Summer.

Glaser, W.A. (1980), Paying the Hospital in Canada, (unpublished), Center for the Social Sciences at Columbia University, New York, November.

Goldberg, L.E. and Greenberg, W. (1977), The Effect of Physician-Controlled Health Insurance: U.S. vs. Oregon State Medical Society, Journal of Health Politics, Policy and Law, Vol. 2, No. 1, Spring.

Grossman, M. (1970), The Demand for Health: A Theoretical and Empirical Investigation, N.B.E.R. Occasional Paper £119, Columbia University Press, New York.

Hall, E.M. (1980), A Commitment for Renewal, Canada´s National-Provincial Health Program for the 1980´s, Report of the Special Commission, Health Services Review ´79, appointed by the Minister of National Health and Welfare, Saskatoon, Saskatchewan, August.

Hammond, P.J. (1980a), Ex-Ante and Ex-Post Welfare Optimality Under Uncertainty, University of Essex, Economics Discussion Paper £83.

Hammond, P.J. (1980b), Some Uncomfortable Options in Welfare Economics Under Uncertainty, Given at Symposium on Social Choice, Caen, September.

Havighurst, C.C. and Hackbarth G.M. (1979), Private Cost Containment, New England Journal of Medicine, Vol. 300, No. 23, June 7.

Hirschman, A.O. (1970), Exit, Voice, and Loyalty, Harvard University Press, Cambridge, Mass.

Horne, J.M. and Beck, R.G. (1981), Further Evidence on Public vs. Private Administration of Health Insurance, Journal of Public Health Policy, Vol. 2, No. 3, September.

Krashinsky, M. (1981), User Charges in the Social Services: An Economic Theory of Need and Inability, Ontario Economic Council Research Study £22, University of Toronto Press, Toronto.

Lancaster, K. (1979), Variety, Equity and Efficiency, Columbia, New York.

Lewin and Associates Inc. (1976), Government Controls on the Health Care System: The Canadian Experience, Washington, D.C., January 31.

Lindsay, C.M. (1969), Medical Care and the Economics of Sharing, Economica, Vol. 36, No. 144, November.

Marmor, T.R., Wittman, D.A. and Heagy, T.C. (1976), Politics, Public Policy, and Medical Inflation, in Zubkoff, M. (ed.) Health: A Victim or Cause of Inflation?, Prodist for the Milbank Memorial Fund, New York.

Marmor, T.R. and Bridges, A. (1980), American Health Planning and the Lessons of Comparative Policy Analysis, Journal of Health Politics, Policy and Law, Vol. 5, no. 3, Fall.

Martin, A.R., et al. (1980), A Trial of Two Strategies to Modify the Test-Ordering Behaviour of Medical Residents, New England Journal of Medicine, Vol. 303, No. 23, December 4.

Mossin, J. (1968), Aspects of Rational Insurance Purchasing, Journal of Political Economy, Vol. 76, No. 4, Part 1, July/August.

Needleman, J. (1980), The Management of Medical Technology in Canada, in United States Congress, Office of Technology Assessment, The Implications of Cost-Effectiveness Analysis of Medical Technology, Background Paper £4: The Management of Health Care Technology in Ten Countries, U.S. Government Printing Office, Washington D.C., October.

Pauly, M.V. (1968), The Economics of Moral Hazard: Comment, American Economic Review, Vol. 58, No. 3, June.

Pauly, M.V. (1969), A Measure of the Welfare Cost of Health Insurance, Health Services Research, Vol. 4, No. 4, Winter.

Pauly, M.V. (1974), Overinsurance and Public Provision of Insurance: The Roles of Moral Hazard and Adverse Selection, Quarterly Journal of Economics, Vol. 88, No. 1, February.

Preston, T.A. (1977), Coronary Artery Surgery: A Critical Review, Raven Press, New York.

Rothschild, M. and Stiglitz, J.E. (1976), Equilibrium in Competitive Insurance Markets: An Essay on the Economics of Imperfect Information, Quarterly Journal of Economics, Vol. 90, No. 4, November.

Satterthwaite, M. (1979), Consumer Information, Equilibrium Industry Price, and the Number of Sellers, Bell Journal of Economics, Vol. 10, No. 2, Autumn.

Schelling, T.C. (1978), Micromotives and Macrobehaviour, Norton, New York.

Schroeder, S.A., Showstack, J.A. and Roberts, H.E. (1979), Frequency and Clinical Description of High-Cost Patients in 17 Acute-Care Hospitals, New England Journal of Medicine, vol. 300, No. 23, June 7.

Spence, M. and Zeckhauser, R. (1971), Insurance, Information, and Individual Action, American Economic Review Papers and Proceedings, Vol. 61, No. 2, May.

Stoddart, G.L. and Barer, M.L. (1981), Analyses of Demand and Utilization through Episodes of Medical Service, in Perlman, M. and van der Gaag, J. (eds.), Health, Economics, and Health Economics, North-Holland, Amsterdam.

Stoddart, G.L. and Woodward, C.A. (1980), The Effect of Physician Extra-Billing on Patients´ Access to Care and Attitudes Toward the Ontario Health System, (unpublished), A Study Commissioned by the Special Commissioner, Health Services Review ´79 (Hall, 1980), McMaster University, Hamilton, Ontario.

Taylor, M.G. (1957), Financial Aspects of Health Insurance, Canadian Tax Papers, £12, Canadian Tax Foundation, Toronto.

Tuohy, C.J. and Wolfson, A.D. (1977), The Political Economy of Professionalism: A Perspective, in Trebilcock, M.J. (ed.), Four Aspects of Professionalism, Consumer Research Council, Department of Consumer and Corporate Affairs, Ottaws.

Williams, A. (1978), Need: An Economic Exegesis, in Culyer, A.J. and Wright, K.G. (eds.), Economic Aspects of Health Services, Martin Robertson, London.

Wilson, C. (1976), A Model of Insurance Markets with Asymmetric Information, Cowles Foundation Discussion Paper £432, Yale University, June 29.

Wolfson, A.D. and Tuohy, C.J. (1980), Opting Out of Medicare: Private Medical Markets in Ontario, Ontario Economic Council Research Study £19, University of Toronto Press, Toronto.

Zeckhauser, R. (1970), Medical Insurance: A Case Study of the Tradeoff Between Risk Spreading and Appropriate Incentives, Journal of Economic Theory, Vol. 2, No. 1, March.

Zook, C.J. and Moore, F.D. (1980), High-Cost Users of Medical Care, New England Journal of Medicine, Vol. 302, No. 18, May 1.

ARNE RYDE SYMPOSIUM ON SOCIAL INSURANCE
L. Söderström (editor)
© Elsevier Science Publishers B.V. (North-Holland), 1983

INFLATION IN THE HEALTH CARE SECTOR
AND THE DEMAND FOR INSURANCE:
A MICRO STUDY

Peter Zweifel*

1. INTRODUCTION

Apart from the U.S., Switzerland is one of the few countries where individuals basically decide themselves about the amount of health insurance. Only a small minority of low-income earners are required to have health insurance by law, yet almost the entire population is covered by at least a basic package providing for ambulatory care and free stationary care in a public ward. A great majority has even opted for supplementary hospital insurance granting access to semi-private and private wards of both public and voluntary hospitals. Here, the dynamics of what has become known as the cost-insurance spiral are most clearly observed. The spiral was probably triggered in the mid-sixties by an amendment to the Law on Health and Disability Insurance requiring the sick funds to cover stationary care costs up to 720 consecutive days within three years. This boosting of demand exerted an upward pressure on daily room rates and treatment fees, jeopardizing the insurers' financial equilibrium. Their typical reaction has been to increase the premium for the basic package but leaving the marginal price of supplementary hospital insurance unaffected. Nevertheless, an adjustment of the insurance policy to the higher financial risk associated with hospitalization does cost more. If the insured shy away from the certain cost of additional insurance, they will bear some of the higher expected costs of the sickness episodes. Demand is curtailed, and the cost-insurance spiral comes to a stop. If, however, the insured shy away from the higher risk, they will opt for increased coverage. Since the variance of cost for medical treatment typically increases, they are likely to overshoot in their adjustment. When physicians realize that their patients are even more sheltered from the actual price of medical care, they are less constrained than ever by cost considerations in their choice of treatment. Hence, the spiral may go into its next turn.

This process has been described by Feldstein (1973) in his pioneering study of the dynamic feedbacks between insurance, demand, and inflation in the U.S. health care sector. This paper purports to construct a microeconomic model laying the theoretical basis for the link from cost inflation to the demand for insurance presupposed by Feldstein. The focus will be on a European institutional setting where insurance density has been high for a long time. Hence, the cost-insurance spiral can be studied in its pure form, without being fueled by the growth of the insurance market. In the same vein, a distinction is made between patient-controlled demand for ambulatory care and physician-determined utilization of hospital services. This model is presented in the following section and compared with previous work in the economics of health insurance. The necessary conditions for an optimum are interpreted in another section. The comparative static implications of a price increase in the health care sector are then worked out and shown to depend on the degree of risk aversion. The empirical part begins with a description of the micro data base developed for this study, consisting of some 1,600 individual observations over the years 1976-1980. Refined hypotheses bearing on two jointly dependent variables are also formulated. The econometric results are discussed in the sequel. The concluding section contains a preliminary answer to the question of whether the postulated cost-insurance spiral might exist at all in Switzerland.

2. A MODEL OF INSURANCE DEMAND ASSUMING BOUNDED RATIONALITY

In this section a model of the demand for supplementary health insurance coverage is sketched, which incorporates the assumption of bounded rationality of the insured on the one hand and some peculiarities of policies written by Swiss sick funds on the other hand. The individual is assumed to maximize expected utility defined over net income and healthy leisure time in the following way.

$$E(U) = \int_0^c U[Y(s),H(s)]f(s,\bar{s})ds + \int_c^m U[Y(s),H(s)]f(s,\bar{s})ds$$

$$+ \int_m^1 U[Y(s),H(s)]f(s,\bar{s})ds$$

$$\rightarrow \quad \text{max. S.T.}$$

$$Y = w[W - g \cdot t \cdot M] - r \cdot q \cdot M - R \tag{1a}$$
$$H = T - L(M,s) - W \tag{1b}$$
$$0 \leq s < c(M) \quad \text{state 1}$$

$$Y = \bar{Y} - [q \cdot K(X,s) - X] - R \tag{2a}$$
$$H = T - L[K(X,s),M(s),s] \tag{2b}$$
$$c \leq s < m \quad \text{state 2}$$

$$Y = \bar{Y} - [(q-b) \cdot M(s)] - [q \cdot K(s) - X] - R \tag{3a}$$
$$H = T - L[K(s),M(s),s] \tag{3b}$$
$$m \leq s \leq 1 \quad \text{state 3}$$

$$R = (1 + \theta) \left\{ \int_0^c [(1-r)[q \cdot M] f(\bar{s})d\bar{s} + \int_c^m [q \cdot M(\bar{s}) + X] f(\bar{s})d\bar{s} \right. \tag{4}$$
$$\left. + \int_m^1 [b \cdot M(\bar{s}) + X] f(\bar{s})d\bar{s} \right]$$

Decision variables

b : Daily room charge covered by policy

M : Medical services demanded, in fractionals of physician days (only in state 1 with ambulatory care; exogenous in states 2 and 3)

W : Working time, in days, including time spent on ambulatory care

X : Costs of stationary treatment covered by the policy

Derived decision variables

c : Critical symptom level of the ambulatory care physician, marking the beginning of hospitalization

L : Days lost due to illness (only in states 1 and 2; exogenous in state 3)

H : Healthy days, net of working time

R : Premium paid to the sick fund

Y : Wage income, net of sick fund premium and out-of-pocket expenditures for medical care

Exogenous variables

g : Share of working time lost due to ambulatory care which is deducted in the calculation of income

K : Stationary treatment, in fractionals of hospital physician days

M : Length of stay in the hospital, in days (in states 2 and 3)

m : Emergency level of symptom intensity

q : Implicit wage rate of the physician in charge (private or hospital-based), or daily room rate.

r : Average coinsurance rate applied to ambulatory services

s : Symptom level, random variable, $0 \leq s \leq 1$

$\bar{s}$: Parameter characterizing the density function $f(s)$, e.g. "mean symptom level"

t : Patient's time input per physician day of ambulatory care

w : Wage rate of the insured

$\bar{Y}$: Transfer income, effective when insured is hospitalized

θ   :   Loading factor for covering administrative costs and
        accumulation of reserves

In this model, the individual decides to what extent he wants to purchase
supplementary insurance granting access to semiprivate and private accommodation.[1] In doing this, he has to weigh three states of the world. In the
first state, depicted by eqs. (1a) and (1b), he works, being basically
healthy. He demands ambulatory medical care (M) in the economic sense of
the term. This demand requires time input which is deducted from gross
working time (W) to the extent that the parameter (g) is different from
zero. For example, g = 1 for a blue collar worker, while g = 0 for a public
employee. Net income (Y) is further reduced because the fraction (r) of the
medical bill, amounting to (q·M), must be borne by the insured.[2] Besides
net income (Y), healthy leisure time (H) also enters the individual´s utility function. This is given by the total time available minus working time
(W) minus time lost due to illness (L). This loss is reduced by the use of
ambulatory medical care (M) but is primarily a function of symptom level
(s), a random variable.

In state 2, this symptom level exceeds a critical threshold (c) where the
physician refers his patient to a hospital. But there is still time enough
to search for a bed where the daily room rate (denoted by (q) again for
parsimony of notation) is covered by the benefit (b) contracted in the policy. Patients in semiprivate and private wards are billed separately for
stationary treatment, again at a price (q) per time unit of (K).[3] Therefore, the insured runs a risk of being less than fully covered on that
account if he opts for a low benefit level (X). Since he does not work when
in the hospital, he receives an income transfer (Ȳ) instead of his earned
wage income (Y). Swiss law traditionally requires sick funds to offer a
minimum daily transfer payment as part of their health insurance package.
This part of the policy is very rarely modified; therefore, it is not expected to contribute to the dynamics of the cost-insurance spiral and will
not be analyzed as a separate decision variable. Out of his transferred income the individual must cover any difference between the treatment costs
incurred in the hospital, given by q·K(s), and the insured upper limit (X).
Board and room charges leave his net income unaffected because in state 2
he is able to select a hospital whose rate is fully covered by his insurance policy. Finally, the change of notation should be noted. The decision
variable (M) of the first state has been replaced by the random variable
M(s), which is not under the individual´s control according to this model.
Accordingly, the number of healthy days (H) has become a fully stochastic
variable.

State 3 describes an emergency where the individual cannot influence the
choice of the hospital anymore. He may therefore find himself in an institution whose daily room rate will be only partially covered by his policy.
This means that the difference (q-b) will be his daily out-of-pocket expense, for a period of (M) days. Finally, the individual counts on hospital
physicians to do all that is necessary to keep him alive, regardless of insurance status. For this reason, loss (L) is independent of (X) in state 3.

For an insurance to maintain its long-run financial equilibrium, the premium (R) paid by an individual member would have to equal the expected value
of cost attributed to him. This is the pricing principle associated with
the notion of actuarially fair insurance, see Phelps (1976); for other
pricing rules, see Borch (1974); for different interpretations of equiva-

lence in insurance, see Eisen (1979). Equation (4) is a much weaker condition, saying that premiums are set as to cover the costs generated by an
individual that could be drawn from any of the populations at risk, each of
these populations being characterized by some value of mean symptom level
($\bar{s}$). Thus, there is no individual experience rating, only community experience rating (for the basic package) and rating according to age of entry
(for supplementary hospital coverage as well). Differentiation according to
sex is limited to a 10% surcharge for female members throughout; in return,
the sick funds receive a per capita subsidy amounting to some 20% of their
income. Since profit and loss statements need not be published by line of
business, there is ample room for cross-subsidization from the basic
package (covering ambulatory care as well as accommodation and treatment in
a public ward) to supplementary hospital insurance (where funds compete
with private insurance companies). In short, eq. (4) may be considered as
an approximation to premium setting by sick funds, which cannot be examined
more closely within the scope of this paper. The formulation chosen implies
that sick funds may not be viable on the long run. In fact, their number
has decreased from 898 in 1966 to 469 in 1980 (Swiss Statistical Yearbook
1982, pp. 315, 316).

This model is one of bounded rationality for three reasons. First, the decisionmaker does not consider ex ante the relationship between his choice
of coverage and the fact that he will incur higher expected costs in the
future due to his own moral hazard. Second, the decision to go to the hospital lies in the hands of the physician; he, not the patient, sets the
critical symptom level that governs hospitalization. Third, the insured
considers his medical bill to be a random variable as soon as he is
referred to the hospital. All three assumptions deviate from the received
literature on the demand for health insurance, represented e.g. by Phelps
(1976). But they may well mirror the subjective decision framework of an
individual who has been highly insured for a long time compared to American
standards. He has therefore been taught to fully delegate decisions to the
physician in charge. Moreover, hospital-based physicians often assume control even when the patient has opted for semi private accommodation. This
makes for a very much reduced influence of the patient on the size of the
hospital bill. All of this is of course not meant to deny that patients as
a group may influence the behavior of physicians inside and outside the
hospital.[4] But of these facts and relationships, only two are deemed to be
relevant to the individual: He does suspect that calling upon the ambulatory care physician more often increases the probability of being sent to the
hospital; critical symptom level (c) is therefore made an inverse function
of demand (M) in the first state. The insured also expects that physicians
in the hospital will treat him more intensively if insurance coverage
allows. Hence, input of treatment hours (K) is a function of treatment
outlays coverage (X) in state 2.

3. NECESSARY CONDITIONS FOR OPTIMAL COVERAGE

In this section, we study the choice of supplementary health insurance coverage of a typical individual on the assumption that eqs. (1) to (4)
adequately depict his objectives and binding constraints. Out of the four
decision variables (b,X,M,W) we simultaneously analyze two (b,X), postu-
lating demand for ambulatory care (M) and supply of hours worked (W) to be
predetermined when the individual decides about the values of (b) and (X)
written into his insurance contract. In contradistinction to private health
insurance, the rate of coinsurance (r) is fixed by law and therefore exoge-

nous to the model.[5] In turn, these parameters of his policy are fixed when he becomes ill and considers seeing the doctor or reducing his working time. Under these assumptions, we have at an interior optimum,

$$\frac{\partial EU}{\partial b} = 0, \frac{\partial EU}{\partial X} = 0; \quad \begin{bmatrix} \dfrac{\partial^2 EU}{\partial b^2} & \dfrac{\partial^2 EU}{\partial b \partial X} \\ \\ \dfrac{\partial^2 EU}{\partial b \partial X} & \dfrac{\partial^2 EU}{\partial X^2} \end{bmatrix} \text{ negative definite.} \tag{5}$$

Using eqs. (1a) to (3a) and (4) we obtain for the first necessary condition

$$\frac{\partial EU}{\partial b} = \frac{\partial}{\partial b} \left[\int_0^c U(\cdot)f(\cdot)ds + \int_c^m U(\cdot)f(\cdot)ds + \int_m^1 U(\cdot)f(\cdot)ds \right] \tag{6}$$

$$= \int_0^c \frac{\partial}{\partial Y}[U(\cdot)]\frac{\partial Y}{\partial b} f(\cdot)ds + \int_c^m \frac{\partial}{\partial Y}[U(\cdot)]\frac{\partial Y}{\partial b} f(\cdot)ds + \int_m^1 \frac{\partial}{\partial Y}[U(\cdot)]\frac{\partial Y}{\partial b} f(\cdot) \ ds$$

$$+ \int_0^c 0 \cdot f(\cdot)ds + \int_c^m 0 \cdot f(\cdot)ds + \int_m^1 0 \cdot f(\cdot)ds$$

$$= 0.$$

EU : Expectation of the utility index, $= E(U)$

$f(\cdot)$: Density function defined over (s), $= f(s,\bar{s})$

$U(\cdot)$: Utility function, $= U[Y(s), H(s)]$

The three vanishing terms at the end of the equation mirror the fact that varying (b) has no influence on the number of healthy days (H). For in state 1 $(0 \leq s \leq c)$, there is no relationship whatsoever between (H) and (b), cf. eq. (1b). In states 2 and 3 $(c \leq s \leq 1)$, the number of healthy days is determined by the symptom level (s) and therefore a random variable independent of (b), cf. eq. (2b) and (3b). We now turn to the partial relationship between net income (Y) and the insured daily room rate (b). Again, the three states are distinguished by the individual as well as by the sick fund (cf. eq. (4)):

$$\frac{\partial Y}{\partial b} = \begin{cases} -\dfrac{\partial R}{\partial b} = -(1+\theta)\int_m^1 M(\bar{s})f(\bar{s})d\bar{s} < 0 & 0 \leq s < c \\ \\ -\dfrac{\partial R}{\partial b} = -(1+\theta)\int_m^1 M(\bar{s})f(\bar{s})d\bar{s} < 0 & c \leq s < m \quad (7) \\ \\ M(s) - \dfrac{\partial R}{\partial b} = M(s) - (1+\theta)\int_m^1 M(\bar{s})f(\bar{s})d\bar{s} > 0 & m \leq s \leq 1 \end{cases}$$

The sign of the third expression of eq. (7) would be self-evident if individuals were identical in terms of their distribution of $M(s)$ in state 3. But here we allow individual expectations concerning this distribution to differ from the evaluation by the sick fund, which is in terms of entire populations ($\bar{s}$). Nevertheless, there is no reason why a majority of insureds should think of themselves as belonging to a population characterized by a value of ($\bar{s}$) that is lower than the value used for premium setting. It is therefore reasonable to posit

$$M(s) - \int_{m}^{1} M(\bar{s})f(\bar{s})d\bar{s} > 0. \qquad\qquad m \leq s \leq 1 \qquad (8)$$

Together, eqs. (6) and (7) yield

$$\frac{\partial EU}{\partial b} = \int_{0}^{c}[-U_Y(1+\theta)EM]f(\cdot)ds + \int_{c}^{m}[-U_Y(1+\theta)EM]f(\cdot)ds \qquad (9)$$
$$\phantom{\frac{\partial EU}{\partial b} =}\ \ {}_{(-)}\ \ {}_{(-)}$$

$$+ \int_{m}^{1}U_Y[M(s) - (1+\theta)EM]f(\cdot)ds = 0.$$
$$\phantom{+ \int_{m}^{1}U_Y[M(s) - }{}_{(+)}$$

U_Y : Marginal utility of income, $= \partial U/\partial Y$

EM : Expectation of $M(\bar{s})$ as estimated by the sick fund,
$$= \int_{m}^{1} M(\bar{s})f(\bar{s})d\bar{s}$$

When selecting his preferred coverage of the daily room rate (b), the individual must therefore weigh three aspects against each other. As long as he is basically healthy or at least has some liberty in planning his admission to the hospital (states 1 and 2), he loses income by opting for a higher value of (b). In the optimum, this expected loss is matched by the avoided loss of income due to insufficient insurance coverage in the emergency state 3. It is remarkable that the restriction (8), together with the requirement that (θ) be small, is sufficient for the existence of an optimum with $b > 0$.[6] In similar manner, the first-order optimum condition with regard to maximum treatment costs covered by the policy is

$$\frac{\partial EU}{\partial X} = \int_{0}^{c}\frac{\partial}{\partial Y}[U(\cdot)]\frac{\partial Y}{\partial X} f(\cdot)ds + \int_{c}^{m}\frac{\partial}{\partial Y}[U(\cdot)]\frac{\partial Y}{\partial X} f(\cdot)ds \qquad (10)$$

$$+ \int_{m}^{1}\frac{\partial}{\partial Y}[U(\cdot)]\frac{\partial Y}{\partial X} f(\cdot)ds$$

$$+ \int_{0}^{c}0\cdot f(\cdot)ds + \int_{c}^{m}\frac{\partial}{\partial H}[U(\cdot)]\frac{\partial H}{\partial X} f(\cdot)ds + \int_{m}^{1}0\cdot f(\cdot)ds$$

$$= 0.$$

The effect of a change of (X) on net income, $\partial Y/\partial X$, is again state-dependent, due to eqs. (1a), (2a) and (3a):

$$
\frac{\partial Y}{\partial X} = \begin{cases}
- \dfrac{\partial R}{\partial X} = -(1+\theta) \int\limits_{c}^{1} f(\bar{s})d\bar{s} < 0 & 0 \leq s < c \\[4mm]
-q\cdot\dfrac{\partial K(X,s)}{\partial X} + 1 - \dfrac{\partial R}{\partial X} = 1 - q\cdot\dfrac{\partial K(X,s)}{\partial X} - (1+\theta) \int\limits_{c}^{1} f(\bar{s})d\bar{s} > 0 & c \leq s < m \\[4mm]
1 - \dfrac{\partial R}{\partial X} = 1 - (1+\theta) \int\limits_{c}^{1} f(\bar{s})d\bar{s} > 0 & m \leq s \leq 1
\end{cases}
\tag{11}
$$

The sign restrictions are plausible in view of the small value of (θ) noted above and the fact that the premiums set by the sick fund do not take into account the increase in intensity of stationary treatment due to improved coverage, see the discussion of the variable CSTAY in the empirical part of the paper.

In contradistinction to the other states, there is an indirect influence of (X) on the number of healthy days in state 2:

$$
\frac{\partial H}{\partial X} = \frac{\partial L(\cdot,s)}{\partial K} \cdot \frac{\partial K}{\partial X} > 0.
\tag{12}
$$

Substituting eqs. (11) and (12) into eq. (10), we obtain

$$
\frac{\partial EU}{\partial X} = \int\limits_{0}^{c} [-U_Y(1+\theta)F]f(\cdot)ds + \int\limits_{c}^{m} [-U_Y\{1-q\cdot\frac{\partial K}{\partial X} - (1+\theta)F\}] \ f(\cdot)ds
\tag{13}
$$
$$
\phantom{\frac{\partial EU}{\partial X} =}{\scriptstyle(-)}{\scriptstyle(+)}
$$

$$
+ \int\limits_{c}^{m} [-U_H\cdot\frac{\partial L}{\partial K}\cdot\frac{\partial K}{\partial X}]f(\cdot)ds + \int\limits_{m}^{1} [U_Y\{1 - (1+\theta)F\}]f(\cdot)ds
$$
$$
{\scriptstyle(+)}{\scriptstyle(+)}
$$

$$
= 0.
$$

F : Probability of $(\bar{s})$ exceeding the critical level (c),

$$
= \int\limits_{c}^{1} f(\bar{s})d\bar{s}.
$$

This condition is easy to interpret. The income loss due to the additional premium payable for a marginal increase in (X) must be balanced against two advantages. The first is the assurance that the hospital physician will be less constrained by cost in his choice of treatment. Although only relevant in state 2, this may carry a great weight in terms of marginal utiliy. The other advantage is the decreased risk of out-of-pocket expenditures in states 2 and 3, where costs of stationary treatment may exceed the limit (X). The location of the optimum depends on the premium schedule of the sick fund which defines the marginal cost of insurance. It also depends on the characteristics of the insured. If he thinks of his personal distribution of symptom levels as being skewed towards low values, he will select a low value of (X). Another subjective component is the marginal utility of income (U_Y) in the three states, about which no generally valid statement seems possible. For on the one hand, a sick person cannot enjoy additional income very much for consumption purposes. This would make for comparatively low values of U_Y in states 2 and 3. On the other hand, a major illness may still result in economic distress for many so that additional net income would be of particular benefit. Individuals emphasizing this aspect will opt for rather extensive health insurance.

4. RISING PRICES FOR HEALTH CARE: COMPARATIVE STATICS

For the study of the dynamics of the cost-insurance spiral, the nexus between the price of health care and the demand for coverage is crucial. The price change is indicated by the common symbol (dq) for simplicity. In reality, there has been a steady upward drift in the implicit wage rate of private practitioners whereas daily room rates are adjusted rather infrequently. Outlays on stationary treatment ($q \cdot K$) are again subject to creeping inflation. For the time being, we disregard such divergences, as they are likely to fade away in the long run. They do play a role, however, in the context of fixing of the premium (r), see the section, "Description of variables and operational hypotheses" below, in particular CSTAY and CTREAT and the derivation of Hypotheses 4 and 5.

Now let the individual´s optimum solution be disturbed by the price change (dq). If the individual is to balance this disturbance by adjusting his decision variables (b) and (X), with demand for ambulatory care (M) and working time (W) fixed, we must have

$$\frac{\partial}{\partial b}\left[\frac{\partial}{\partial b}EU\right]db + \frac{\partial}{\partial X}\left[\frac{\partial}{\partial b}EU\right]dX + \frac{\partial}{\partial q}\left[\frac{\partial}{\partial b}EU\right]dq = 0$$

$$\frac{\partial}{\partial b}\left[\frac{\partial}{\partial X}EU\right]db + \frac{\partial}{\partial X}\left[\frac{\partial}{\partial X}EU\right]dX + \frac{\partial}{\partial q}\left[\frac{\partial}{\partial X}EU\right]dq = 0.$$

Using vector notation and marking sign restrictions, we obtain

$$
\begin{bmatrix}
\dfrac{\partial^2 EU}{\partial b^2} & \dfrac{\partial^2 EU}{\partial b \partial X} \\
(-) & (+/-) \\
\dfrac{\partial^2 EU}{\partial b \partial X} & \dfrac{\partial^2 EU}{\partial X^2} \\
(+/-) & (-)
\end{bmatrix}
\begin{bmatrix}
db \\
\\
dX
\end{bmatrix}
= -
\begin{bmatrix}
\dfrac{\partial^2 EU}{\partial b \partial q} \\
(+/-) \\
\dfrac{\partial^2 EU}{\partial X \partial q} \\
(+/-)
\end{bmatrix}
dq .
\tag{14}
$$

The diagonal elements of the Hessian are necessarily negative if the conditions specified in eq. (5) are assumed to hold (Chiang, 1974, pp. 329-331). Restrictions on the remaining elements of the equation system require further elaboration. For simplicity, cross partials of the utility function will be disregarded ($U_{YH} = 0$). The expression $\partial^2 EU/\partial b \partial q$ appearing in the impulse vector on the right hand side of eq. (14) then becomes

$$\frac{\partial^2 EU}{\partial b \partial q} = \frac{\partial}{\partial q} \int_{0}^{c} [-U_Y(1+\theta)EM]f(\cdot)ds \qquad (15)$$

$$+ \frac{\partial}{\partial q} \int_{c}^{m} [-U_Y(1+\theta)EM]f(\cdot)ds$$

$$+ \frac{\partial}{\partial q} \int_{m}^{1} [U_Y\{M(s) - (1+\theta)EM\}]f(\cdot)ds \; ; \; \text{cf. eq. (7)}$$

EM : Expected value of $M(\bar{s})$ in state 3 as seen by the sick fund,

$$= \int_{m}^{1} M(\bar{s})f(\bar{s})d\bar{s}.$$

The nature of the variable (M) is of some importance in this context. Symbolizing length of stay associated with an emergency hospitalization, it appears in the third term of eq. (15) above. If (M) were to be strictly interpreted as demand deployed by the individual, then the reaction $\partial M/\partial q < 0$ would have to be taken into account by a truly rational decisionmaker. However, length of stay is interpreted as a random variable beyond the individual's control.[7] This is documented by the choice of notation, M(s). It also has the consequence that the change (dq) has no impact on the number of healthy days, (H). Its partial influence on net income, on the other hand, is given by

$$\frac{\partial Y}{\partial q} = \begin{cases} -r \cdot M & 0 \le s < c \\ -K(X,s) & c \le s < m \\ -[M(s) + K(s)] & m \le s \le 1 \end{cases} \qquad (16)$$

Since the decision variables (M) and (W) are assumed predetermined at the time the decision about insurance coverage is made, all terms in (H), involving (U_{HH}, U_{YH}) can be disregarded in the evaluation of eq. (15), yielding

$$\frac{\partial^2 EU}{\partial b \partial q} = \int_{0}^{c} [U_{YY} \cdot rM(1+\theta)EM]f(\cdot)ds \qquad (17)$$
$$\qquad\qquad (-)$$

$$+ \int_{c}^{m} [U_{YY} \cdot K(X,s)(1+\theta)EM]f(\cdot)ds$$
$$\qquad\qquad (-)$$

$$+ \int_{m}^{1} [U_{YY}\{M(s) + K(s)\}\{M(s) - (1+\theta)EM\}]f(\cdot)ds$$
$$\qquad\qquad (+)$$

U_{YY} : Rate of change of marginal utility of income with increasing gain or loss of income,

$$= \partial^2 U/\partial Y^2 < 0,$$

$$= -R_A/U_Y$$

R_A : Coefficient of absolute risk aversion,

$$= -U_{YY}/U_Y.$$

The first term of eq. (17) is negative. It can be large, despite the fact that cost-sharing for ambulatory treatment is very limited in Switzerland and that (M), measured in fractionals of physicians days, will be small in state 1. But for most members of the fund, symptom levels in the interval [0,c) will make up for the lion´s share of the entire distribution. The second term of eq. (17) is negative as well. The sign of the third term depends on the sign of [M(s) - (1+θ)EM]. This difference was found to be positive, cf. the optimum condition (9). Since price is defined per day of stay or treatment throughout, the multiplier [M(s) + K(s)] is rather large compared to the patient-controlled (M) of state 1. Both of these bracketed expressions loom large with individuals who subjectively evaluate their health prospect rather pressimistically. Therefore, the second and third terms of eq. (17) will tend to outweigh the first, resulting in $\partial^2 EU/\partial b \partial q > 0$. Others, who are confident that they will not need hospitalization, let alone as an emergency case, will attribute little weight to the second and third terms of eq. (17) and will thus be characterized by $\partial^2 EU/\partial b \partial q < 0$. Hence, no general sign restriction can be expected to hold with respect to $\partial^2 EU/\partial b \partial q$, but rather the binary set,

$$\frac{\partial^2 EU}{\partial b \partial q} = \begin{cases} < 0 & \text{for subjectively good risks} \\ \\ > 0 & \text{for subjectively bad risks or strong risk averters regarding state 3.} \end{cases} \tag{18}$$

Sparing the reader an analogous argument relating to the second element of the impulse vector appearing on the right hand side of the equation system (14), we note that

$$\frac{\partial^2 EU}{\partial X \partial q} = \begin{cases} < 0 & \text{for subjectively good risks} \\ \\ > 0 & \text{for subjectively bad risks or strong risk averters regarding states 2 and 3} \end{cases} \tag{19}$$

The restrictions (18) and (19) have an intuitive basis. An increase in the price of health services (dq) certainly implies a loss of expected utility on the part of the insured, i.e. $\partial EU/\partial q < 0$. A further increase of insurance coverage would only add to this loss for those subjectively healthy individuals who do not want to pay the additional premium for stationary services they do not count on consuming. Hence, we have $\partial^2 EU/\partial b \partial q < 0$, $\partial^2 EU/\partial q \partial X < 0$ for them. The other members of the fund assign a possibly exaggerated probability to the interval [c,1] of the symptom density function. By increasing coverage, they can alleviate the loss of expected utility stemming from hospitalization even if they have to pay a higher premium. For them, it may be true that $\partial^2 EU/\partial b \partial q > 0$, $\partial^2 EU/\partial q \partial X > 0$.

Finally, it can be shown that the interactive impact of the two decision variables upon expected utility should differ according to the subjective evaluation of the individual's health. The restrictions are

$$\frac{\partial^2 EU}{\partial b \partial X} = \begin{cases} > 0 & \text{for subjectively good risks} \\ \\ < 0 & \text{for subjectively bad risks or strong risk} \\ & \text{averters regarding states 2 and 3.} \end{cases} \tag{20}$$

These preliminaries enable us to place some qualitative restrictions on the solution of the equation (14). Applying Cramer's rule and using the inequalities (17) to (20), we obtain

$$\frac{db}{dq} = \begin{cases} \dfrac{-1}{|H|} \begin{vmatrix} \dfrac{\partial^2 EU}{\partial b \partial q} & \dfrac{\partial^2 EU}{\partial b \partial X} \\ (-) & (+) \\ \dfrac{\partial^2 EU}{\partial X \partial q} & \dfrac{\partial^2 EU}{\partial X^2} \\ (-) & (-) \end{vmatrix} & < 0 \text{ for subjectively good risks} \\ \\ \dfrac{-1}{|H|} \begin{vmatrix} \dfrac{\partial^2 EU}{\partial b \partial q} & \dfrac{\partial^2 EU}{\partial b \partial X} \\ (+) & (-) \\ \dfrac{\partial^2 EU}{\partial X \partial q} & \dfrac{\partial^2 EU}{\partial X^2} \\ (+) & (-) \end{vmatrix} & \gtrless 0 \text{ for subjectively bad risks or} \\ & \text{strong risk averters regarding} \\ & \text{state 3.} \end{cases} \tag{21}$$

The implication $db/dq > 0$ for subjectively bad risks, while not being unambiguous, receives some support from the negative definiteness of the Hessian. This property constitutes a certain dominance of the diagonal elements, cf. Goldberger (1964, p. 36). Therefore, the absolute value of $\partial^2 EU/\partial X^2$ will exceed the one of $\partial^2 EU/\partial b \partial X$ as long as $\partial^2 EU/\partial X^2$ and $\partial^2 EU/\partial b^2$ are of comparable magnitude. The determinant in the lower part of eq. (21) would then tend to be negative. The prediction of the model can be formulated as follows: When prices for health care services rise and the sick fund adjusts premiums accordingly, subjectively good risks will tend to decrease rather than increase coverage of the daily room rate. Subjectively bad risks - who may well be a majority of the insured - may react either way because they assign some probability to the event of a hospitalization - planned or emergency. There is some presumption, to be tested empirically, that they will adjust their insurance coverage upwards due to the price increase.

We now turn to the coverage of costs arising from stationary treatment. Again using inequalities (17) to (20), we obtain, in full analogy to (21),

$$
\frac{dX}{dq} =
\begin{cases}
\dfrac{-1}{|H|}_{(-)} \;
\begin{vmatrix}
\dfrac{\partial^2 EU}{\partial b^2} & \dfrac{\partial^2 EU}{\partial b \partial q} \\[2mm]
(-) & (-) \\[3mm]
\dfrac{\partial^2 EU}{\partial b \partial X} & \dfrac{\partial^2 EU}{\partial X \partial q} \\[2mm]
(+) & (-)
\end{vmatrix}_{(+)}
\; < 0 \text{ for subjectively good risks} \\[18mm]
\dfrac{-1}{|H|}_{(-)} \;
\begin{vmatrix}
\dfrac{\partial^2 EU}{\partial b^2} & \dfrac{\partial^2 EU}{\partial b \partial q} \\[2mm]
(-) & (+) \\[3mm]
\dfrac{\partial^2 EU}{\partial b \partial X} & \dfrac{\partial^2 EU}{\partial X \partial q} \\[2mm]
(-) & (+)
\end{vmatrix}_{(-/+)}
\; \gtrless 0 \text{ for subjectively bad risks or} \\
\qquad\qquad\qquad\qquad\qquad\qquad\quad \text{strong risk averters regarding} \\
\qquad\qquad\qquad\qquad\qquad\qquad\quad \text{states 2 and 3.}
\end{cases}
\tag{22}
$$

These implications correspond to those derived previously for db/dq. Again, subjectively good risks will shy away from the increased cost of coverage. This reaction to rising prices in the health care sector cannot be entirely excluded for the subjectively mediocre and bad risks. But the more probable reaction certainly is an increase in the coverage of outlays due to treatment in the hospital.

The ambiguity of the model´s predictions has two rather basic reasons. Both an increase of the covered daily rate (db) and of covered treatment costs (dX) serve to reduce net income in state 1, which has by far the highest probability for most decisionmakers. The net effect of (db,dX) on expected income therefore cannot be established unambiguously, a result also found by Phelps (1976, pp. 120-122). Moreover, the two insurance instruments compete for the marginal income unit very much like two ordinary goods compete for the household´s budget. In a two-goods world, substitution is the dominant relationship (Henderson and Quandt, 1971, p. 37). It is somewhat attenuated in this model because changes in (b) and (X) have different effects on income and health in the three states considered. It also may be worth noting that the model contains no indication to the effect that an individual who has opted for db/dq > 0 is more likely to opt for dX/dq < 0. In the theory of consumer demand under certainty, by contrast, the fact that a consumer increases his purchase of the first commodity makes a reduction of purchases of the other commodity more likely.[8]

5. DESCRIPTION OF VARIABLES AND OPERATIONAL HYPOTHESES

The data base for this study consists of three parts. Part one comes from mailed questionnaires. Following a pretest, 6,400 members of Krankenkasse KKB, a major Swiss sick fund, were asked to provide 21 items of supplementary socioeconomic data in November 1980. Members of prime working age were oversampled to correct for their lower response rate. Of some 2,300 responses, 1,654 were retained for this study.[9]

Visual analog scales were used throughout for continuous numerical variables. For the delicate items dealing with income and financial wealth in particular, there is reason to believe that respondents prefer merely marking a scale to writing down a number or putting themselves into a bracket.[10] Part two of the data base consists of insurance status information pertaining to the period 1976 to 1980. Part three is a billings file containing some 23,000 items, starting in 1975 but fully complete only from 1977 on. Both of these files were supplied by the sick fund Krankenkasse KKB.[11] Together, the three files assemble a host of information about the development of insurance coverage, health care utilization, and socioeconomic characteristics of 1,654 respondents over the years 1976-1980. Table 1 shows the summary statistics of those variables actually used here.

They are discussed in alphabetical order. Where appropriate, a binary set of specific hypotheses is stated, the first relating to BDAILY, the covered daily room rate (=b of the theoretical model, see eq. (3a)), and the second to XTREAT, the covered cost of stationary treatment (=X).

AGE, AGE^2. The second of these two variables is included in view of Grossman's (1972) model of the demand for health. For with increasing age, demand for health itself should first increase and then decrease whereas the productivity of medical services relative to the individual's own time in the production of health steadily increases. Since the demand for health insurance can be derived from these demands, it should also follow a nonlinear age pattern. We accordingly have the

Hypotheses 1: A : $\partial BDAILY/\partial AGE > 0,$ $\partial^2 BDAILY/\partial AGE^2 < 0;$

                B : $\partial XTREAT/\partial AGE > 0,$ $\partial^2 XTREAT/\partial AGE^2 < 0.$

BDAILY. This is the first dependent variable, reflecting insurance status at the end of the current year. In 1976, some 16% of the individuals in the sample had no insurance covering the daily charge for semiprivate or private accommodation, at least not with the sick fund Krankenkasse KKB. By 1980, the share of those opting for the public ward or having purchased supplementary insurance from a private company has dropped to 8%[12]. Because of this heterogeneity of non-buyers, buyers and non-buyers are not necessarily divided by some characteristic, in particular, income. Accordingly, the choice of the estimation method (OLS or Limited Dependent Variable) should not make much difference for this variable. The individuals of this sample have adjusted their coverage beyond the rate of hospital cost inflation; in 1980, BDAILY amounted to 72.5 Swiss francs per day (up by 32% from 1976), whereas the average daily room rate increased by 17% for women and by 27% for men between 1976 and 1980, see Krankenkasse KKB (1981), p. 17.

CLAUSE. When a member of the fund applies for higher coverage, the fund may specify health conditions for which only the previously contracted coverage will apply. Between 4 and 5% of the individuals of this sample faced such reservation clauses in a given year. If there is any correspondence between officially perceived risk and subjective judgment, these members should in their own view be characterized by a particularly high mean symptom level (s). These considerations lead to the formulation of

Table 1. Descriptive statistics, all complete observations
(n = 1654)

Variable	Symbol in model	Explanation	Year	Mean	SD	Skew-ness
AGE	$\bar{s}$	Age as of January 1, 1981	1980	44.4	16.2	0.622
BDAILY	b	Covered daily room rate, in Sfr.	1976 1980	55.2 74.1	41.1 41.9	0.437 -0.0475
CLAUSE	$\bar{s}$, R_A	=1: Reservation clause in effect	1976 1980	0.0442 0.0453	0.205 0.208	4.44 4.37
COMMERCE	$f(s,\bar{s})$	=1: Graduate of a school of commerce	1976	0.126	0.332	2.25
CAMB	M,c	Cost sharing for ambulatory care services, in Sfr.	1976 1980	48.0 38.9	72.0 54.4	2.27 2.03
CSTAY	q·M	Gross billings for room and board at a hospital, in Sfr.	1977 1980	11.1 53.5	121 332	15.8 10.9
CTREAT	q·K	Gross billings for stationary treatment, in Sfr.	1977 1980	24.9 32.8	171 235	9.16 10.6
EMPLOYEE	$f(s,\bar{s})$	=1: Employee, public or private	1976	0.187	0.389	1.60
INCOME	Y	Total income (labor, social security, property), in 10^3 Sfr. per month	1976 1980	2.48 3.06	1.39 1.55	1.23 1.02
LXTREAT	X	Natural logarithm of covered stationary treatment costs, in Sfr.	1976 1980	4.896 6.704	4.10 3.88	-0.309 -1.075
PRIVATE	Y, R_A	=1: Member is in P2 or P3 class (see text)	1976 1980	0.133 0.128	0.340 0.334	2.16 2.27
RATING	q	Premium class according to community rating, min.=0, max.=8	1976 1980	3.42 3.83	2.20 1.93	0.347 0.468
SEXF	$\bar{s}$	=1: Individual is female	1976	0.53	0.499	-0.124
SUBSID	Y, $\frac{\partial Y}{\partial q}$	=1: Individual qualifies for a premium subsidy	1976 1980	0.0514 0.0399	0.221 0.196	4.07 4.71

<u>Hypotheses 2:</u>   A : $\partial BDAILY/\partial CLAUSE > 0$;

              B : $\partial XTREAT/\partial CLAUSE > 0$.

COMMERCE. This is a dummy variable which takes on the value of one if the insured has graduated from a commercial school. Such individuals should have particularly good knowledge of insurance as a means for coping with risks. At the same time, they may also be able to estimate risks more accurately than others - in this case, the actual probability of hospitalization, possibly over-estimated by many. Hence, a priori hypotheses about the partial effects of COMMERCE on BDAILY and LXTREAT do not seem possible.

CAMB. Costs of ambulatory care are defined as the sum of deductibles and coinsurance payments made to the sick fund within a year. This is an indicator of demand for medical care (M) in state 1, which, according to eqs. (1a) and (1b), tends to decrease the physician´s critical symptom level (c) and thus to increase the probability of hospitalization. Due to considerable delay in billings processing, a recognition lag of several months must be allowed for. Moreover, the request for an adjustment of a policy may take months again to become effective. Therefore, a total lag of one year is postulated throughout.[13] Since no distinction between states 2 and 3 (nonemergency and emergency hospitalization) can be made, we have to limit ourselves to the formulation of

<u>Hypotheses 3:</u>   A : $\partial BDAILY/\partial CAMB_{-1} > 0$;

              B : $\partial XTREAT/\partial CAMB_{-1} > 0$.

CSTAY. This variable reflects the gross value of billings for hospital accommodation. For the great majority of the individuals in the sample, it is zero in a given year. The minority who was exposed to the cost of a hospital stay was a mere 1.5% in 1977, rising to 3.8% in 1980. This is far below the average frequency of hospitalization calculated by the sick fund, which amounted to about 0.09 for men and 0.18 for women in 1980. It is evident that those willing and able to supply data on all the socioeconomic variables used in this study are low users of hospital care. This bias highlights the basic assumption underlying the use of actual cost experience data for explaining demand for insurance. The assumption clearly is that the healthy derive their estimates of the financial risk to be covered from observing the less fortunate few. As an alternative, age and sex specific probabilities of hospitalization and costs of stay given hospitalization were assigned to each individual, based on internal compilations by the sick fund Krankenkasse KKB. However, the explanatory power of these variables turned out to be virtually nil. Finally, using CSTAY as a regressor implies that the product $[q \cdot M(s)]$ rather than price (q) itself serves as the relevant impulse. But this is entirely justified in view of eq. (17), where M(s) is an important element in the determination of $\partial^2 EU/\partial b\partial q$.

In keeping with ineq. (21), no unambiguous prediction regarding $\partial BDAILY/\partial CSTAY_{-1}$ can be made. However, as a matter of fact the sick fund Krankenkasse KKB has deviated from the equivalence condition stated in eq. (4). While adjusting premiums for coverage of ambulatory care costs (state 1) in 1978 and 1980, it left premiums for supplementary hospital insurance unaltered. This stability contrasts sharply with the rise of the probability of hospitalization, from 0.074 in 1976 to 0.089 for men in 1980 and from

0.162 to 0.175 for women. Moreover, treatment costs increased steadily in the same period. These considerations show that supplementary hospital insurance became cheaper relative to other goods and services in general and the financial risk of hospitalization in particular, as well as relative to the basic insurance package. Referring to our model, a term like $\partial^2 EU/\partial q \partial b$ would turn positive for almost all individuals, with the consequence that the behavior predicted for the bad risks becomes the prevalent one, cf. eqs. (18) and (21), for example.

Hence, we have

Hypotheses 4:　A　:　$\partial BDAILY/\partial CSTAY_{-1} > 0$;

　　　　　　　B　:　$\partial XTREAT/\partial CSTAY_{-1} = 0$.

CTREAT. These are the gross billings for stationary treatment. Since again only some 3% of the sample were exposed to these costs in 1980, the remarks made in the context of CSTAY apply here as well. Again, there was an unsuccessful attempt to assign age and sex specific values relevant for the entire population at risk to each individual. In analogy to above, we postulate

Hypotheses 5:　A　:　$\partial BDAILY/\partial CTREAT_{-1} = 0$;

　　　　　　　B　:　$\partial XTREAT/\partial CTREAT_{-1} > 0$.

EMPLOYEE. Whenever the sampled individual is an employee, this categorical variable takes on the value of one. Since the sick fund Krankenkasse KKB has its stronghold in and around the city of Bern, the Swiss capital, the category will consist mainly of public employees. Taking the choice of a public employer as a sign of increased risk aversion, we may deduce

Hypotheses 6:　A　:　$\partial BDAILY/\partial EMPLOYEE > 0$;

　　　　　　　B　:　$\partial XTREAT/\partial EMPLOYEE > 0$.

INCOME. In the questionnaire, one item was labor income, another, income from other sources. Aggregating the two allows us to keep retired members of the sick fund in the sample, for whom social security payments are the most important and often only source of income. For these members, labor income in state 1 should be supplemented by old age transfer income ($\overline{Y}$), whereas the marginal wage rate (w) should remain positive in eq. (1a), according to the findings of the questionnaire. These modifications are of little consequence in this context. More important, the theoretical model abstracts from the amenities a higher room rate may buy, for income (Y) influences demand for hospital insurance only through its effect on the marginal utility of income (U_Y), cf. eqs. (7) and (10). In reality, however, amenity is a choice variable. It is reasonable to assert that the hotel characteristics of a hospital are reflected by CSTAY (billings for room and board) rather than CTREAT (billings for treatment). Accordingly, we have, writing $\varepsilon(\cdot,\cdot)$ for a partial elasticity,

Hypotheses 7:　A　:　$\partial BDAILY/\partial INCOME > 0$;

　　　　　　　B　:　$\partial XTREAT/\partial INCOME > 0$,
　　　　　　　　　$\varepsilon(XTREAT, INCOME) < \varepsilon(BDAILY, INCOME)$.

PRIVATE. The sick fund Krankenkasse KKB distinguishes three membership classes in ambulatory care insurance. The general P1 class comprises individuals with medium to low family incomes. The well-to-do are requested to be in the P2 class, where premiums for the basic package are about 30% higher. On the other hand, physicians are allowed to bill a 45% surcharge for the ambulatory treatment of a P2 patient. Even the very rich can remain in social health insurance by registering as quasi-private patients (P3). Here, physicians are basically free to charge for their ambulatory services what the market will bear, or more precisely, what the member via his coinsurance (r=0.1, but see fn. 2) will bear. Thus, P2 and P3 members enjoy a certain priority access to ambulatory care. This is an important advantage to a high wage earner or an individual who considers himself not too good a health risk. Either characteristic probably results in a demand for high quality accommodation and high intensity of care in particular. Since there are very few individuals in the P3 category, we aggregate the two groups, obtaining the

Hypotheses 8: A : $\partial BDAILY/\partial PRIVATE > 0$;

               B : $\partial XTREAT/\partial PRIVATE > 0$,
                      $\varepsilon(XTREAT, PRIVATE) > \varepsilon(XTREAT, INCOME)$.

RATING. Swiss sick funds rate communities when setting their premiums for the basic package. If an individual lives in a region rated high (RATING=8), the hospital he would be admitted to is likely to be an expensive city hospital. Being exposed to a high price (q), he should opt for particularly high coverage. Although RATING is a nominal variable varying between 0 and 8, it is used like a cardinal entity for simplicity. We clearly have

Hypotheses 9: A : $\partial BDAILY/\partial RATING > 0$;

               B : $\partial XTREAT/\partial RATING > 0$.

SEXF. This categorical variable is equal to one if the respondent is female. Since insurance contracts cover maternity on the same terms as other hospitalization (barring only pregnant women from opting for higher coverage), women can be viewed as a population characterized by a higher mean symptom level ($\bar{s}$). Given a common critical level (c) applied by physicians, women are exposed to a higher risk of hospitalization. This suffices for the formulation of

Hypotheses 10: A : $\partial BDAILY/\partial SEXF > 0$;

                B : $\partial XTREAT/\partial SEXF > 0$.

SUBSID. This categorical variable characterizes individuals whose premium for the basic package, including ambulatory care and stationary care in a public ward, is subsidized by the State. Although this subsidy is not tied to any restrictions regarding the purchase of supplementary insurance, we predict the partial relationship between BDAILY and XTREAT on the one hand and SUBSID on the other to be negative. First, the individual must live in a low-income household to be eligible for the subsidy, and second, most of the individuals in this category did not have much of an incentive to adjust their coverage in the past, being fully protected for all expenses in the public ward. Hence, we have

Hypotheses 11: A : $\partial BDAILY/\partial SUBSID < 0$;

B : $\partial XTREAT/\partial SUBSID < 0$.

XTREAT. This is the second decision variable, indicating the covered limit of stationary treatment outlays for a hospital episode of not more than 720 days´ length. In 1976, about 41% of the individuals in the sample did not have this supplementary insurance, lowering the average value of XTREAT to 3,330 francs. Four years later, only 27% were not insured, and mean coverage had more than doubled, exceeding 7,600 francs. These developments call for the simultaneous explanation of transition to the insured category as well as to higher coverage within the insured category. This can be accomplished by limited dependent variable estimation methods. Since the options are defined by the set of values (1,000, 2,000, 3,000, 5,000, 10,000, 20,000, 50,000, 100,000), transition from one option to another is likely to involve a doubling of the covered amount. A log transformation of the dependent variable, symbolized by LXTREAT, takes this feature into account.

6. ECONOMETRIC RESULTS

Since ineqs. (21) and (22) imply that individuals may react differently to a price change, a number of interactions was examined, e.g. between $CSTAY_{-1}$ and SEXF. If indeed female insureds consider themselves to be rather bad risks, then a given impulse ($CSTAY_{-1}$) ought to have a stronger impact on their demand for insurance than the demand of male insureds. Interactions inevitably lead to a considerable amount of specification search, with deleterious consequences for the distribution of estimated parameters (Bock et al. (1973); Leamer (1978, ch. 5)). In an effort to safeguard against the risk of misinterpretation of statistical tests, odd-keyed respondents were set aside from the very beginning. Results of a Tobit estimation of BDAILY on the basis of the even-keyed sub-sample are shown in Table 2.[14]

The availability of data suggests the choice of 1976 as the base year from which to start the process of adjustment. However, information concerning $CSTAY_{-1}$ and $CTREAT_{-1}$ was still lacking then.

All qualitative hypotheses concerning BDAILY are borne out, except for 11A. In the 1978 equation, the effects of direct ($CAMB_{-1}$) and hearsay ($CSTAY_{-1}$) cost experience do not attain statistical significance, contrary to Hypotheses 3A and 4A. As to the dynamics of adjustment, unchanged personal characteristics like sex and age are already reflected in the value of $BDAILY_{-1}$. They should therefore make a minimal independent contribution to the explanation of BDAILY when $BDAILY_{-1}$ is included as a regressor. In the Tobit equation shown, $BDAILY_{-1}$ is replaced by its predicted value. For preliminary regressions revealed positive autocorrelation of residuals generated by a sequence of static equations ($\hat{\rho} \geq 0.85$).[15] Otherwise, the specification used for the year 1978 was retained. The results shown in the third column of Table 2 indicate that unchanged personal characteristics are in fact nonsignificant, with the possible exception of SEXF. In a next step, these static regressors were dropped, together with lagged treatment outlays ($CTREAT_{-1}$), in keeping with Hypotheses 5A, cf. the fourth column of Table 2.

In the equation for 1980, $CAMB_{-1}$, the indicator of hospitalization risk

Table 2. Tobit estimation of BDAILY, even-keyed subsample (n_1 = 846)

Explanatory variable	1976	1978	1979	1979	1980
AGE	1.45* (0.627)	0.771 (0.615)	0.107 (0.631)	-	-
AGE^2	-0.0122* (0.0063)	-0.00529 (0.00625)	0.00072 (0.00063)	-	-
$\widehat{BDAILY}_{-1}$	-	-	0.715** (0.185)	0.971** (0.0686)	0.915** (0.0651)
CLAUSE	19.2** (6.67)	16.1* (6.59)	0.585 (7.28)	-	-
COMMERCE	13.6** (4.30)	15.1** (4.30)	5.07 (5.15)	-	-
$CAMB_{-1}$	0.123** (0.040)	0.0805* (0.0225)	0.0181 (0.0202)	0.0132 (0.0190)	-0.0096 (0.0184)
$CSTAY_{-1}$	-	0.0108 (0.0188)	0.0177 (0.007)	0.0181** (0.0057)	0.0058* (0.0021)
$CTREAT_{-1}$	-	0.0175 (0.0093)	-0.00067 (0.00064)	-	-
EMPLOYEE	8.57* (3.68)	8.10* (4.12)	-	-	-
INCOME	3.22** (1.15)	3.16** (1.08)	1.86 (1.19)	-	-
PRIVATE	23.6** (4.43)	26.9** (4.44)	5.22 (6.61)	-	-
RATING	5.64** (0.689)	4.95** (0.726)	-0.0356 (1.10)	-	-
SEXF	7.41** (2.88)	7.94** (2.90)	6.40* (3.25)	-	-
SUBSID	-8.86 (6.41)	-12.5 (7.3)	-12.5 (7.7)	-	-
CONSTANT	-24.0 (13.6)	-4.20 (13.6)	7.50 (13.4)	8.88* (4.25)	8.89* (4.62)
log likelihood	3,798	3,926	4,034	4,040	4,090
S.E.	39.7	39.7	39.6	40.0	38.6

Note: Asymptotic standard errors in parentheses. Single asterisks (*)
denote a significance level of 0.05 or better, double asterisks (**),
of 0.01 or better (two-tailed test). The value of the lagged
dependent variable is given by the previous year's Tobit estimate
of the variable's expected value.

does not exert a recognizable influence on BDAILY whereas $CSTAY_{-1}$, reflecting largely indirect cost experience, turns out to be significant. The slight increases of the log value of the likelihood function and of the standard error of the equation suggest that this simplification of the model is compatible with the data.[16]

In Table 3, the analogous estimation sequence for LXTREAT is shown. Again, stable personal characteristics are important for explaining the level of insurance chosen in 1978 and 1976. All hypotheses are confirmed, with the exception of Hypothesis 5B, concerning $CTREAT_{-1}$. As expected, unvaried characteristics contribute little to the explanation of the dynamics of adjustment. When reducing the set of explanatory variables to the cost impulses, $CTREAT_{-1}$ can be retained as a significant predictor of LXTREAT both in 1979 and 1980.

BDAILY. We now proceed to test the hypotheses stated in the previous section using the full sample of 1,654 observations. Referring to Table 4 and comparing it to Table 2, we see that the estimates of the 1976 equation for BDAILY are equal for all practical purposes.[17] In particular, both estimates imply that, ceteris paribus, insurance coverage tends to rise until the age of about 54 and to be reduced thereafter.[18] Both females and employees (SEXF, EMPLOYEE) have 8 Sfr. or 14% more coverage of daily room rates compared to others. Another important aspect is the rating of the community, the maximum difference (RATING=8 vs. RATING=0) being associated with a difference in BDAILY of 51 Sfr., or more than 90% of the mean value.

The equations tracing the adjustment of BDAILY from 1977 to 1980 seem to mirror a semi-stable process, judged by the coefficients of the lagged dependent variable. The 1978 point estimate of 1.05 (0.0507) is compatible with the view that the cost-insurance spiral may be explosive temporarily. However, in that same year the sick fund Krankenkasse KKB launched a major special offer for increased supplementary hospital insurance. This highly successful special offer was found to induce other parameter changes (lasting for not more than a year, cf. Zweifel, 1982b). It may also be the cause of the lack of significance found for the cost variables $CAMB_{-1}$ and $CSTAY_{-1}$ in 1978. On that interpretation, the adjustment process would have returned to its normal course by 1980. But even then, exogenous shocks are estimated to have repercussions for up to 21 years (21 = 1/(1-0.952), see $BDAILY_{-1}$ in Table 4). Regarding the cost impulses as one type of exogenous shock, $CAMB_{-1}$ (the indicator of the risk of hospitalization) tends to lose statistical significance to $CSTAY_{-1}$ (the indicator of board and room cost in the hospital). Also, the estimated elasticity of BDAILY with respect to $CAMB_{-1}$ decreases from 0.146 in 1976 to 0.020 in 1979, even turning negative in 1980; cf. Table 6 for a set of elasticity estimates. On the other hand, the elasticity with respect to $CSTAY_{-1}$ remains stable with values between 0.10 and 0.18. Hence, a 10% increase of daily room rates seem to be sufficiently noticed to trigger a mean adjustment of 1.8% in the following year and of more than 30% in the very long run (37.5 = 1.8/(1-0.952)).

XTREAT. The full sample estimates of LXTREAT, shown in Table 5, correspond again rather closely to those displayed in Table 3 above. Here, insurance coverage is found to increase up to age 50, ceteris paribus. There are rather pronounced differences among classes of insureds. For example, members subject to clauses due to health reasons (CLAUSE) have an estimated 230% higher limit on covered treatment outlays, amounting to 10,960 Sfr., compared to 3,320 Sfr. for the grand mean of the sample. The differential is almost 200% for the well-to-do members of the private category

Table 3. Tobit estimation of LXTREAT, even-keyed subsample (n_1 = 846)

Explanatory variable	1976	1978	1979	1979	1980
AGE	0.252** (0.092)	0.182* (0.082)	0.0133 (0.079)	-	-
AGE^2	-0.0029* (0.00093)	-0.0022* (0.00084)	-0.00034 (0.00090)	-	-
CLAUSE	3.060** (0.951)	2.54** (0.874)	0.274 (0.895)	-	-
COMMERCE	1.30* (0.614)	0.985 (0.570)	0.694 (0.537)	-	-
CAMB$_{-1}$	0.0216** (0.0058)	0.0115* (0.0030)	0.0074** (0.0024)	0.0012 (0.00062)	-0.00062 (0.0022)
CSTAY$_{-1}$	-	0.0030 (0.0025)	0.0011 (0.00083)	-	-
CTREAT$_{-1}$	-	0.0021 (0.0012)	0.00057 (0.00076)	0.0049* (0.0022)	0.00065* (0.00031)
EMPLOYEE	0.821 (0.531)	1.22* (0.487)	0.720 (0.471)	-	-
INCOME	0.478** (0.167)	0.295* (0.145)	0.191 (0.136)	-	-
$\widehat{\text{LXTREAT}}_{-1}$	-	-	0.445* (0.190)	0.880** (0.0812)	0.932** (0.0088)
PRIVATE	2.38** (0.630)	2.55** (0.587)	0.830 (0.685)	-	-
RATING	0.643 (0.100)	0.559* (0.0976)	0.150 (0.120)	-	-
SEXF	1.58** (0.426)	1.35** (0.393)	0.775 (0.414)	-	-
SUBSID	-3.59** (1.070)	-3.81** (1.12)	-2.18* (1.02)	-	-
CONSTANT	-6.55** (2.01)	-3.61 (1.83)	1.42 (1.65)	0.982* (0.438)	0.537 (0.537)
log likelihood	1,862	1,965	2,080	2,087	2,118
S.E.	5.55	5.18	4.65	4.69	4.49

Notes: cf. Table 2.

Table 4. Tobit estimation of BDAILY, entire sample (n = 1654)

Explanatory variable	1976	1977	1978	1979	1980
AGE	1.69** (0.415)	-	-	-	-
AGE^2	-0.0158** (0.0041)	-	-	-	-
$\widehat{BDAILY}_{-1}$	-	1.00** (0.0474)	1.05** (0.0507)	1.00** (0.0504)	0.952** (0.0497)
CLAUSE	21.7** (4.82)	-	-	-	-
COMMERCE	15.2** (3.04)	-	-	-	-
$CAMB_{-1}$	0.169** (0.030)	0.0647** (0.0147)	0.0196 (0.0165)	0.0255 (0.0144)	0.0157 (0.0138)
$CSTAY_{-1}$	-	-	0.0085 (0.0083)	0.0095** (0.0035)	0.0061** (0.0020)
EMPLOYEE	7.89** (2.64)	-	-	-	-
INCOME	3.08** (0.814)	-	-	-	-
PRIVATE	22.9** (3.22)	-	-	-	-
RATING	6.38** (0.479)	-	-	-	-
SEXF	7.87** (2.05)	-	-	-	-
SUBSID	-9.85* (4.64)	-	-	-	-
CONSTANT	-31.7* (9.14)	-4.31 (2.65)	-2.45 (2.85)	5.58 (3.05)	5.47 (3.39)
log likelihood	7,333	7,428	7,591	7,815	7,926
S.E.	39.6	39.5	40.5	40.5	39.4
$\widehat{Pr}$(BDAILY = 0)	0.087	0.078	0.069	0.045	0.035
Pr(BDAILY = 0)	0.16	0.15	0.13	0.10	0.079

Notes: Asymptotic standard errors in parentheses. Single asterisks (*) denote a significance level of 0.05 or better, double asterisks (**), of 0.01 or better (two-tailed test). The value of the lagged dependent variable is given by the previous year's Tobit estimate of the variable's expected value.

P. Zweifel

Table 5. Tobit estimation of LXTREAT, entire sample (n = 1654)

Explanatory variable	1976	1977	1978	1979	1980
AGE	0.304** (0.071)	-	-	-	-
AGE^2	-0.0034** (0.00071)	-	-	-	-
CLAUSE	2.28** (0.694)	-	-	-	-
COMMERCE	1.53** (0.440)	-	-	-	-
$CAMB_{-1}$	0.0286** (0.0044)	0.0087** (0.0021	0.0038 (0.0022)	0.0042* (0.0017)	-0.0012 (0.0016)
$CTREAT_{-1}$	-	-	0.0016* (0.00077)	0.00079 (0.00048)	0.00075** (0.00027)
EMPLOYEE	0.645 (0.386)	-	-	-	-
INCOME	0.402* (0.121)	-	-	-	-
$\widehat{LXTREAT}_{-1}$	-	1.35** (0.0786)	1.30** (0.0785)	1.10** (0.0712)	1.11** (0.0752)
PRIVATE	1.95** (0.465)	-	-	-	-
RATING	0.720** (0.071)	-	-	-	-
SEXF	1.43** (0.306)	-	-	-	-
SUBSID	-2.63** (0.760)	-	-	-	-
CONSTANT	-7.95** (1.56)	-3.43** (0.413)	-2.56** (0.406)	-0.578 (0.386)	-0.973 (0.462)
log likelihood	3,618	3,688	3,821	4,049	4,120
S.E.	5.60	5.42	5.25	4.77	4.58
$\widehat{Pr}$(XTREAT = 0)	0.12	0.10	0.088	0.052	0.040
Pr(XTREAT = 0)	0.41	0.39	0.35	0.27	0.24

Notes: cf. Table 4.

(PRIVATE). At the other extreme, the mean predicted value of XTREAT is practically zero for those insureds receiving a subsidy (SUBSID). The dynamic adjustment of XTREAT must be qualified as overshooting in the years 1977 and 1978. There, the coefficient of $LXTREAT_{-1}$ is significantly greater than unity. This result is the more impressive as the estimated elasticity of XTREAT with respect to $CTREAT_{-1}$ tends to exceed unity as well, cf. Table 6.

Table 6. Selected short-run elasticity estimates.

Elasticity	1976	1977	1978	1979	1980
$\varepsilon(BDAILY, CAMB_{-1})$	0.146	0.084	0.016	0.020	-
$\varepsilon(BDAILY, CSTAY_{-1})$	-	-	0.101	0.182	0.132
$\varepsilon(BDAILY, INCOME)$	0.138	-	0.141^a	-	-
$\varepsilon(BDAILY, PRIVATE)$	0.414	-	0.469^a	-	-
$\varepsilon(XTREAT, CAMB_{-1})$	1.36	0.645	0.191	0.236	-
$\varepsilon(XTREAT, CTREAT_{-1})$	-	-	1.34	0.908	1.50
$\varepsilon(XTREAT, INCOME)$	0.997	-	0.811^a	-	-
$\varepsilon(XTREAT, PRIVATE)$	0.259	-	0.326^a	-	-

[a] Based on even-keyed subsample

Notes: Elasticities evaluated at the means; at the means of nonzero observations in the case of $CSTAY_{-1}$ and $CTREAT_{-1}$.

Summing up, we can say that the great majority of the hypotheses formulated above are confirmed. The one systematic exception is the prediction that the income elasticity of BDAILY should be greater than the income elasticity of XTREAT. It was argued that the daily room rate reflects hotel amenities of a hospital to a greater extent than treatment outlays, hotel services being a luxury good. According to Table 6, neither BDAILY nor XTREAT qualifies as a luxury good. But the income elasticity of XTREAT is the higher one, approaching unity. This result is not compatible with Hypothesis 7B. The estimated equations can also be faulted for predicting too low a share of individuals having no complementary hospital insurance. In general, the results presented in this section do not constitute an exhaustive test of the model's implications. For ineqs. (21) and (22) clearly state that the adjustment of coverage to a cost surge should depend on the degree of perceived risk as well as the intensity of risk aversion. This hypothesis calls for interaction terms of the type $(SEXF \cdot CSTAY_{-1})$ in an equation for BDAILY, say. Since females generally run a higher risk of being hospitalized, they should react to a given increase of room and board costs more sharply than males. Despite of intensive search, interaction regressors could not be shown to significantly contribute to either status or adjustment of insurance coverage. The problem with such interaction terms is that they take on a value different from zero only for those few individuals who were in hospital during the year under consideration. The empirical evidence presented therefore supports the theoretical model but in rather broad terms.

CONCLUSIONS

Demand for health insurance is an important element in the cost-insurance spiral suspected to turn in the health care sector. Only if the insureds overshoot in their adjustment to an increase of the price of medical services by increasing their relative coverage despite higher premiums does such a spiral continue to turn. Previous international research was the starting point for the formulation of a formal economic model of demand for coverage of costs associated with semiprivate and private stationary care. In an attempt to take the institutional conditions prevailing in Switzerland (and to some extent in Austria, France, and The Netherlands) into due account, two decision variables were introduced: (b), the daily room rate of hospital covered by the policy, and (X), the costs of treatment in the hospital covered by the policy. Since the coinsurance rate applicable to ambulatory care outlays is set at the legal maximum of 0.1 by all Swiss sick funds, this variable can be considered exogenous. At the time when the individual selects his coverage, demand for ambulatory care (M) and working time (W), reflecting the amount of sick-leave, are viewed as predetermined as well. The model was employed for predicting the likely reaction of the insured to an increase of prices in the health care sector, depending upon whether they subjectively conceive of themselves as good or bad health risks and whether they are particularly risk averse when suffering from bad health. This binary set of implications could not be fully tested because premiums for supplementary hospital insurance were not adjusted to inflation during the period of observation, 1976-1980. Hence, there was a clear incentive to contract for higher coverage. Based on individual data of some 1,600 insureds, it was found that the process of adjustment tended to be stable with regard to (b), but temporarily explosive with regard to (X). Also, the estimated short-run elasticity of (X) with regard to hospital treatment cost exceeds unity, which is evidence in favor of the overshooting hypothesis stated above. However, as long as the causal link from insurance status to demand and utilization remains to be demonstrated, this only means that one necessary condition for the existence of a cost-insurance spiral is satisfied. Preliminary estimates suggest that this other link is not very strong at the individual level, reducing the likelihood of an explosive cycle.

FOOTNOTES

*   Institute for Empirical Research in Economics, Zurich. The author would like to thank Karl Borch, Roland Eisen, Jörg Finsinger, Alberto Holly, and Barbara Wolfe for helpful comments and criticisms. Thanks are also due to two anonymous referees, especially one whose painstaking review has resulted in a significant improvement of the paper. Financial support by the Swiss National Science Foundation under Grant No. 4.349-079.08 of the National Research Program No. 8 is gratefully acknowledged.

1)   Sick funds governed by the Law on Health and Disability Insurance must offer a basic package covering ambulatory care (except for a small deductible and coinsurance, see fn. 2 below) and all outlays associated with treatment in the public ward of a hospital in the member State of residence of the insured. The funds are free to offer supplementary hospital insurance for accommodation and treatment in semiprivate and private wards. The amenity aspects that have caused a majority of insureds to buy such a supplement are not dealt with in the model. For the analysis focuses on the adjustment of coverage over time, taking the selected level of amenities as given.

2)   It is very difficult to determine the ex ante relevant rate of coinsurance for an individual insured by a Swiss sick fund. Under general membership (rather than semiprivate or private), he contributes a deductible of 30 francs per quarter of ambulatory care, or 10% of the bill, whichever is greater. This means that the marginal coinsurance rate is 100% in the interval [0,30], 0% in the interval (30,300], and 10% above 300 Sfr. The expected coinsurance rate therefore depends on the severity of the illness, symbolized by the symptom level (s). For further details, cf. Zweifel (1982a, ch. 8).

3)   In practice, only the product ($q \cdot K$) will be observed, (q) being the implicit wage rate of the surgeon, e.g. For a theoretical and empirical study illustrating the relevance of the implicit physician wage rate, see Zweifel (1981). The use of the common symbol (q) for the prices of ambulatory and stationary services is of no consequence as long as these prices move together. For this parallel movement can be represented by the single shift (dq), as in eq. (14).

4)   Evidence to the effect that patients as a group influence physician behavior is accumulating. Steinwald and Sloan (1974) find statistically significant relationships between the share of high income and high age patients on the one hand and the average fee charged by physicians in general practice on the other. Sloan and Lorant (1977) successfully introduce similar variables (along with physician-related ones, of course) in their study of waiting time for a visit. The critical symptom level (c), a latent decision variable governing referral and hospitalization, is found to be related to average symptom intensity ($\bar{s}$) and average patient income in the work of Zweifel (1982a, ch. 9).

5)   Private health insurers in Switzerland are free to offer policies with variable coinsurance rates and deductibles. However, they mostly write policies with no coinsurance and deductibles of no more than 500 Sfr. per year (some 175 US dollars at 1980 exchange rates). Swiss social insurance law specifies an upper limit of 10% for cost-sharing in ambulatory care, see fn. 2. This limit is applied throughout by sick funds.

6)   Administrative costs and reserve accumulation together amount to 9.5% of total accounting outlays of the Krankenkasse KKB in 1979, with little variation since 1976. The corresponding estimate of average θ (0.095/(1-0.095) = 0.105) may conceal variations among different divisions and membership classes (general, semiprivate, private), and age-region segments.

7)   This view contrasts in particular with Phelps' (1973, 1976) formulation in which no distinction is made between ambulatory and stationary care. All services, from the initial physician visit to treatment in a high intensity care unit, are aggregated into a common demand variable there.

8)   Let the two consumption goods be x and y, with prices p_x and p_y. For the case of an exogenous change of the consumption budget, dB, we have (Chiang, 1974, p. 398),

$$\frac{dx}{dB} \underset{+}{=} \frac{1}{|J|} \begin{vmatrix} -p_x & U_{xy} \\ -p_y & U_{yy} \end{vmatrix} \quad , \quad \frac{dy}{dB} \underset{-}{=} \frac{-1}{|J|} \begin{vmatrix} -p_x & U_{xx} \\ -p_y & U_{xy} \end{vmatrix}$$

In these expressions, J is the bordered Hessian, of positive sign. One instance of dx/dB > 0 is given when $U_{yy} < 0$, $U_{xy} < 0$ but p_y is small. Such a combination does not leave dy/dB unaffected, however. It increases the chances of the minor in the second expression above being positive, and hence of dy/dB < 0. The observation that an individual has stepped up his purchase of x in reaction to an increase of his income would therefore lead one to expect a decrease in his purchase of y. Such a relationship is absent from inequalities (21) and (22) of this model.

9)   The file contains 2,065 partially complete observations, with data on income and financial wealth most frequently missing. When income was recognized as an important predictor of supplementary health insurance, the sample had to be restricted to the 1,692 fully complete observations. Since the model predicts a tendency to reduce coverage for good risks, individuals having less coverage in 1980 than in 1976 were carefully analyzed. With few exceptions, 1980 values for BDAILY and XTREAT were zero. This is an almost sure sign of dropping out of this particular sick fund in favor of another fund or a private insurer. These individuals probably increased rather than reduced coverage, albeit by an unknown amount. Their exclusion from the sample resulted in a final set of 1,654 individuals.

10) Visual analog scales have been in frequent use for testing a new drug with prospective consumers, based on psychological research (McKelvie, 1978). But there, only endpoints are defined, e.g. "does not bother at all" and "unbearable" in the case of a drug's side effects. The modified visual analog scale used for measuring labor income is shown below.

Q5. Your employer spends a certain wage on you every month (or you reckon your own wage if self-employed). This amount is the sum of the monthly payment plus the pro rata shares of bonuses payable at the end of the year.

Please mark the approximate total amount in <u>thousands of Sfr.</u>:

```
├──┼──┼──┼──┼──┼──┼──┼──┼──┼──┼──┼──┼──┼──┼──┤
0   1   2   3   4   5   6   7   8   9  10  11  12  13  14  15
```

(Example: A designer costs his firm Sfr. 3,000.- in terms of his monthly wage. If this wage is payable 13 times a year and his Christmas bonus is Sfr. 100.- (say), then the scale below should be marked as shown:

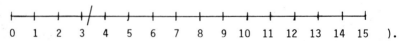

```
├──┼──┼──┼─/┼──┼──┼──┼──┼──┼──┼──┼──┼──┼──┼──┤
0   1   2   3   4   5   6   7   8   9  10  11  12  13  14  15   ).
```

11) At this point, thanks are due to Dr. H. Schmid, director of the Krankenkasse KKB, for his continuing support of this project. Mr. P. Haas, head of the EDP division, did a splendid job in coordinating the mailing and coding of the questionnaires and making the insurance records available.

12) Basically, there are two health insurance options in Switzerland. One is provided by the sick funds, the other, by for-profit insurance companies. But having purchased the basic package from sick fund A, the individual may still buy supplementary hospital insurance from fund B or from company C.

13) Preliminary OLS regressions showed that cost variables lagged two and more years contributed little to the explanation of BDAILY and XTREAT. Current cost variables were estimated to have effects comparable to lagged ones. They were not retained in order to avoid problems of simultaneity, which arise because of the suspected causal link running from insurance status to utilization.

14) Tobit estimation is a maximum likelihood method which takes into account that the dependent variable cannot vary continuously between negative and positive infinity. The method is due to Tobin (1958) and has been generalized by Nelson (1976). The macro &LIMDEP (dated July 1976) of the TROLL system was used for estimation. Preliminary analysis revealed that is was not necessary to distinguish more than two intervals, one with zero value of the dependent variable, the other, with positive values. The actual threshold structure is more refined than this, with steps of 10 Sfr. for BDAILY and 8 different classes ranging from 1,000 Sfr. to 100,000 Sfr. for XTREAT.

15) When the error component of the dependent variable is correlated over time, the lagged dependent variable cannot be introduced as a usual regressor. One possible solution is to replace the lagged dependent variable by an estimate of its conditional expected value, which is presumably purged of the error component. Using the full set of lagged endogenous variables amounts to instrumental variable estimation, a possibility discussed by Griliches (1967) and analyzed by Dhrymes (1971, pp. 109-111). After replacing the lagged dependent variables by their predicted values, first-order correlation of residuals decreased substantially ($\hat{\rho} \leq 0.2$ in preliminary regressions).

16) At first sight, log likelihoods in the thousands seem to indicate very poor statistical fit. However, the value of the likelihood function increases monotonically with sample size (cf. Tobin (1958)), and 846 is a rather large size, let alone the 1,654 observations of the entire sample. Incidentially, the OLS regression used for finding starting values as input to the limited dependent variable estimation procedure has R^2 values between 0.2 to 0.3. On the usual normality assumption, the deterioration of goodness of fit in Table 2 can be tested for its significance. For two times the increase of the value of log likelihood is asymptotically distributed as a chi-square variate, cf. Dhrymes (1970, pp. 34-35). Referring to the two 1979 equations, we have $2\cdot(4040-4034) = 12$, which is less than the critical value with 9 degrees of freedom (=16.9 at a significance level of 0.05).

17) A formal test of the equality of estimated coefficients contained in the 1976 equations of Tables 2 and 4 (and Tables 3 and 5) can be con-

structed following again Dhrymes (1970, pp. 34-35) and Theil (1971, p.
147). It amounts to a comparison of the log likelihood calculated on the
basis of the entire sample with the sum of the log likelihood based on the
even-keyed (n_1=846) and odd-keyed (n_2=808) subsamples. Twice the difference
is asymptotically distributed as a Chi-square variate with d.f. equal to
the number of regressors (=12). The appropriate calculations are shown
below for 1976:

Log likelihoods	BDAILY	LXTREAT
even-keyed subsample (cf.Tables 2,3)	3,798	1,862
odd-keyed subsample (not shown)	3,527	1,751
Total without equality restrictions	7,325	3,613
Total with equality restrictions (entire sample, cf. Tables 4,5)	7,333	3,618
twice the difference	16	10
critical value (12 d.f., 0.05 level of sign.)	22.4	22.4

These results imply that the equality hypothesis concerning the two
subsample Tobit estimates need not be rejected.

18) The point where BDAILY starts to decrease with AGE is given by the
equation, ∂BDAILY/∂AGE = 1.69 - 2·0.0158·AGE = 0; see Table 4, 1976 column
for the coefficients. The solution to this equation is AGE = 53.5.

REFERENCES

Bock, M.G., Yancey, T.A. and Judge, G.W. (1973), The Statistical Consequences of Preliminary Test Estimators in Regression, Journal of the American Statistical Association 68, 109-116.

Borch, K. (1974), The Mathematical Theory of Insurance. An Annotated Selection of Papers on Insurance Published 1960-1972, Heath & Co., Lexington,
Mass.

Chiang, A.C. (1974), Fundamental Methods of Mathematical Economics, 2nd
ed., McGraw-Hill International Student Edition, Tokyo.

Dhrymes, P.J. (1970), Econometrics. Statistical Foundations and Applications, Harper & Row, New York.

Dhrymes, P.J. (1971), Distributed Lags. Problems of Estimation and Formulation, Holden-Day, San Fransisco.

Eisen, R. (1979), Theorie des Versicherungsgleichgewichts (The Theory of
Insurance Equilibrium), Duncker & Humblot, Berlin.

Feldstein, M.S. (1973), The Welfare Loss of Excess Health Insurance, Journal of Political Economy 81 (2) Part II, 251-280.

Goldberger, A.S. (1964), Econometric Theory, J. Wiley & Sons, New York.

Griliches, Z. (1967), Distributed Lags: A Survey, Econometrica 35 (1), 16-49.

Grossman, M. (1972), On the Concept of Health Capital and the Demand for Health, Journal of Political Economy 80 (2), 223-255.

Henderson, J.M. and Quandt, R.E. (1971), Microeconomic Theory. A Mathematical Approach, 2nd ed., McGraw-Hill International Student Edition, Tokyo.

Krankenkasse KKB 111, (1981), Jahresbericht, 1. Januar bis 31. Dezember 1980 (111th Annual Report), Bern.

Leamer, E.E. (1978), Specification Searches. Ad hoc Inference with Nonexperimental Data, J. Wiley & Sons, New York.

McKelvie, S.K. (1978), Graphical Rating Scales: How many Categories?, British Journal of Psychology 69, 185-202.

Nelson, F.D. (1976), On a General Computer Algorithm for the Analysis of Models with Limited Dependent Variables, Annals of Economic and Social Measurement 5 (4), 493-510.

Phelps, C.E. (1973), Demand for Health Insurance: A Theoretical and Empirical Investigation, R-1054, OEO, Rand Corporation, Santa Monica, Cal.

Phelps, C.E. (1976), Demand for Reimbursement Insurance, in Rosett, R.N. (ed.), The Role of Health Insurance in the Health Services Sector, Universities-NBER Conference Series No. 2, Neale Watson, New York, 115-155.

Sloan, F.A. and Lorant, J. (1977), The Role of Waiting Time: Evidence from Physicians´ Practices, Journal of Business 50 (Oct.) 486-509.

Steinwald, B. and Sloan, F.A. (1974), Determinants of Physicians´ Fees, Journal of Business 47 (Oct.), 493-507.

Theil, H. (1971), Principles of Econometrics, J. Wiley & Sons, New York.

Tobin, J. (1958), Estimation of Relationships for Limited Dependent Variables, Econometrica 26 (1), 24-36.

TROLL Experimental Programs (1976), Qualitative and Limited Dependent Variables, MIT Information Processing Services, Boston, Mass.

Zweifel, P. (1981), Supplier-induced Demand in a Model of Physician Behavior, in Perlman, M. and van der Gaag, J. (eds.), Health, Economics, and Health Economics, North Holland, Amsterdam.

Zweifel, P. (1982a), Ein ökonomisches Modell des Arztverhaltens (An Economic Model of Physician Behavior), Lecture Notes in Economics and Mathematical Systems No. 198, Springer Verlag, Heidelberg.

Zweifel, P. (1982b), Demand for Supplementary Health Insurance in Switzerland: A Theoretical and Empirical Investigation, The Geneva Papers on Risk and Insurance, 7 (24), July 1982, 207-236.

ARNE RYDE SYMPOSIUM ON SOCIAL INSURANCE
L. Söderström (editor)
© Elsevier Science Publishers B.V. (North-Holland), 1983

PUBLIC PENSIONS AND PRIVATE SAVING:
A BRIEF REVIEW OF THE SWEDISH SYSTEM

Ann-Charlotte Ståhlberg*

1. INTRODUCTION

After Feldstein published his article on the negative effects of the social
security system on private saving in 1974, a great deal has been written on
this subject, both supporting and opposing his hypothesis. Numerous explanations have been offered as to why the expected negative effect is not
always obtained. In recent years critical studies have been increasingly in
evidence and the life cycle hypothesis has been questioned in many quarters. However, it is not necessary to assume that the inconsiderable savings effect obtained in certain empirical studies implies that the life
cycle hypothesis is not relevant. On the contrary, if the premises of the
model are adapted to more realistic conditions, it may well be that a weak
savings effect is consistent with the life cycle model. Accordingly, I introduce a number of new assumptions into the traditional life cycle model,
such as the presence of credit constraints, voluntary transfers from parents to children, and changed life cycle incomes due to the introduction of
the pension system. Using simulations I then show if these more realistic
conditions, taken individually, cause the savings effect in the life cycle
model to be considerably smaller. I also examine how well the life cycle
model relates to the experiences of the Swedish ATP system. Furthermore, I
calculate the pension claims actually earned by Swedish households. These
alone amount to 80 000 million dollars, or an average of 20 000 dollars per
household (which is more than double their traditional wealth). If we add
expected, though not yet earned, pension claims to this amount, the result
will be an even larger sum. It is my opinion that this wealth to some
extent replaces other kinds of saving.

2. THE PUBLIC PENSION WEALTH IN SWEDEN

In Sweden, as in many other countries, the non-private pension systems have
grown in importance over the years. The basic pension was introduced in
1913. Initially, the pension amounts were extremely modest but later
reforms have given the basic pension the character of a general basic security which, together with certain means-tested supplements, is supposed to
ensure a minimum standard of living. In 1960 the Swedish supplementary pen-

sion system (the ATP) was introduced; together with the basic pension this system was intended to give the pensioner an economic standard comparable to the one he had during his years of gainful employment. In addition to these public pension systems there are negotiated pension systems which supplement the ATP in certain respects. Finally, there are private pension schemes; the importance of these is, however, small in comparison with that of the public pensions.

Many people no doubt consider the right of a public old-age pension their most valuable wealth. If these public pension systems had not existed, the individual would have had to provide for his old age himself either by saving or by taking out a private insurance policy. Since public pension rights are not marketable there is a problem of valuation, but it is quite possible to make certain estimates of the actuarial value of the pension right. In the next few pages I shall calculate the value of the ATP wealth of Swedish households. My purpose in doing so is to show both how one should proceed in order to estimate this kind of not yet realized wealth correctly and how considerable this wealth is in comparison with more traditional types of wealth such as bank savings, real estate and so on.

Under the Swedish ATP system every individual over 16 years of age who has earned pension points is guaranteed the right of an ATP pension. The size of the pension that he or she will receive depends both on the size of previous incomes from employment and on the number of years he or she has been gainfully employed. Normally, a period of 30 active years is required for receiving a full pension. Those who have worked for fifteen years only receive half a pension and so on. The rule is that when a full pension is received the annual old-age pension from the ATP should amount to 60% of the average pensionable income during the 15 best-paid years of gainful employment. The pensionable income is considered to be the total labour income earned between 16 and 64 years of age and between a base amount of 1 and 7.5. The base amount follows, with certain exceptions, the consumers' price index, thus making the pension inflation indexed.

The pension points are calculated on the basis of the pensionable income and the social insurance offices register for each year how many pension points the individual has earned. These points determine the size of the pension amount; in other words, the pension points earned make the individual eligible for a certain pension in the future. One might say that the individual has a pension claim due to him under the ATP system and this claim increases in size as the individual earns more and better pension points and grows older. The claim (F(t)) due to an individual under the ATP system for a certain year (t) equals

$$F(t) = 0.60 \times \frac{t}{N} \times \bar{p}(t) \times B(t) \sum_{i=M}^{T} (1+r)^{-(i-m)} \times \pi(m,i) \qquad \begin{array}{l} \text{for } t=1\text{--}\bar{t} \\ \quad m < M \\ t=\bar{t} \text{ if } m=M-1 \end{array}$$

$$F(t) = 0.60 \times \frac{t}{N} \times \bar{p}(\bar{t}) \times B(t) \sum_{i=1}^{T-m} (1+r)^{-i} \times \pi(m,m+i) \qquad \begin{array}{l} \text{for } t > \bar{t} \\ m = M\text{---}T \end{array}$$

$t/N = 1 \forall t \geq N$

p̄(t) is the average of the 15 highest p(t) values during the period 1....t.

p(t) = (y(t) - B(t))/B(t)

B(t) < y(t) ≤ 7.5 B(t)

N is the number of years required for a full pension.[1] M is the pensionable age, m the individual´s age, and π(m,i) is the probability that a person aged m years will reach the age of i years. r is the real rate of interest and T indicates the maximum life span; B is the base amount and y is the income.

All the information necessary for determining each individual´s ATP wealth is available in the Swedish ATP register, in which his/her annual pension points, number of pensionable years and other similar data are entered. I have calculated the pension claim due to each household under the ATP for the year 1978.[2] The pension wealth calculated in this way is shown in tables 1 and 2. Since age is an important factor in this context, I have divided the population into a number of age groups; the figures for these age groups are shown separately in tables 4 and 5. In table 3 a comparison is made with the traditional wealth of the households.

The amounts in question are by no means small. I find it unlikely that the households would disregard forced saving of this magnitude and save money for their old age as though the ATP system did not exist. Still, the figures shown in the tables refer only to the ATP wealth earned so far. It must also be remembered that the households expect the ATP wealth to increase accordingly as their incomes increase. However, objections may be raised against the methods of calculation employed. In the critical discussion two reasons in particular have been adduced for why one should proceed cautiously in interpreting the figures obtained. The first is that the estimates are sensitive to the rate of interest at which future income streams are discounted. At a low rate of discount the pension claims, especially those of young people, are worth more than they would be at a high rate of discount. The second reason is the uncertainty about the construction of the pension system in the future. There may be people who even at this moment expect the system to become less advantageous and assess their claims accordingly. In addition, there is the fact that the pension wealth is not part of a person´s liquid assets; for this reason it may be worth less than the corresponding private means.

To state the correct rate of interest for a forecast period of up to 70 or 80 years, as in this case, is an impossibility. However, in a study such as this one it is generally considered reasonable to assume that the real rate of interest will be between 2 and 4%. As for the rest, one is obliged to rely on sensitivity analyses.

In principle, the ATP system is a pay-as-you-go system, whose relevancy is dependent on the individual wage-earner´s belief that the policy of the system will remain unchanged in the future. In today´s discussion concerning the ATP system it is often asserted that the cost of maintaining the system will increase at such a rate that it will prove impossible in the future to expect unchanged pension benefits. If young people today doubt that the pension committments will be met when they are old, their ATP wealth decreases in value. The natural reaction to any suspicion that the regulations now in operation will be changed to one´s disadvantage is

Table 1. The ATP wealth of Swedish households when the
         discount rate is 2%.

ATP wealth (dollars)	Percentage of households
100 000 -	0.7
60 000 - 100 000	5.3
50 000 - 60 000	3.4
40 000 - 50 000	6.8
30 000 - 40 000	9.6
20 000 - 30 000	11.7
10 000 - 20 000	17.0
2 000 - 10 000	21.3
0 - 2 000	9.3
0	14.9

Table 2. The ATP wealth of Swedish households when the
         discount rate is 4%.

ATP wealth (dollars)	Percentage of households
100 000 -	0.2
60 000 - 100 000	2.5
50 000 - 60 000	1.8
40 000 - 50 000	3.2
30 000 - 40 000	6.7
20 000 - 30 000	10.2
10 000 - 20 000	17.3
2 000 - 10 000	25.5
0 - 2 000	17.6
0	14.9

Table 3. The traditional wealth of Swedish households.

Traditional wealth (dollars)	Percentage of households
100 000 -	0.4
60 000 - 100 000	1.1
50 000 - 60 000	1.1
40 000 - 50 000	1.6
30 000 - 40 000	3.2
20 000 - 30 000	6.6
10 000 - 20 000	15.9
2 000 - 10 000	22.5
0 - 2 000	10.3
0	21.1
-0	16.0

Table 4. The ATP wealth of different age groups at a
discount rate of 2%.

Age group [3]	Percentage of households	Average in dollars
20 - 24	1.0	2 055
25 - 29	3.1	6 248
30 - 34	6.4	12 402
35 - 39	8.4	19 778
40 - 44	8.4	23 975
45 - 49	9.1	27 646
50 - 54	11.0	33 940
55 - 59	17.3	38 005
60 - 64	17.5	49 297
65 - 69	11.6	29 998
70 - 74	5.3	16 340
75 - 79	0.7	2 465
80 -	0.0	0

Table 5. The ATP wealth of different age groups at a
         discount rate of 4%.

Age group[3]	Percentage of households	Average in dollars
20 - 24	0.5	774
25 - 29	1.9	2 586
30 - 34	4.3	5 609
35 - 39	6.1	9 799
40 - 44	6.7	13 086
45 - 49	8.1	16 643
50 - 54	10.7	22 488
55 - 59	18.6	27 688
60 - 64	20.8	39 766
65 - 69	14.5	25 444
70 - 74	6.8	14 164
75 - 79	1.0	2 162
80 -	0.0	0

to try to think of other ways of ensuring that one´s old age will be economically safe. Is it in fact possible to discern such tendencies in the
available statistics?

The sale of private pension schemes has increased in recent years but it is
hard to say if this is because the annual cost of private pension schemes
is tax-deductible or because the ATP system is being questioned. The increased interest in owner-occupied houses is, in my opinion, more likely to
be caused by our present housing policy and by the tax and credit policies
subsidizing the system of owner-occupied houses than by a desire for
tolerable economic conditions in one´s old age. As to the creation, at the
beginning of the 1970s, of a negotiated pension for blue-collar workers,
the STP, which is a pension scheme by union contract, this is intended to
be complementary to the ATP and cannot guarantee an acceptable standard of
living by itself. (The STP amounts to about 10% of terminal pay.)

There is, in other words, no strong evidence suggesting that people in general act as though the ATP system was worthless; hence, there are no well-
grounded reasons to assume that the average citizen doubts that the present
regulations will be valid in the future as well. As I see it, there is
hardly any need for introducing more sophisticated expectation mechanisms
into the analysis of the ATP, at least not into the discussion of the 20
years which have passed since the ATP was introduced. The concern which
people feel about the future design of the system is a relatively new
phenomenon.

3. THE LIFE CYCLE MODEL: A PERSONAL VARIANT

The life cycle model has been subjected to a great number of econometrical
tests in many countries. The best-known of these are Feldstein´s (1974,
1976a, 1979, 1980) estimates of the consumption function made with the help
of American time series data. According to these, a decrease in private

savings by 30-50% would not be unreasonable. Even if there are many studies which support his results[4] there are also some which oppose them.[5] Danzinger, Haveman and Plotnick (1981), in their survey, are of the opinion that the effect on saving is considerably lower, between 0 and 20%, "with", as they say, "the most likely estimate lying near the lower end of this range."

There is a growing mistrust of the capacity of the life cycle hypothesis to predict how the pension system affects household saving. However, the weak savings effect obtained in some empirical studies need not imply that the life cycle hypothesis is not relevant here. On the contrary, it may well be that a weak savings effect is consistent with the life cycle model if the premises of the model are adapted to more realistic conditions. In order to examine this I shall introduce a number of new assumptions into the traditional life cycle model, such as the presence of credit constraints, voluntary transfers from parents to children and changed life cycle incomes due to the introduction of the pension system. With the help of simulations I shall then show if these more realistic conditions, taken individually, cause the savings effect in the life cycle model to be considerably lower than it would otherwise have been.

Old age saving is primary in the life cycle model in those cases where old age pensions are inconsiderable or do not exist. If a public pension system exists, it replaces private old age saving. The substitution is perfect if the capital market is perfect and if the life cycle income is not affected by there being or not being a pension system. This is the life cycle hypothesis in its purest form. If the pension system is actuarially fair the life cycle income is not affected. Actuarially fair means that an individual's pension benefits equal his pension costs including the interest. However, the public pension systems do not function according to such principles; they are so-called pay-as-you-go systems. This term means that the pensions paid out during a certain year are financed by those gainfully employed on the understanding that future generations will attempt to do the same for them. As there is no unambiguous relation between individual benefits and costs in a system of this kind, both intragenerational and intergenerational income redistributions are possible, and the system also encourages people to choose a lower pensionable age. For this reason the life cycle income may well be affected by a pay-as-you-go system.

A perfect capital market is hardly something which exists in real life. Credit rationing occurs frequently. If an individual's future income increases because of the pension system, he is not allowed to react to this by consuming more in times of credit rationing. This may be the case even if he happens to possess some private wealth since this can be more or less liquid. Part of the household's wealth may consist in home ownership, for example, but the credit rationing makes it difficult to borrow money with the houses as security.

Perhaps we must also assume that parents try to compensate their children to a certain extent for paying their pensions in a pay-as-you-go system. If a small part only of a person's income is pensionable, the effect on saving is moderate. The decrease which occurs because of the introduction of the pension system in that case represents a small share of the total household saving. Transfers from parents to children need not be pensionable. As examples of such transfers one could mention the (taxfree) economic support which parents give their children while they are still at school or university, or the fact that parents sometimes lend their children money at

a rate of interest which is lower than the market rate, or that they give
their children gifts of various kinds.

Table 6 offers a summary of possible situations and of the effects we may
assume the pension system to have a priori. In order to estimate what the
effect on private saving should be according to the life cycle hypothesis
if the various conditions set forth in table 6 are met, I have simulated
the life cycle saving in the different cases. An advantage of the simulation model is that it is possible to isolate the effects of the various
parameter changes obtained. Still, it has its limitations too since the
parameter changes are studied in a partial analysis only. In a non-partial
analysis attention must be paid to the indirect effects of the pension system, how the labour supply and the individual´s choice of education and occupation are affected, and how these factors change the pattern of the
lifetime income.

The simulation model which I have used is as follows. In its very simplest
form individual saving is determined by age and expected life cycle income
in the following manner:

$$c(v,m) = \alpha(v,m)W(v,m) \tag{1}$$

$$W(v,m) = \sum_{t=0}^{T-m} y(v,t)(1+r)^{-t} + k(v,m-1) \tag{2}$$

$$s(v,m) = y(v,m-\bar{m}) + rk(v,m-1) - c(v,m) \tag{3}$$

$$k(v,m) = k(v, m-1) + s(v,m) \tag{4}$$

$$k(v,\bar{m}-1) = 0 \tag{5}$$

$$m = \bar{m}...T$$

$$v = 0....$$

m stands for the individual´s age and v denotes his cohort. The life-span
is assumed to be known, equalling T. c(v,m) denotes the desired (real) consumption of an m-year-old individual in cohort v. W(v,m) is the sum total
of his (real) net worth and the expected present value of his future (real)
income. r stands for the (real) rate of interest. s(v,m) denotes (real)
saving and k(v,m) (real) net worth. $\alpha(v,m)$ is the proportion of W(v,m) consumed by an m-year-old in cohort v. $\alpha(v,m)$ is derived by maximizing the individual utility function

$$\sum_{t=0}^{T-m} u(c(v,t+m))(1+\rho)^{-t}; \quad m=\bar{m}...T \tag{6}$$

subject to the budget constraint

$$\sum_{t=0}^{T-m} c(v,t+m)(1+r)^{-t} = \sum_{t=0}^{T-m} y(v,t)(1+r)^{-t} + k(v,m-1); \quad m=\bar{m}...T \tag{7}$$

ρ in equation (6) is the subjective discount rate over time. The aggregate
saving during a particular year i, S_i, is obtained by ascertaining how much

Table 6. The effect of a public pension system on private saving according to the life cycle hypothesis.

Conditions	Private saving	
1. Perfect credit market. Unchanged life cycle income.	Pensions form a perfect substitute for private saving. Private saving decreases by A%.	
2. Credit constraints. Unchanged life cycle income.	Pensions do not form a perfect substitute for private saving. Private saving decreases by B%. B < A.	
3. Perfect credit market. Changed life cycle income.	a) All income is pensionable.*	b) Part of the income is not pensionable.
	Private saving decreases by C%.	Private saving decreases by D%. D < C.
4. Credit constraints. Changed life cycle income.	a) All income is pensionable.*	b) Part of the income is not pensionable.
	Private saving decreases by E%. E < C.	Private saving decreases by F%. F < D.

* Up to the stipulated maximum limit.

an individual in cohort v saves: this figure is then multiplied with the number of individuals in the cohort, and the final value is obtained by adding the cohorts together.

$$S_i = \sum_{v=\tau}^{\tau+T-\bar{m}} s(v,m_i) \; f(v,m_i) \; B_i \qquad\qquad (8)$$

where m_i is the age of the cohort v in the year i, B_i is the adult population in the year i, and $f(v,m_i)$ is the m_i-year-old individual's share in it.

The household saving ratio in the year i is obtained by dividing aggregate household saving in the year i, S_i, with the aggregate household incomes in the year i, Y_i where

$$Y_i = \sum_{v=\tau}^{\tau+T-\bar{m}} y(v,m_i-\bar{m}) \; f(v,m_i)B_i \qquad\qquad (9)$$

Credit constraints are introduced into the model by assuming either

$$c(v,m) \leq y(v,m-\bar{m}) + rk(v,m-1) + k(v,m-1) \qquad\qquad (7*)$$

or

$$c(v,m) \leq y(v,m-\bar{m}) + rk(v,m-1) + ny(v,m-\bar{m}) + k(v,m-1); \; m=\bar{m}...T \qquad (7**)$$

Should there be no publicly-administered pensions, the individual having to provide for his old age himself, his wage income over the life cycle is

$$y(v,t) \qquad\qquad \text{for } t = 0...h \text{ and}$$
$$\qquad\qquad\qquad\qquad\qquad\qquad\qquad\qquad\qquad (10)$$
$$y(v,t) = 0 \qquad\qquad \text{for } t > h$$

When a person's old-age maintenance is taken care of by means of public pensions, his wage income is

$$y^-(v,t) = y(v,t) \; (1-\theta(v,t)) \qquad\qquad \text{for } t = 0...h$$
$$\qquad\qquad\qquad\qquad\qquad\qquad\qquad\qquad\qquad (11)$$
$$y^-(v,t) = P(v,t) \qquad\qquad\qquad \text{for } t > h$$

$\theta(v,t)$ is the sacrifice, in terms of lower wages/salaries or a lower rate of wage increase, made by the individual today in order to ensure future pension benefits. $\theta(v,t)$ is stated as a percentage of the wage/salary.

I have tried to describe cases 3b and 4b in Table 6 by assuming that transfers of a non-pensionable type occur only once in a person's lifetime and then from those who are I years of age to those who are J years of age. Let us furthermore assume that the transfers are not expected. In that case the (positive or negative) transfers which an individual makes in the year t are added to his lifetime budget that year and thus affect both consumption and saving in all future periods.

In that model equations (2) and (3) have consequently been altered so that

$$W(v,m) = \sum_{t=0}^{T-m} y(v,t)(1+r)^{-t} + k(v,m-1) + Tr(v,m) \qquad \text{for } m=J \qquad (2^*)$$

$$s(v,m) = y(v,m-\bar{m}) + rk(v,m-1) - c(v,m) + Tr(v,m) \qquad \text{for } m=J \qquad (3^*)$$

and

$$W(w,m) = \sum_{t=0}^{T-m} y(v,t)(1+r)^{-t} + k(v,m-1) - Tr(v,m) \qquad \text{for } m=I \qquad (2^{**})$$

$$s(v,m) = y(v,m-\bar{m}) + rk(v,m-1) - c(v,m) - Tr(v,m) \qquad \text{for } m=I \qquad (3^{**})$$

where $Tr(v,m)$ stands for the transfers.

In order to be able to calculate household saving in the different cases the parameters must be determined numerically. The utility function is given the simple form

$$u(c(v,m)) = \frac{c(v,m)^{1-\sigma}}{1-\sigma} \quad ; \sigma > 0, \sigma \neq 1 \tag{12a}$$

$$u(c(v,m)) = \ln c(v,m); \sigma = 1 \tag{12b}$$

From equations (6), (7), (12a) and (12b) $\alpha(m)$ is derived

$$\alpha(m) = \frac{1}{\sum_{t=0}^{T-m} (\frac{1+r}{1+\rho})^{t/\sigma} (1+r)^{-t}} \quad ; m=\bar{m}...T \tag{13}$$

Further it is assumed that $\alpha(v,m)$ is independent of cohort v so that $\alpha(v,m) = \alpha(m)$. The age distribution, $f(v,m)$, is determined in the following manner:

$$B_i = \sum_{t=\bar{m}}^{T} \xi B_{i-t} \tag{14a}$$

$$B_i = (1+\beta)^i B_0 \tag{14b}$$

B_i is the size of the adult population in the year i, ξ is the birth rate, and β the population growth rate. Together, (14a) and (14b) yield

$$B_i = \xi B_0 \frac{(1+\beta)^{T-\bar{m}+1} - 1}{\beta} \tag{15}$$

this being the size of the (adult) population in the year i. In the year i the number of $(\bar{m}+n)$-year-olds is

$$\xi[1+\beta]^{i-\bar{m}-n} B_0 \tag{16}$$

and the proportion of $(\bar{m}+n)$-year-olds in the population

$$f(v,m) = \frac{\beta[1+\beta]^{T-\bar{m}-n}}{[1+\beta]^{T-m+1}-1} \tag{17}$$

$n = 0....(T-\bar{m})$

The retirement age is assumed to be exogenously determined and the same for everyone. The pension benefit amount, $P(v,t)$, is taken to be dependent on earlier income from employment according to given rules. I have chosen to use the rules of the Swedish ATP system, partly because I want to be able to examine how well the results of the simulation model tally with the experiences of the Swedish ATP system. The size of the annual ATP pension is fixed as a certain percentage of the average income during a maximum of 15 years. Those are the 15 best-paid years. Normally, 30 years of earning a pensionable income are required for a full pension. During a transitional stage, however, other and more generous rules are applied. The first persons to be eligible for pensions are those who have taken part in the system and have had pensionable incomes for three years. They receive 3/20 of the full pension. Next year´s beneficiaries will receive 4/20, etc. Those who have had pensionable incomes for 20 years or longer receive full pensions.

An individual´s income is assumed to develop over the life cycle in the following way:

$$y(v,t) = A(1-De^{-Gt})(1+\gamma)^{V} \qquad \text{for } t = 0...h$$

$$y(v,t) = 0 \qquad \text{for } t > h \tag{18}$$

In order to be able to calculate $y´(v,t)$ in the equation (11) numerically $\theta(v,t)$ must be derived. This is done in equation (19) where

$$\sum_{v=\tau}^{\tau+h} y(v,m_i-\bar{m})\theta_i f(v,m_i)B_i = \sum_{v=\tau+h+1}^{\tau+T-\bar{m}+1} P(v,m_i-\bar{m})f(v,m_i)B_i \tag{19}$$

m_i is the age of cohort v in the year i.

This gives the value of θ_i when the analysis is partial, the pension system is a purely pay-as-you-go one and the employees as a group bear the cost of the pensions.[6]

If the required values are given to the model parameters, the aggregate household saving can be simulated. First this is done for an economy without a public pension system. Then it is assumed that a pension system of the Swedish type is introduced and successively established. In consequence, the expected lifetime incomes are altered, which leads to changes in household saving as well. Aggregate household saving is then simulated for different years during the build-up years of the pension system.

The values of the population growth, the real pay growth, and the rate of interest are fixed. In the year $\bar{i}$ no public pensions exist. In the year $\bar{i}+1$ the ATP system is introduced and during a transitional period regulations of varying kinds are in operation.[7] The pension costs $\theta(i)$ keep growing as more and more people receive pensions and ever-increasing numbers draw full pensions.[8] At the point where all living cohorts can include the ATP from their very first consumption plan onwards, the system is considered to be in full-scale operation. In the model this happens after T-m̄ years.

The Results of the Simulations

The Swedish ATP system has only existed for about 20 years and so has not yet been fully implemented. I wish to be able to compare the results of the simulations with the actual experiences of the ATP system. Therefore, I account for how big the simulated savings effect will be during the first 20 years after ATP´s introduction into the model. Obviously the results are sensitive to the parameter values chosen. I mean that at least cases 1, 2, 4 and 6 below appear reasonable for Swedish conditions.

Table 7. The parameter values in the different cases.

Case	r	ρ	σ	β	γ	A*	D	G
1	0.04	0.02	2	0	0.02	30 000	0.5	0.07
2	0.04	0.02	2	0.01	0.02	30 000	0.5	0.07
3	0.04	0.02	2	0.02	0.02	30 000	0.5	0.07
4	0.04	0.02	2	0.01	0.01	30 000	0.5	0.07
5	0.04	0.02	2	0.01	0.03	30 000	0.5	0.07
6	0.02	0.02	1	0.01	0.02	30 000	0.5	0.07

* 1960 prices.

I shall account for the simulations according to the following pattern: In table 8 and table 9 allowance has been made only for the fact that the life cycle incomes change because of the pension system. In table 8 the pensionable age is given. In table 9 the pensionable age varies. In table 10 and table 11 allowance has been made for the fact that the life cycle in-

Table 8. The decrease of the average private saving ratio during the first 20 years after the introduction of the ATP system

Case	Decrease of the private saving ratio
1	37.0
2	30.5
3	27.7
4	58.5
5	17.6
6	67.0

come changes when the pensionable age is fixed. In table 10 credit rationings are added. In table 11 credit rationings have not been included.
Instead it is assumed that the older generation transfers incomes to the
younger in the form of gifts, etc.

The saving decreases in the model by 20 to 70%. Nowhere is the decrease as
low as only a few percent.

We have observed that the pension system diminishes the need for private
saving. But if the system causes the pensionable age to become lower at the
same time, this may in its turn counteract saving and thus have a positive
effect on it. The individual must now compensate for a loss of income
during a longer period than if he had retired at a higher age.[9] To simulate
that effect I have allowed the pensionable age to vary in the model.

Table 9. The decrease of the average private saving ratio
         during the first 20 years after the introduction of
         the ATP system. Different ages for retirement.

Case	Decrease of the private saving ratio when the pensionable age is			
	65	63	60	58
1	37.0	27.1	11.5	0.5
2	30.5	18.7	0	12.9 (increase)
4	58.5	52.5	43.5	37.4
6	67.0	43.5	8.1	15.7 (increase)

If everybody were to cut their work contribution by as much as 5 years or
more, the effect would be a big one. In that case the negative effect of
the pension system on household saving may be moderate. However, it is
disputable whether it is realistic to assume that the amount of work done
will be cut by as much as 5 years. I do not think so.

In Sweden it is possible to receive a full pension even though one continues to work after reaching the pensionable age. This may have helped to
moderate the retirement effect. But other factors may have induced an
earlier retirement age and thus an increase in individual saving. The
transitional generations may not have had an opportunity to qualify for a
full pension. Still, as more and more people are offered this possibility,
the need to supplement one´s pension with income from employment decreases;
in addition, the chances of doing so may have been made smaller by the
labour market situation of older people. However, there are no empirical
studies which can verify this.

Where American conditions are concerned a number of studies[10] point to a
strong negative connection between the American pension system and the pensionable age. In spite of the older labour force having improved their
health status and there being comparatively good possibilities of finding
employment the labour supply of older people has decreased at the same time

as their pension benefits have become better. To a certain extent this effect is due to the American tax system, which provides very little incentive to go on working once the pensionable age has been reached. Other studies[11] find a more interdependent relation between health and financial factors. The results vary but nowhere is it argued that the decrease of labour supply is so considerable as to make the simulated savings effect of less than 10% seem reasonable.

The effect of credit rationing is big in case 6 only. Consumption is assumed to be evenly distributed over the entire life cycle in this particular instance; in all the others it is assumed to be growing. In case 6 the desired consumption is big in comparison with the income people earn when they are young. For this reason young people want to borrow money, but the credit rationing stops them from doing so. They are forced to consume less and save more. With the utility function underlying cases 1 to 5 the individual's need for borrowing money is considerably lower. In spite of the severe credit terms obtaining in 7* the difference in decreased saving is fairly small - not more than 1 to 2 percentages - in comparison with the case "no credit rationing".

Table 10. The decrease of the average private saving ratio during the first 20 years after the introduction of the ATP system. Credit rationing.

Case	No credit rationing	Credit rationing in accordance with equation 7*	Credit rationing in accordance with equation 7** $\eta = 0.25$
1	37.0	36.4	37.0
2	30.5	28.9	30.2
3	27.7	25.4	26.8
4	58.5	56.7	58.0
5	17.6	16.3	17.1
6	67.0	47.2	50.3

Table 11. The decrease of the average private saving ratio during the first 20 years after the introduction of the ATP system. Transfers from the old generation to the young one.

Case	$J = 25$ $I = 50$ $Tr=1000(1+\gamma)^V$	$J = 25$ $I = 50$ $Tr=2000(1+\gamma)^V$	$J = 30$ $I = 60$ $Tr=1000(1+\gamma)^V$	$J = 25, 30$ $I = 50, 55$ $Tr=1000(1+\gamma)^V$
1	36.2	35.3	36.2	35.5
2	29.6	28.6	29.5	28.8
4	56.9	55.7	57.1	55.8
6	64.1	61.5	64.3	61.9

The transfer effect, as I have described it, is small. In addition, the effect becomes smaller when there is credit rationing. Transfers from old people to young people reduce the effect of credit rationing on consumption and saving. In order to have a considerable effect, gifts and other types of financial support must obviously form an important part of the lifetime budget.[12]

It is an old question whether the old generation tries to compensate the children when the pension system is constructed as a pay-as-you-go one and increases the bequests in terms of both human and physical capital. Barro (1974, 1976)[13] thinks that transfers between the generations even out one another so that every generation in fact pays its own pensions. Feldstein (1976b) believes that there is no reason to compensate the young generation as every generation benefits from a pay-as-you-go system. Everybody receives a pension amount which is larger than the amount they contributed to the older generation when they themselves were young. The condition is that the population growth or the productivity growth is greater than zero and that the pension system exists ad infinitum.[14]

Buiter and Tobin (1980) have made a survey of the debt-neutrality discussion from Adam Smith onwards. They think that the theoretical models and empirical studies available today are no more than tentative in their conclusions and that more empirical work is needed before it is possible to say which of the two - Feldstein or Barro - has provided the most accurate answer. Until this problem is solved I prefer to side with Feldstein.

Comment

The results of the simulations have not convinced us that a life cycle model adapted to more realistic conditions is capable of explaining why the pension system does not make the households cut their saving by more than 0 to 20%. I have to admit that I had expected the effect of credit rationing and intergenerational transfers to be considerably higher. Nevertheless, the conclusion must not be that the life cycle model is insufficient. There can be purely methodological reasons why many empirical estimates show a weak savings effect. Leymer and Lesnoy (1980), for example, think that the results are heavily dependent on the assumptions underlying the construction of the pension variable in the consumption function.

4. THE EXPERIENCES OF THE SWEDISH ATP SYSTEM

I want to dwell somewhat on the Swedish experiences of the ATP system and compare these with the results of the simulations. In this context there is reason to look more closely at the way in which the pension wealth has been defined in the Swedish surveys. Ettlin (1976) uses the AP fund as a measure of the pension wealth of the households. Actually, the AP fund has not very much to do with the pension wealth of the households. It was built up during the initial stage as a compensation for the expected loss of savings within the household sector. The pension claims of the households have increased constantly at the same time as the increase of the fund expressed as a percentage has decreased each year and is now almost zero. Today the pension claims are 80 000 million dollars, according to the calculations shown in Tables 1 and 2. When the ATP system is completely built up, they will be even bigger, maybe twice as big.[15]

Figure 1. The development of the pension wealth as estimated by
          Benzel and Berg (1980) and Ettlin (1976) respectively

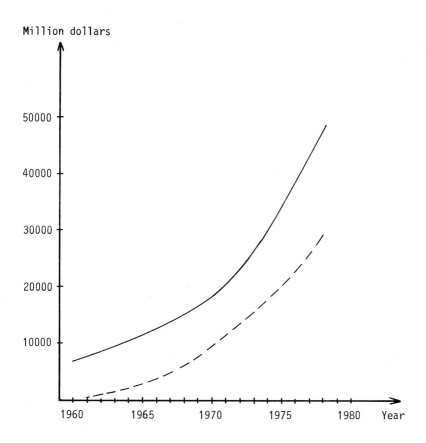

Million dollars

The development of the pension wealth, as estimated by
Benzel & Berg (1980).

– – –The development of the pension wealth, as estimated by
Ettlin (1976)

Benzel and Berg (1980) have worked out a pension wealth variable on
Feldstein´s pattern. An individual´s pension wealth is assumed to equal the
present value of his future pension benefits, the size of the future pensions being determined in the same way as now. Since the pension from the
ATP is calculated on the basis of the wage income earned during the 15
best-paid years of gainful employment, the calculation of the expected pension wealth must be based on a forecast of the future incomes of the households. Benzel and Berg approximate the expected incomes of the households
during a given year with the average pensionable income during that year,
which is not age-specific but the same for all age groups. Presumably, the
pension wealth has been underestimated since the real income normally grows
annually and the pension is calculated on the basis of the average of the
15 best-paid years of employment.

It is hard to say if this will be of decisive importance if the trend in
the development of pension wealth is correct. The development of the pension wealth is more or less the same in Benzel´s and Berg´s study, on the
one hand, and Ettlin´s, on the other, although the level differs. This is
shown by Figure 1.

Figure 2. The savings ratio of the households according to old
          data and to new, revised data

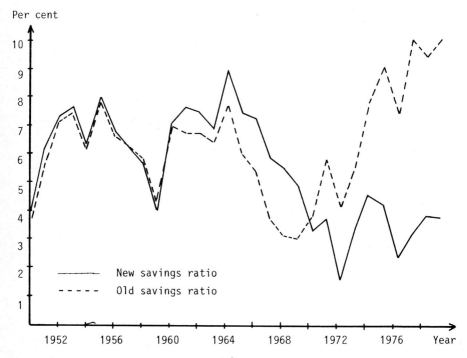

Source: Swedish National Accounts and Benzel & Berg (1980).

Benzel and Berg have been able to use revised national account data in their study. Such a revision was made as late as 1980. According to it, the savings ratio of the households has been considerably lower during the 1970s than earlier data has shown. Figure 2 shows the savings ratio of the households both according to old and to new revised data.[16]

Ettlin´s savings variable increases from the end of the 1960s onwards. This is not the case in Benzel´s and Berg´s study, however, which appears from figure 2. Nevertheless, it is Ettlin who has been able to demonstrate a decrease in private saving due to the ATP. Benzel and Berg find no significant support for the idea that the ATP may have affected saving negatively. This appears to me to be somewhat confusing. For this reason it is difficult to draw any conclusion other than that the results of the two Swedish studies are fairly uncertain.

Markowski and Palmer (1980) assume that the value of each year´s expected pension benefits are proportional to all pension incomes. In contradistinction to Feldstein and others, they do not use any wealth variable but a permanent income variable for the expected pension benefits. They found that the ATP has had a negative effect on household saving and that the average savings ratio during the period 1960-1975 has been about 25% lower or more because of the ATP.

The material is too contradictory for us to be able to draw any specific conclusions. However, I have permitted myself to speculate a little with the help of the simulation model. The decrease of savings generated in the life cycle model varies heavily with the parameter values and so it is of course difficult to be more precise. My ideas on the subject can be summarized as follows. The ATP system received its definitive design after a long period of commission work, negotiations, and settlements by compromise. Let us assume that the system that was finally adopted was considered to be the optimal one. If so, a utility function such as the one in case 1-5 is suited to the analysis. This would mean that at a rate of real pay growth of 2% and a rate of population growth of between 0 and 1% we should expect a decrease in savings of between 20 and 30%. In this case the actual savings ratio would have been 1.3 to 2.3 percentages higher on the average if the ATP had not existed.[17] Whether this is a correct estimate or not is, in the last instance, an empirical question.[18]

FOOTNOTES

* University of Lund. This study has been made possible through the financial support of The Bank of Sweden Tercentenary Foundation and Sparbankernas forskningsstiftelse.

1) During an initial stage certain transitional regulations are in operation. A lower number of pensionable years than 30 is required of those born between 1896-1923 for a full pension.

2) The calculation is based on a sample comprising some 10 000 households. The sample is the same as in SCB´s HINK survey.

3) In households where there is no man the woman´s age has been used.

4) See Munnell (1976) among others.

5)   See Leimer and Lesnoy (1980) among others.

6)   In a small open economy such as Sweden's it may be assumed that the
rate of interest will be equal to the international rate in the long run.
If so, the employees as a group bear the entire cost of the pensions. In
the short run, however, it is possible that the capital must bear part of
the costs.

7)   See the previous page.

8)   When a pension system of the pay-as-you-go type is introduced, the effect on the lifetime incomes of the transitional generations is more favourable than that on the incomes of later generations. Those who are
middle-aged or older when the system is introduced make contributions
towards it only for a small number of years; furthermore, the regulations
employed to determine the size of their pensions are more generous than
those to be employed later on when the system has been in operation for
some time.

9)   This is the so-called induced retirement effect introduced into the
discussion by Feldstein (1974). However, in the long run a reduced labour
supply may lead to higher pension contributions and lower lifetime income
than would otherwise have been the case.

10) Boskin (1977), Bowen and Finegan (1969).

11) Quinn (1977), Barfield and Morgan (1974).

12) Kotlikoff and Summers (1980) think that transfers of this kind are
very important in the USA. This is something which is very difficult to
test empirically.

13) See also Becker (1974) and Blinder (1976).

14) A decrease in saving results in a lower rate of growth in the long run
and constitutes a threat to future generations. Theoretically, Feldstein
thinks, this might be a reason for not decreasing saving but an individual
is hardly likely to be so foresighted.

15) See Ståhlberg (1980).

16) The differences were due primarily to three sources: 1) a change in
the method of estimating the income of family houses, 2) the introduction
of a new principle for calculating net interest income, and 3) the extension of pension incomes from collective pension funds.

17) It should not be forgotten that transfers from the younger generation
to the older actually occurred even before there were any public pension
systems. In those days the transfers took place within the families in that
the children provided for their parents' old age. The introduction of public pensions thus need not have as dramatic an effect on private saving as
that simulated in the life cycle model.

18) That this decrease may have been more than compensated for by the
building up of the ATP fund is another matter.

REFERENCES

Barfield, R.E. and Morgan, J.N. (1974), Early Retirement: The Decision and the Experience and a Second Look, University of Michigan, Survey Research Center.

Barro, R.J. (1974), Are Government Bonds Net Wealth?, Journal of Political Economy 6, 1095-1117.

Barro, R.J. (1976), Reply to Feldstein and Buchanan, Journal of Political Economy 2, 343-349.

Becker, G.S. (1974), A Theory of Social Interactions, Journal of Political Economy 6, 1063-1093.

Benzel, R. and Berg, L. (1980), The Role of Demographic Factors as a Determinant of Savings, University of Uppsala, Department of Economics, working paper No. 2.

Blinder, A.S. (1976), Intergenerational Transfers and Life Cycle Consumption, American Economic Review 2, 87-93.

Boskin, M.J. (1977), Social Security and Retirement Decisions, Economic Inquiry 1, 1-25.

Bowen, W.G., and Finegan A.T. (1969), The Economics of Labor Force Participation, Princeton University Press.

Buiter, W., and Tobin, J. (1980), Debt Neutrality: A Brief Review of Doctrine and Evidence, in von Furstenberg, G. (ed.), Social Security versus Private Saving.

Danzinger, S., Haveman, R. and Plotnick, R. (1981), How Income Transfer Programs Affect Work, Savings and the Income Distribution: A Critical Review, Journal of Economic Literature XIX, 975-1028.

Ettlin, F. (1976), Hushållens konsumtion och sparande under två decennier. Ett försök att bestämma orsaken till deras förändringar, Skandinaviska Enskilda Bankens Quarterly Review 3-4, 94-104.

Feldstein, M. (1974), Social Security, Induced Retirement and Aggregate Capital Accumulation, Journal of Political Economy 5, 905-926.

Feldstein, M. (1976a), Social Security and Saving: The Extended Life Cycle Theory, American Economic Review 2, 77-86.

Feldstein, M. (1976b), Perceived Wealth in Bonds and Social Security: A Comment, Journal of Political Economy 2, 331-336.

Feldstein, M., and Pellechio, A. (1979), Social Security and Household Wealth Accumulation: New Microeconomic Evidence, The Review of Economics and Statistics 3, 361-368.

Feldstein, M. (1980), Social Security, Induced Retirement and Capital Accumulation: A Correction and Update, National Bureau of Economic Research, Cambridge, Mass., working paper No. 579.

Kotlikoff, L.J., and Summers, L. (1980), The Role of Intergenerational Transfers in Aggregate Capital Accumulation, National Bureau of Economic Research, Cambridge, Mass., working paper no. 445.

Leimer, D.R., and Lesnoy, S.D. (1980), Social security and Private Saving: A Reexamination of the Time Series Evidence using Alternative Social Security Wealth Variables, US Department of Health, Education and Welfare, working paper No. 19.

Markowski, A., and Palmer, E.E. (1980), Social Insurance and Saving in Sweden, in von Furstenberg, G. (ed.), Social Security versus Private Saving.

Munnell, A. (1976), Private Pensions and Saving: New Evidence, Journal of Political Economy 5, 1013-1032.

Quinn, J.F. (1977), Microeconomic Determinants of Early Retirement: A Cross-sectional View of White Married Men, Journal of Human Resources 3, 329-346.

Ståhlberg, A. (1980), De offentliga pensionssystemens betydelse för förmögenhetsfördelningen (Effects on the Distribution of Wealth of the National Swedish Pension Schemes), Statistisk Tidskrift 2, 129-138.

ARNE RYDE SYMPOSIUM ON SOCIAL INSURANCE
L. Söderström (editor)
© Elsevier Science Publishers B.V. (North-Holland), 1983

ON THE CONCEPT OF NON-EMPLOYABILITY WITH RESPECT TO A NON-HOMOGENEOUS LABOR FORCE

Bernard van Praag
and
Han Emanuel*

1. INTRODUCTION

One of the most intriguing relatively new phenomena in the Western economy is that of social security.

Originating from charity in recent years it has grown considerably and it has become based on law. Vast parts of the population are involuntary contributors and also vast parts of the population are potential or actual beneficiaries of such systems. The legal cause for eligibility may be either sickness, disability or unemployment. Economically the cause seems to be a single one. People who temporarily or permanently lack the earning capacity to support their own living have to be supported by their more fortunate fellow-citizens. Therefore a transfer system is constructed. The beneficiaries receive benefits from a fund that is fed by the contributions or social premiums from the contributors. Such systems have the character of a pay-as-you-go system although there are numerous variants. In previous decades it was implicitly assumed that the existence of such a social security system (SSS) either did not have an impact on other macro-economic variables like unemployment or only a positive one via the Keynesian multiplier process. As history progresses, there seems to be a tendency that those systems get more and more beneficiaries and that, consequently, the ratio of social security benefits to the national income increases. In the Netherlands, for example, the number of families on benefit already equal the number of families that live on earned income.

The question may be raised whether this tendency is likely to stop or that the whole working population might crowd out and go on the dole, if the SSS would not be changed in time. There seem to be three fundamental factors which may cause this tendency:

(1) In our societies wages are no longer flexible, but rather rigid. The majority of wage schedules are negotiated between employers and unions. Wages are a function of some rather rough characteristics like schooling,

age and experiences. Wages are not adapted to personal talents. It follows that some people are not worth their wage and as it is impossible to reduce their wage the employer tries to get rid of them either by straightforward firing, or by early retirement, disability declaration, etc. In short such a person is <u>non-employable</u>.

The contributions to the SSS are usually in the form of a payroll tax, partly levied from the employer, partly levied from the employee.

(2) If the employer has to pay a payroll tax it implies a wage increase, which according to classical notions will lead to a reduction of the employed labor force.

(3) If the payroll tax has to be paid by workers it reduces their net wage, and hence they will become less eager to supply their labor. (At least if there is a positive labor supply elasticity; compare Fullerton (1982), Boskin (1973), Hausman (1981)).

In this paper we try to analyze the question in what way a social security system, implanted in a market economy, tends to affect the labor market equilibrium. This study is on the basis of a simple model, which is illustrated by numerical simulations. Our conclusion will be that the impact cannot be neglected.

In Section 2 we describe heterogeneous labor supply in terms of a labor quality vector and we define the labor-productivity ratio ϕ, that is the value per dollar wage of each worker. By ordering the workers according to their labor-productivity ratio, workers are differentiated according to their attractivity for firms and consequently an order of hiring and firing is defined.

In Section 3 we study the hiring behavior of firms and we define the non-employability concept in a heterogeneous labor market. Labor demand is derived on the basis of a Cobb-Douglas production function and the possibility of a labor market equilibrium is investigated in the context of a market economy <u>without</u> a social security system. In Section 4 we study the impact of an <u>SSS</u>, where the SSS is assumed to be financed by a payroll tax paid by employers. The employers behavior will be affected by the incurred cost increase. In Section 5 the effect of an SSS on the labor market is studied, where it is assumed that the SSS is supported from a wage tax, paid by the workers.

In Section 6 an SSS which has a mixed finance structure is studied. In Section 7 some conclusions are drawn, the qualifications for this research are spelled out and indications for future research directions are discussed.

2. QUALITIES, LABOR EFFICIENCY UNITS AND LABOR PRODUCTIVITY

It is a matter of fact that the labor force is not homogeneous like assumed in textbook economics. Basically, the labor force is just like the mass of capital. Workers may replace each other but they are not perfect substitutes. This is caused by the fact that workers are of different quality levels. Quality is a more-dimensional concept. We may differ by age, schooling, etc. In general quality is desribed by a vector q, which we assume to be positive.

Moreover we shall assume that one worker of quality q_1 represents $a(q_1)$ efficiency units and the worker of quality q_2 is equivalent to $a(q_2)$ units. Hence one q_1 worker may be substituted by $a(q_1)/a(q_2)$ workers of type q_2.

Wages are also quality-differentiated. There is a wage-function $w(q)$. In a complex modern society such a wage-function is a product of institutional negotiations, which of course are influenced by market conditions, but which are too rigid to reflect them completely. The obvious variable in which the employer is interested is the efficiency per money unit, that is $a(q)/w(q)$. This ratio will be called the labor-productivity ratio and be denoted by $\phi(q)$. In the classical situation that wages reflect market conditions the market would equalize any temporal differences in ϕ. In other words, in the classical equilibrium situation $\phi(q)$ would be constant. Due to the rigidity of wages according to institutionally fixed patterns $\phi(q)$ varies over quality classes.

Finally we assume that for each quality level q and wage $w(q)$ there is a specific labor supply. Hence for the labor force as a whole there is a quality distribution of supply, described by the density function $g(q)$. The total labor force consists of N individuals. The following example will be used for simulation purposes. Let q be the 2-vector (age, schooling) and let us assume both components are statistically independent and distributed according to lognormal distributions. More specifically we assumed that $\ln$ (age) is normally distributed $N(3.5, 0.3)$ and $\ln$ (schooling) is a $N(2.7, 0.3)$ variate where we add a restriction "school < age - 7", specifying that any individual starts going to school at the age of seven.

Productivity is assumed to depend on q in the following way

$$\ln(a(q)) = \alpha_1 \ln q_1 + \alpha_2 \ln q_2 + \alpha_3 (\ln q_1)^2 \tag{1}$$

where the coefficients in this example are specified as

$$\alpha_1 = 3.35 \qquad \alpha_2 = 0.21 \qquad \alpha_3 = -0.45$$

Wages are assumed to obey a similar relation

$$\ln(w(q)) = \beta_1 \ln q_1 + \beta_2 \ln q_2 + \beta_3 (\ln q_1)^2 \tag{2}$$

where the coefficients are chosen to be

$$\beta_1 = 3.00 \qquad \beta_2 = 0.20 \qquad \beta_3 = -0.40$$

The specific values have been selected in order to get somewhat realistic outcomes. The model appears to be rather sensitive to changes in the parameter values.

As a result we find

$$\ln(\phi(q)) = \ln(a(q)) - \ln(w(q)) = \gamma_1 \ln q_1 + \gamma_2 \ln q_2 + \gamma_3 (\ln q_1)^2 \tag{3}$$

where $\gamma_i = \alpha_i - \beta_i$.

The contour lines of $\phi(q)$ in (ln age, ln school) - space are sketched in Figure 1. Those lines are parabolas due to the specification in (1) and

Figure 1. Labor-productivity ratio contour lines

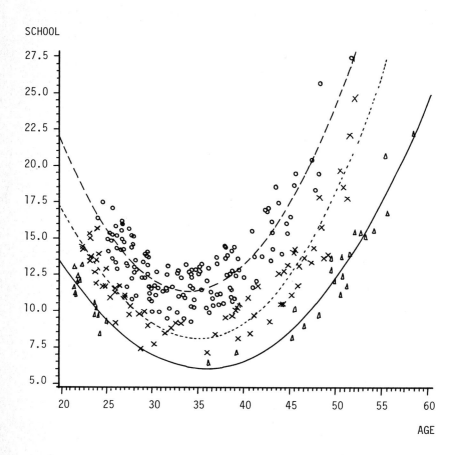

SCHOOL

AGE

(2). Their shape depends on the parameters α and β, that is the technical productivity relation and the institutional wage relation. By (3) each worker is classified on a specific parabola in Figure 1, where a higher parabola corresponds to a higher labor-productivity ratio. The assumption is that less (formal) schooling can be compensated by somewhat higher age if one is young but that for high age it is just the reverse.

The frequency of each class is given by the number of dots in the figure. It follows from the q-distribution assumed.

3. THE ORDER OF HIRING AND FIRING AND THE DEMAND FOR LABOR

The variation in $\phi(q)$ over quality space is the reason that some workers are more attractive than others. The order of attractiveness is defined by the order of ϕ or $\ln(\phi)$.

Notice that $\phi(q)$ depends on the wage pattern $w(q)$. A change of wage will generally imply a change in the ordering that ϕ defines on the quality space. There is a specific lower bound ϕ_{min}, such that workers with $\phi < \phi_{min}$ are non-employable. The employed labor force is denoted by $L(\phi_{min})$. In formula we get

$$L(\phi_{min}) = N \int_{\phi_{min}}^{\infty} h(\phi)d\phi \qquad (4)$$

where $h(\phi)$ is the density function of ϕ.

The average productivity $\bar{a}(\phi)$ in a class ϕ is defined by

$$\bar{a}(\phi) = \frac{1}{h(\phi)} \int_{\phi(q)=\phi} a(q)g(q)dq \qquad (5)$$

and the average wage $\bar{w}(\phi)$ for the class ϕ is simply

$$\bar{w}(\phi) = (1/\phi)\bar{a}(\phi) \qquad (6)$$

It follows that the cumulated efficiency units in $L(\phi_{min})$ are given by

$$A(\phi_{min}) = N \int_{\phi_{min}}^{\infty} \bar{a}(\phi)h(\phi)d\phi \qquad (7)$$

while the wage sum is given by

$$W(\phi_{min}) = N \int_{\phi_{min}}^{\infty} \phi^{-1} \bar{a}(\phi)h(\phi)d\phi \qquad (8)$$

Consider now the demand for labor by firms. We assume a Cobb-Douglas function

$$Y = F(A(\phi_{min}),K) = cA^{\delta}(\phi_{min})K^{\varepsilon}. \qquad (9)$$

We assume a fixed sales price p. The marginal condition states that marginal money productivity is equal to the wage of the marginal worker. We get

$$pcK^{\varepsilon}.\delta A^{\delta-1}(\phi_{min}).\bar{a}(\phi_{min})h(\phi_{min}) = \bar{w}(\phi_{min})h(\phi_{min}) \qquad (10)$$

Using (6) we rewrite the labor market equilibrium equation as

$$pcK^{c}.\delta.A^{\delta-1}(\phi_{min}) = \phi_{min}^{-1} \qquad (11)$$

From (7) it follows that $A(\phi)$ is decreasing in ϕ.

However, this implies that $A^{\delta-1}$ is increasing in ϕ, provided that $\delta < 1$, which is a classical assumption. It can be shown that (11) has a unique non-zero solution.

The upshot of this analysis is that if $g(\phi)$ is a non-zero continuous density there will always be a fraction of the labor force which is unemployable. The unemployability does not depend only on $a(q)$ but also on $w(q)$, the
wage demanded. It follows that everybody is employable if his wage $w(q)$ is
low enough. The quality ranking vanishes only if the classical assumption
holds, i.e., when $a(q)/w(q) = \phi(q)$ is constant. When we assume (2) and (3)
to hold it implies that the set of employed people E would be described by

$$E = \{q | \gamma_1 \ln q_1 + \gamma_2 \ln q_2 + \gamma_3 (\ln q_1)^2 \geq \ln \phi_{min}\} \tag{12}$$

while the set of the unemployable is described by

$$U = \{q | \gamma_1 \ln q_1 + \gamma_2 \ln q_2 + \gamma_3 (\ln q_1)^2 < \ln \phi_{min}\} \tag{13}$$

where ϕ_{min} is the solution to (11). Assuming $\gamma_3 > 0$ it implies that the old
and young people will belong to U.

Figure 2. Employment equilibrium in a market without social security.

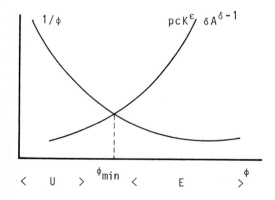

It can be shown that the $A^{\delta-1}$-curve shifts upwards if either capital K or
the labor elasticity δ is increased. This would yield a lower ϕ_{min} and thus
less unemployment.

4. AN EMPLOYER-FINANCED SOCIAL SECURITY SYSTEM

Let us assume that the set U has to get social security benefits. The benefit is described by the function $b(q)$. It may be that $b(q)$ is related to
$w(q)$, for instance $b(q)=\psi.w(q)$, or that $b(q)$ is a constant. It may also be
that $b(q)$ depends on age, family size etc. In any case the total sum B of
benefits is given by

$$B(U) = \int_U b(q)g(q)dq \tag{14}$$

neglecting the scale factor N.

This amount has to be financed out of social security premiums. If social premiums are collected by means of a payroll tax, there are three usual systems. Either the premium is paid by the employer or by the employee or by both. There are authors like Brittain who defend the thesis that the distinction is only formal since the employer´s share plus net wage will remain constant. We do not choose party in this debate, but we shall study both cases. We assume in this section that social security is financed exclusively by firms. The premium is $\pi(q)$, so the total premium revenue is

$$P(E) = \int_E \pi(q)g(q)dq. \tag{15}$$

The premium $\pi(q)$ may depend on wage $w(q)$, for instance, proportionally such that $\pi(q) = \pi.w(q)$, but it may also depend on other factors, which do not influence wages, like family size.

For employers the distinction between wage and premium is purely formal; they decide on wage costs $\tilde{w}$, where

$$\tilde{w}(q) = w(q) + \pi(q). \tag{16}$$

We notice that by the introduction of social premiums the whole order of hiring and firing will be changed, for firms will base themselves now on the real labor productivity ratio

$$\tilde{\phi}(q) = \frac{a(q)}{\tilde{w}(q)} = \frac{a(q)}{w(q) + \pi(q)} = \phi\{\frac{1}{1 + \pi(q)/w(q)}\}. \tag{17}$$

It follows that the ϕ-order changes, except if $\pi(q)/w(q)$ is constant. In this paper we shall assume such a constant rate, which is denoted by π_1.

Neglecting the operational cost of the system, the equilibrium condition of the social fund is B=P, or

$$B(U) = P(E) \tag{18}$$

$$= \pi W(E)$$

where $W(E)$ is the wage sum of the employed, that is

$$W(E) = \int_E w(q)g(q)dq.$$

Since U and E are determined by ϕ_{min} we may rewrite (18) more explicitly as

$$B(\phi_{min}) = \pi_1 W(\phi_{min}) \tag{19}$$

where B is an increasing function and W a decreasing function in ϕ_{min}. It follows that for a fixed premium/wage rate π_1 the minimal employable wage/labor productivity ratio ϕ_{min} is uniquely determined. It is easily seen from (19) that π_1 is an increasing function g_1 in ϕ_{min}, viz., $\pi_1 = B(\phi_{min}) /W(\phi_{min}) = g_1(\phi_{min})$. We have $g_1(0) = 0$.

Figure 3. Social security link and productivity link

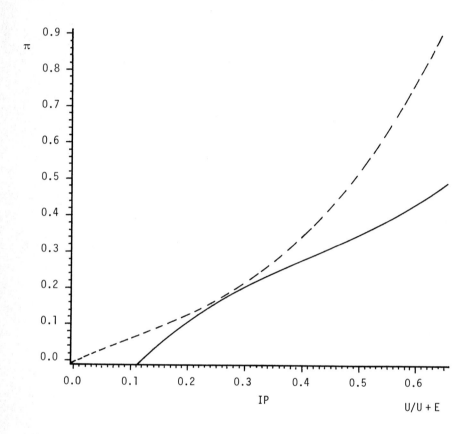

On the other hand $\lim\limits_{\phi_{min} \to \infty} g_1(\phi_{min}) = \infty.$

We call $\pi_1 = g_1(\phi_{min})$ the <u>social security link</u>.

However, there is a second relationship g_2 between π and ϕ_{min} via the labor demand behavior of the firm. In the previous section it was described by equation (11), now it has to be replaced by

$$pcK^\varepsilon \cdot \delta A^{\delta-1}(\phi_{min}) = \frac{1 + \pi}{\phi_{min}}. \qquad (20)$$

Equation (20) yields the relation $\pi_1 = g_2(\phi_{min})$ which is also increasing in ϕ_{min} as implicit differentiation of (20) shows. We call the latter relation the <u>productivity link</u> between π_1 and ϕ_{min}. Notice, however, that for $\pi=0$ $\phi_{min}>0$ in (20). In Figure 3 both relations are sketched for $\delta=0.8$ and K=11.

Figure 4a. The premium π_1 as a function of capital for various benefit/income ratios under a firm financed system.

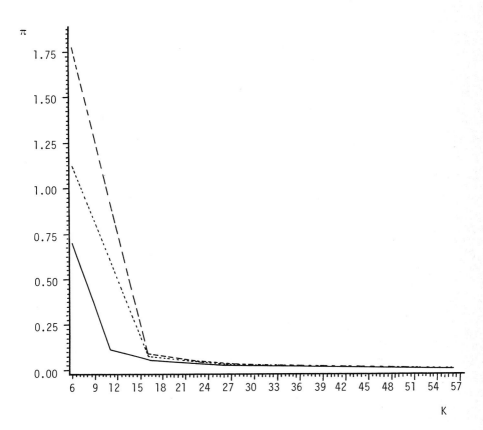

It seems that no specific statement can be made about the behavior of the two curves in Figure 3. However, one thing is clear. Only at intersection points, where $g_1(\phi_{min}) = g_2(\phi_{min})$, an equilibrium is possible. It implies that there may be a finite set of equilibrium points or even no equilibrium at all. The latter situation is sketched in Figure 3.

Whether there exists an equilibrium depends on the structure of the benefits tariff $b(w(q))$, the structure of the premium tariff $\pi(w(q))$ and the capital stock.

Now we analyze the problem in the context of the numerical example given in Section 2. Let us assume as before that the premium tariff and benefit tariff are proportional, that is

$$\pi_1(w) = \pi_1 w \qquad b(w) = \psi.w$$

Figure 4b. The unemployment rate as a function of capital for various
benefit/income ratios under a firm financed system.

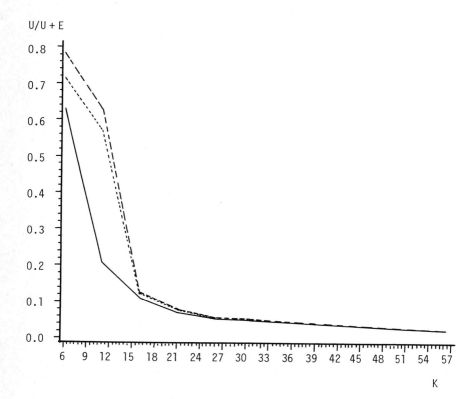

U/U + E

Assuming $\delta = 0.8$ we calculated the premium π_1 and unemployment U/U+E for three benefit/income ratios $\psi = 0.7$, 0.8 and 0.9 and for various values of the factor $pcK^{\varepsilon}\delta$. Those relationships are sketched in Figures 4a and 4b (where $pc\delta$ is set at 1). From Figure 4a we see that there is a strong dependency between capital and the premium π_1. The curves stop at the left where π_1 would exceed 50%. It is seen that for high values of capital premiums and unemployment are rather low and that the level of ψ does not make too much of a difference. If capital decreases, premiums and unemployment rise steeply. The most interesting point is that π_1 and the unemployment ratio U/U+E are functions of ψ and K, say G_1 and H_1, where both G_1 and H_1 are increasing in ψ and decreasing in K. It follows, that if K is fixed, fixation of the benefit/income ratio ψ implies fixation of the premium π_1 and of unemployment as well. We doubt whether the crucial role of ψ in this second respect is properly recognized by policy-makers. In our numerical setting we also found that the technical parameter δ is rather critical. With $\delta < 0.75$ an equilibrium becomes rather implausible. However, let us now look at the other well-known finance structure, where workers finance social security.

5. A LABOR-FINANCED SOCIAL SECURITY

In the previous section it was assumed that employers had to finance the social security system. An alternative is that the employed workers support the unemployable.

In that case the sum of benefits $B(U)$ is covered by premiums $\pi_2(w(q))$, levied from employees. It implies that we have to distinguish between gross wages $w(q)$ and net wages $\tilde{w}(q) = w(q) - \pi_2(w(q))$.

In this system wage-costs do not change for the firm. We may expect, however, a reaction of labor supply.

At prevailing wages the supply of type q is described by the supply density $g(q)$. If we assume that supply is influenced by changes in net wages, it implies that net wages $\tilde{w}$ appear as parameter in $g(q)$. We realize this by changing $g(q)$ in $\tilde{g}(q)$ with

$$\tilde{g}(q) = g(q) \left[\frac{\tilde{w}(q)}{w(q)}\right]^{\eta} \quad \text{with } \eta > 0. \tag{21}$$

The second factor, smaller than one if $\tilde{w}(q)/w(q) < 1$, reflects the disincentive caused by a net wage reduction. If $\eta=0$ such a reduction is absent. Notice that $\tilde{g}(q)$ does not only differ from $g(q)$ in <u>shape</u>, but also in <u>level</u>. Especially

$$\int_A \tilde{g}(q)dq < \int_A g(q)dq \quad (A \subset E),$$

which means that not only the composition has changed but also the total size of labor supply. In the special case of a constant premium fraction $\tilde{w}/w = 1-\pi_2$ the disincentive is identical for all workers. We shall consider this case in more detail.

In this case the <u>social security link</u>, analogous to (18), becomes

$$B(U) = \int_U b(q)g(q)dq$$

$$= \int_E \pi_2 w(q).(1-\pi_2)^{\eta}g(q)dq$$

$$= \pi_2(1-\pi_2)^{\eta}W(E) \tag{22}$$

$$\text{or } B(\phi_{min}) = \pi_2(1-\pi_2)^{\eta}W(\phi_{min}).$$

The <u>productivity link</u> is influenced since labor supply changes. We get $\tilde{g}(q) = (1-\pi_2)^{\eta}g(q)$ and hence $\tilde{h}(\phi) = (1-\pi_2)^{\eta}h(\phi)$. It follows that (5) remains the same, but that (7) changes in

$$\tilde{A}(\phi_{min}) = (1-\pi_2)^{\eta}A(\phi_{min}). \tag{23}$$

In case of a Cobb-Douglas function (11) changes in

$$pcK^{\varepsilon}\delta(1-\pi_2)^{\delta\eta}A^{\delta-1}(\phi_{min}) = \phi_{min}^{-1} \tag{24}$$

Figure 5a. The premium π_2 as a function of capital for various
benefit/income ratios under a labor-financed system.

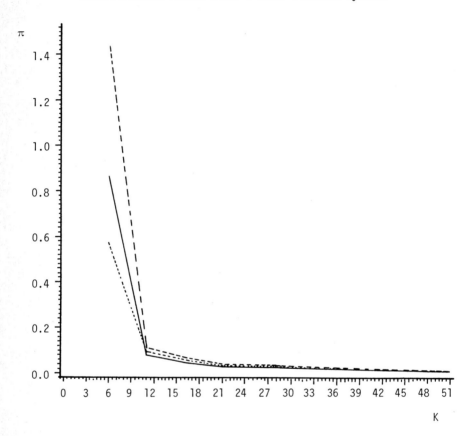

It is seen that the supply reduction has the same influence on the firm as
a lowering of the selling price p. For, the supply reduction implies a reduction of top quality first.

Combination of (22) and (24) yields the system

$$\pi_2(1-\pi_2)^\eta W(\phi_{min}) = B(\phi_{min})$$

$$(1-\pi_2)^{\delta\eta}pcK^\varepsilon \delta A^{\delta-1}(\phi_{min}) = \phi_{min}^{-1}$$

(25)

from which equilibrium solutions (ϕ_{min},π_2) may be derived, if they exist.

Again, this system is investigated for $\delta = 0.8$, while we choose $\eta = 0.5$ for

Figure 5b. The unemployment rate as a function of capital for various
          benefit/income ratios under a labor-financed system.

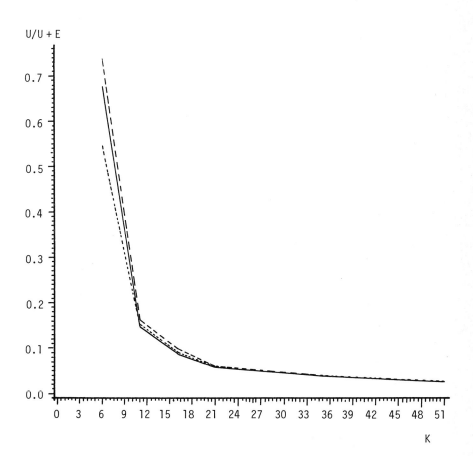

the labor supply elasticity. (cf. Fullerton (1982), p.16 and the literature
reviewed there). Equation (22) implies that all people with $\phi < \phi_{min}$ apply
for social security benefits ψw, while only a fraction $(1-\pi_2)^\eta$ of the
workers with $\phi > \phi_{min}$ remain in the work force to support the non-emloyable.
However the employable who drop out voluntarily do not apply, or/and are
not eligible for benefits.

In Figures 5a and 5b the dependency between π and U/U+E with K is sketched,
analogous to Figures 4a and 4b. We see that a labor financed model may
yield the same difficulties as the employer-financed version. That is
$\pi_2 = G_2(\psi,K)$ and $U/(U+E) = H_2(\psi,K)$ where G_2 and H_2 are increasing in ψ and
decreasing in K.

Figure 6a. The premium π_2 as a function of capital for various
          benefit/income ratios under an employers-labor financed system.

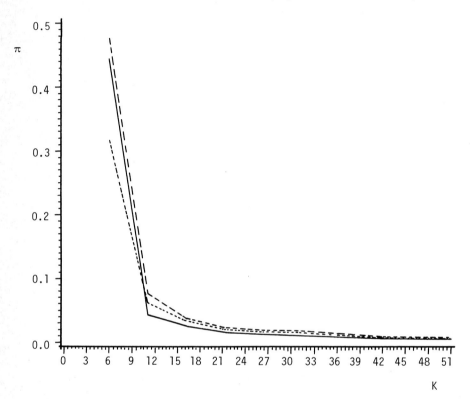

Obviously the value of the labor supply elasticity is rather crucial. In
our numerical context it was found that with an η above 0.5 the system appeared to tend to a full crowding-out situation.

6. A SOCIAL SECURITY SYSTEM FINANCED BY FIRMS AND LABOR

Many systems are a combination of both systems, where a part of the premium, say, $\pi_1(w(q))$ is paid by the employer and a part $\pi_2(w(q))$ by the employee. In that case the system (25) becomes

$$B(\phi_{min}) = (\pi_1+\pi_2)(1-\pi_2)^{\eta}W(\phi_{min})$$

$$(1-\pi_2)^{\delta\eta}pcK^{\varepsilon}{}_{\delta}A^{\delta-1}(\phi_{min}) = (1+\pi_1)/\phi_{min}$$

(26)

Figure 6b. The unemployment rate as a function of capital for various
         benefit/income ratios under an employers-labor financed system.

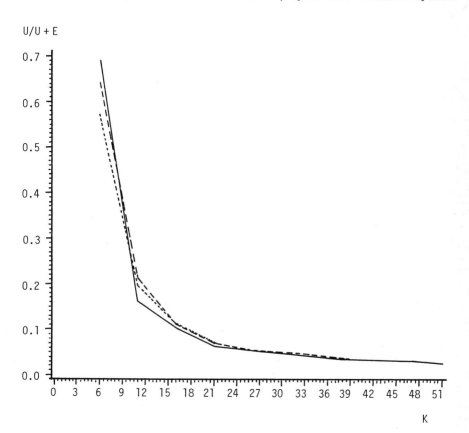

U/U + E

In this case we have three unknowns π_1, π_2 and ϕ_{min} but only two equations.
Of course, this degree of freedom vanishes if a third restriction is introduced, for example that $\pi_1=\pi_2$, or in words that employer and employee pay
equal shares. Such relations are in general fixed by law. More generally,
we may specify

$$\pi_2 = \alpha\pi_1 \tag{27}$$

where α may be any positive scalar, fixed by law.

The system (26) can be considered as a generalization of the previous
models. If $\pi_1=0$ and $\pi_2=0$, the system with no security results. If $\pi_2=0$ we
have a firm-financed system, if $\pi_1=0$ the system is labor-financed. A mixed
system with $\pi_1=\pi_2$ has also been simulated. The results have been sketched
in Figures 6a and 6b. Not unexpectedly the curves look like a convex

mixture of Figures 4 and 5.

So the conclusion can be repeated. The equilibrium $(\pi, U/(U+E))$, if it exists, is a function of the benefit/income ratio ψ and the capital stock K.

7. CONCLUSIONS AND DISCUSSION

The theoretical model presented in this paper is still far from reality, as the level of abstraction has been chosen in order to concentrate on the main structure of the model. A number of shortcomings will be pointed out in a moment.

However, this simple model is already rather disconcerting with respect to the problem at issue in this paper. The main findings are:

(1) an SSS is not a neutral transfer system, which has no influence on other variables.

(2) The finance structure and the benefit/wage ratio influence the level of employment.

(3) The higher the benefit/wage ratio, the higher the unemployment will be; the higher the capital equipment the lower unemployment will be.

(4) If the benefit/wage ratio increases and/or capital decreases they may exceed critical bounds such that no equilibrium on the labor market exists any more and all workers crowd out on the dole.

(5) The structure of benefits and premiums has an impact on the hiring and firing pattern on the labor market.

If these conclusions have som general validity, these conclusions are certainly relevant for policy issues. Indeed in practice we see in many countries a considerable exodus of the labor force into non-employment with no sign that an end is reached. It might be that in some countries circumstances are such that no finite equilibrium exists any more and that the only remedy would be a restructuring of the SSS.

As already hinted at, the present model is a rather sketchy one. First we assume that the price-level p is fixed. However if wage costs increase, employers will tend to rise their selling prices as well. On the other hand if prices increase, wages will tend to increase as well. If prices and wages rise (or fall) at the same rate, the model still holds as it can be formulated just as well in real wages $\tilde{w} = w/p$.

If people become beneficiaries the total amount of purchase power falls as the national product falls, so a similar argument may be made for a fall of prices and wages. Our preliminary conclusion is that our first assumption on a constant price and wage level is not making our conclusions totally irrelevant.

Other assumptions that can be refined are that of a constant capital stock K and the assumption of profit maximization. The economy might be split up in several sectors, each with their own production functions. Also labor experience and reschooling in the middle of the life span could be brought in. On the side of the SSS the impact of other benefit structures and especially the fixation of a maximum benefit and premium level should be considered. In following papers it will be attempted to extend our model in the ways outlined above.

FOOTNOTES

* Leyden University and Social Security Council, respectively. This research is part of the Leyden Social Security Project. We thank Freek Atsma, Lex Kwee and Aernout Schmidt for their programming assistance at various stages. The sole responsibility for the opinions, expressed in this paper, remains with the authors.

REFERENCES

Boskin, M.J. (1973), The Economics of the Labor Supply, in Cain, G.C. and Watts, H.W. (eds.), Income Maintenance and Labor Supply, Rand McNally, Chicago.

Brittain, J.L. (1972), The Social Security Payroll Tax, Brookings Institution, Washington D.C.

Fullerton, D. (1982), On the possibility of an inverse relationship between tax rates and government revenues, Journal of Public Economics, 3-22.

Hausman, J.A. (1981), Labor Supply in Aaron, J. and Pechman, J.A. (eds.), How Taxes Affect Economic Behavior, The Brookings Institution, Washington, D.C.

Van Praag, B.M.S. and Halberstadt, V. (1978), Towards an Economic Theory of Non-Employability. A First Approach, in Roskamp, K.W. (ed.), Public Choice and Public Finance, Proceedings of the 34th Congress of the International Institute of Public Finance, Hamburg 1978, Editons Cujas, Paris 1980.

ARNE RYDE SYMPOSIUM ON SOCIAL INSURANCE
L. Söderström (editor)
© Elsevier Science Publishers B.V. (North-Holland), 1983

DISABILITY AS AN ECONOMIC PHENOMENON:
A FIRST APPROACH TO ESTIMATE HIDDEN UNEMPLOYMENT
AMONG DISABILITY BENEFICIARIES

Frans A.J. van den Bosch
and
Carel Petersen*

1. INTRODUCTION

In many countries the number of people who withdraw from the labor market as a consequence of becoming entitled to disability benefits has grown very rapidly. In table 1 some key figures are shown for different countries. Although a direct comparison is difficult on account of differences in legal structure, eligibility criteria etc. of the disability programs, these figures indicate the relative importance of the volume and growth rate of disability recipients.[1]

Table 1. Key figures with respect to disability programs
for some selected countries.

	Average annual growth rate of the number of disability recipients 1968-1978	The number of disability recipients expressed as a percentage of the employed 1978
Netherlands	11.3	13.0
Sweden	3.3	11.9
United Kingdom	2.0	7.8
United States	7.0	14.7
West Germany	2.5	11.0[a]

[a] estimated
Source: Victor Halberstadt and Robert Haveman.

Here we will examine the determinants of the growth of the number of disability recipients at a macro level.[2] To this end we present a conceptual

framework in section two. This framework enables us to estimate the share
of disability awards in the private sector of the economy which is granted
solely as a consequence of economic factors. Consequently, the hidden unemployment among disability beneficiaries can be estimated. This is done in
section three. Finally section four gives some concluding comments.

2. THE CONCEPTUAL FRAMEWORK

In various studies (Lando (1974), Lando et. al. (1979), Hambor (1975),
Emanuel, Halberstadt and Petersen (forthcoming)) the importance of economic
variables, notably the unemployment rate, in explaining the number of disability recipients has been stressed. We have developed a more extended
framework by introducing non-economic variables:

$$DR = f (H, PH, OS, E, LS) \tag{1}$$

where DR stands for the disability incidence rate, i.e. the number of disability awards per year per 100 insured, H for health, PH for perceived
state of health, OS for occupational structure, E for economic factors and
LS for legal structure.

Other things being equal a worsening of the state of health (H) of the insured population implies a larger number of disabled persons. The perceived
state of health (PH) reflects the whole set of norms and values with
respect to whether it is socially and personally acceptable to feel oneself
entitled to a benefit. It is commonly agreed that this set of norms and
values changes over time, and can partly explain the increase of the disability rate.[3] As some occupations are of a more physically (e.g. the
building sector) or of a mentally demanding nature than others, it is obvious that account should be taken of a possible changed occupational structure (OS). The economic factors (E) stand for the effects of economic
determinants on the development of the disability incidence rate. We have
assumed that the profit-maximizing behavior of employers constitutes a
suitable basis for analysing the link between economic variables and the
disability incidence rate. For, given the rigid wage structure, employers
will be inclined if the need arise to dismiss those employees first who are
least productive e.g. because they are handicapped (see e.g. van Praag and
Halberstadt (1980)). Since a disability benefit is generally more attractive, both financially and from the point of view of social acceptance,
than an unemployment benefit (at least in the Netherlands), potential unemployed will, if possible, prefer a disability to an unemployment benefit.
The legal structure (LS), notably criteria governing eligibility and benefit determination, may also contribute to the explanation of the level of
the disability incidence rate.

It will be clear that it is difficult to find the appropriate empirical
counterparts for the explanatory variables introduced above. However, it is
not necessary to measure each of these variables separately since our analysis is based on a comparison between the disability incidence rate in the
private sector and the public sector. According to our framework, any
numerical difference between the two disability incidence rates must be attributed to different values of the explanatory variables. At first sight,
the variable (E) differs remarkably between the two sectors. To be precise,
it can be assumed that profit maximizing behavior of employers is significant only for the explanation of the level of the disability incidence rate
in the private sector. In the public sector arguments other than the profit

criterion are used when expansion or contraction of the number of employees is considered. Hence the basic idea is to make the disability incidence rates in both sectors comparable in such a way that the remaining difference between the disability incidence rate in the private sector and the disability incidence rate in the public sector can be attributed only to economic factors. Consequently it will be possible to calculate that part of the disability volume in the private sector, which may virtually be considered as hidden unemployment.

3. THE APPLICATION TO THE NETHERLANDS

In this section some basic features of the Dutch Disability Programs will be described. Secondly, we will illustrate the application of the framework, and thirdly some results will be presented and discussed.

A. The Dutch Disability Programs

In the Netherlands employees in the private sector receive a benefit under the Sickness Benefit Act during the first year of disability because of illness or accident. After one year of disability the Disability Security Act (DSA), introduced July 1967, comes into effect. Depending on the degree of disability the DSA benefit amounts to a maximum of 80% of the previous earnings up to an income ceiling. There is no maximum benefit duration. The required minimum degree of disability is only 15%. As aging is usually correlated with a worsening state of health, this means that especially the older employees will rather easily meet this eligibility criterion.[4] Besides, by the determination of the benefit percentage not only the health status counts, but also the reduced chance on the labour market because of the handicap must be taken into account (see for a discussion of this e.g. van de Water (1979) and, with respect to the Netherlands, Emanuel (1981)).

Employees in the public sector are covered by a separate disability scheme. The only difference between this scheme and the DSA is the period between the first day of absence and the moment when a disability is awarded (the so-called waiting period). In in the public sector this waiting period is variable, because only when it is almost certain that the disability will be permanent is a disability benefit awarded.

In 1968 the disability incidence rates in the private and the public sector amounted to 1.1% resp. 0.5%. Both rates have increased rapidly and reached in 1980 the level of 2.2% and 1.3% respectively.

B. The application of the conceptual framework

In the following the explanatory variables of the disability incidence rate are discussed for the Netherlands. Our aim is to isolate the variables that are on the one hand responsible for the growth of the disability incidence rate in the both sectors and on the other for the discrepancy between them.

The development of the state of health (H) is, because of a lack of more appropriate data, approached by the development of mortality rates (see for a similar approach Doherty (1979) and Parsons (1980)). These mortality rates (standardized for age and sex) have, in the considered period, slightly improved. Because in addition the average age of both insured pop-

ulations has somewhat declined, we must conclude that the state of health
does not contribute to the explanation of the rise of the disability incidence rate in either the private or the public sector. To eliminate the influence of different age structures of the insured populations of both sectors on the respective incidence rates, we have made both rates comparable
by standardizing for age. [5]

Appropriate data about the second variable, the perceived state of health
(PH) are difficult to obtain. We will return to this shortly. It is however
plausible that the gradual evolution of this attitude is an overall social
phenomenon and has thereby contributed to the increase of the disability
incidence rate in both sectors in the same way.

Because in the period under consideration the occupational structure (OS)
has not significantly changed in either the private or public sector, this
variable does not contribute to the explanation of the increase in the disability incidence rate.[6] However, the difference in the occupational structure between the private and public sector can partly explain the difference between the disability incidence rates in both sectors, since the
average occupation in the private sector is thought to be of a more demanding nature as far as health conditions are concerned. The estimated
correction factor which eliminates this influence decreases the disability
incidence rate of the private sector only slightly.[7] This is in accordance
with an analysis of the disability incidence rate per occupation, where it
has been found that the difference in the disability incidence rates per
occupation keeping economic factors constant, can largely be explained by
different age structures of the occupational groups.[8]

As was pointed in section 2, economic factors (E) are only significant for
the explanation of the disability incidence rate in the private sector.[9] As
we already mentioned above, the longer waiting period in the public sector
is the only significant difference between the legal structures (LS) of the
two sectors.[10] To make the disability incidence rates of the two sectors
comparable with respect to this variable, we have to take account of the
number of people in the public sector whose disability lasts longer than
one year, but who are not awarded a disability benefit because the disability is clearly temporary. We have estimated a correction factor to
eliminate this difference.[11]

Finally, it should be remarked that no evidence has been found that other
factors are substantial in explaining either the increase in both disability incidence rates, or the discrepancy between the disability incidence
rates in the two sectors.

Summing up, the above implies that only the changed perceived state of
health (PH) and the development of the economic variables (E) are considered to be the prime factors in explaining the increase of the disability
incidence rate in the private sector. The only factor held responsible for
the growth of the disability incidence rate in the public sector is the
changed perceived state of health.

We have tested these findings with regression analysis for the period 1968-
1980. The disability incidence rate in the private sector (DR1) is explained by the disability incidence rate in the public sector (DR2), as a
proxy for the change in the perceived state of health (PH) - as mentioned
above an overall societal phenomenon - and the real labor cost per unit of
output (LCUO). This last variable, which has steadily increased in the pe-

riod under consideration, is assumed to be a proxy variable for the economic factors (E). It is assumed that as LCUO increases, which implies that
real wages increase faster than labor productivity, the average profitability of employees decreases (see also Morley, 1979). By implication the
least productive employees, such as the handicapped, will be the first to
be confronted with the possibility of dismissal. In this situation these
employees will be inclined to apply for a disability benefit.

The first equation of table 2 shows that the empirical findings are in accordance with the theoretical setting because both DR2 and LCUO have the
expected signs and are statistically significant. Another way to test the
model is with the so called economic disability incidence rate in the private sector (EDR1). This rate is defined as the difference between the disability incidence rate in the private sector (corrected for OS) and the
disability incidence rate in the public sector (corrected for LS and the
difference with respect to the age distribution). Consequently we get an
estimation of that part of the disability incidence rate in the private
sector which is solely related to economic factors. Equation (2) in table 2
shows that the relationship between EDR1 and LCUO is statistically significant too. The remaining two equations try to explain EDR1 by unemployment
rates. Equation (3) contains the official unemployment rate (U) as explanatory variable. Anticipating of the results presented below, equation (4)

Table 2. Estimates of the disability rate model (1968-1980).

Independent Variable	Dependent Variable			
	(1) $DR1_t$	(2) $EDR1_t$	(3) $EDR1_t$	(4) $EDR1_t$
Intercept	-2.201 (-2.14)	-1.772 (-3.25)	0.655 (7.21)	0.677 (11.24)
$DR2_t$	0.866 (3.23)			
$LCUO_{t-1}$	0.028 (2.61)	0.024 (4.92)		
U_{t-1}			0.074 (3.02)	
UHU_{t-1}				0.043 (4.40)
$\bar{R}^2$	0.920	0.681	0.405	0.607
S.E.	0.104	0.101	0.133	0.108
D.W.	1.818	1.648	1.071	1.271

Note: The t-values are shown in parentheses.

shows the results if U includes the hidden unemployment among disability beneficiaries. This gives the much higher unemployment rate UHU. It appears that UHU explains a larger proportion of the total variation in EDR1 in comparison with U. This can be explained by the fact that the official unemployment rate is an underestimation of the development of unemployment.

C. The method of calculation and some results

The method can be explained as follows. For each year we have calculated the economic disability incidence rate. Multiplying this rate by the number of insured yields the annual number of disability awards for economic reasons, the so-called hidden unemployment. Next, the total volume of hidden unemployment can be calculated on the basis of some assumptions with respect to termination pattern of hidden unemployed.[12] The cumulated result is a volume of about 200,000 man-years of hidden unemployment in 1980. This equals 43% of the total volume of disability beneficiaries (also expressed in manyear) in the private sector.[13] Table 3 shows the importance of these findings by relating hidden unemployment to officially registered unemployment. It appears that the official unemployment rate considerably underestimates the development of unemployment.

Table 3. Hidden unemployment and officially registered
         unemployment rate, (The Netherlands, 1968-1981).

	1968	1974	1980	1981[a]
(1) Hidden unemployment among DSA beneficiaries[b]	0.3	2.7	4.7	4.9
(2) Officially registered unemployment[b,c]	1.9	3.3	5.6	6.5
(3) Total unemployment (3) = (1) + (2)	2.2	6.0	10.3	11.4

[a] Projection is based on the assumption that the disability rates remain at their 1980 level and that the insured populaton remains constant.
[b] Expressed as a percentage of the labor force.
[c] These data are based on: Central Economic Plan 1980, and Macroeconomic Projections 1981 (1980), Central Planning Bureau, The Hague (in Dutch).

4. CONCLUDING REMARKS

It is commonly agreed that the worsening economic conditions have positively influenced the number of disability beneficiaries. It is therefore resonable to conjecture that there may be hidden unemployment among the disability beneficiaries. In this paper we have developed as a first approach a conceptual framework to examine this influence. We have applied this framework to the Dutch Disability schemes and have found a considerable volume of hidden unemployment among disability beneficiaries. This means that the disability program partly fulfils the function of an unemployment scheme. Consequently a trade-off between unemployment and disability arises.

It follows that, to a considerable extent, disability is becoming an economic phenomenon. Like other results of research pertaining to the social security system, see e.g. Martin Feldstein (1978), this must have implications for the optimal redesign of social insurance.

FOOTNOTES

*) Erasmus University Rotterdam. The authors wish to thank Victor Halberstadt, Joop Hartog, Pieter Korteweg, and Dick Wolfson for their comments on an earlier draft of this paper. Further we are endebted to Christina Jonung for comments on a draft of this paper during the Arne Ryde Symposium, and to an anonymous referee who provided important suggestions.

1) See for more data Victor Halberstadt and Robert Haveman, (forthcoming), International Labour Office (1979), Social Security Administration (1980).

2) See for an explanation of the growth of the volume of disability beneficiaries per branch of industry, which differs remarkably, at least in the Netherlands, van den Bosch and Petersen (1982) and (1983).

3) This will be due to both a learning process and the fact that as the volume of beneficiaries increases the stigma attaching to the status of beneficiary usually decreases, see Lando (1974) and Schechter (1981).

4) See also Levy, (1980), especially p. 13.

5) The average age in the public sector is approximately 5 years higher than in the private sector. By standardizing with the age distribution of the private sector the disability incidence rate in the public sector decrease about 30%. See for further details of this and the following correction factors: van den Bosch and Petersen (1979).

6) Assuming that jobs in the service sector are of a less demanding nature as far as health conditions are concerned, the slightly increased share of employment in the service sector with respect to total private sector employment means that this could have a negative influence on the private sector disability incidence rate leading to an underestimation of the results reported below. Furthermore, there is no indication available that the type of work per branch of industry was on the average more demanding in 1980 than it was in 1968. See also van den Bosch and Petersen (1982).

7) The calculaton of this correction factor is based on data pertaining to injury at work and industrial disease. This correction lowers the disability incidence rate in the private sector by 0.05 percent.

8) This analysis was entirely based on data pertaining to the disability

incidence rate by occupation within the public sector. Consequently according to our assumptions the effect of economic factors on the disability incidence rate per occupation is nil.

9)   If the awarding of public sector disability benefits is to some extent influenced by economic factors (e.g. by measures reducing the budget), this could lead to an underestimation of our results.

10) It has to be remarked that the variable PH also incorporates the effects of a possible change of the implicit eligibility criteria used by the awarding boards of both sectors, due to social trends with respect to social and personal acceptability to feel oneself entitled to a benefit.

11) This correction factor is based on an estimation of the number of DSA awards, of which the duration of the disability status was only temporary. Consequently the remaining number of DSA awards is permanent and thus comparable with the public sector awards. For the sake of convenience, we have applied this correction factor to the disability incidence rate in the public sector, (increasing this rate with approximately 30%).

12) We have assumed that the termination percentages (τ) of hidden unemployment equal the overall termination percentages. We can illustrate the method of calculation as follows. Let $HU_i(t)$ the hidden unemployment in the year (t) among persons who received an award in year (i), i = vintage 1968, 1969, ...; t = 1968, 1969, ...; $HU(t)$ the total hidden unemployment in year (t); EDR1 the economic disability incidence rate; IP the number of DSA-insured; $\tau(t)$ the percentage of the initial awards whose benefit has been terminated (t) years after entry. So we can define:

(1) $HU_i(t) = EDR1_i \cdot IP_{i-1} \cdot (100 - \tau(t))$

(2) $HU(t) = \sum\limits_{i=1968}^{t} HU_i(t)$.

13) This means that we have estimated the capacity of work of the total number of disability beneficiaries. It follows that 200,000 man-years corresponds with a considerable higher number of partial hidden unemployed persons.

REFERENCES

Bosch, F.A.J. van den and Petersen, C. (1979), Hidden unemployment and disability, Discussion Paper Series 7913/G, Erasmus University Rotterdam, Institute for Economic Research, Rotterdam.

Bosch, F.A.J. van den and Petersen, C. (1982), Incidence of Disability by Sector of Industry: An Explanation, International Social Security Review 35, 196-204.

Bosch, F.A.J. van den and Petersen, C. (1983), An Explanation of the Growth of Social Security Disability Transfers, De Economist 131, 66-78.

Doherty, N.A. (1979), National Insurances and Absence from Work, The Economic Journal 89, 50-65.

Emanuel, H., Halberstadt, V., Petersen, C., Disability Policy in the Netherlands, in Halberstadt, V. and Haveman, R.H. (eds.), The Cross-National Disability Policy Study, forthcoming.

Emanuel, H. (1981), Factors in the growth of the number of disability beneficiaries in the Netherlands, International Social Security Review 33, 41-60.

Feldstein, M. (1978), The Effect of Unemployment Insurance on Temporary Layoff Unemployment, American Economic Review 68, 834-846.

Halberstadt, V., and Haveman, R.H. (eds.), The Cross-National Disability Policy Study, Cornell Un. Press, forthcoming.

Hambor, J.C. (1975), Unemployment and Disability: an Econometric Analysis with Time Series Data, U.S. Department of Health, Education, and Welfare, Social Security Administration, Office of Research and Statistics, Staff paper no. 20.

International Labour Office (1979), The Costs of Social Security, Geneva.

Lando, M.E. (1974), The Effect of Unemployment on Application for Disability Insurance, Proceedings of the American Statistical Association, (Business and Economics Statistics section), 438-442.

Lando, M.E., Coate, M.D. and Kraus, R. (1979), Disability Benefit Applications and Economy, Social Security Bulletin 42, 3-9.

Levy, J.M. (1980), Demographic Factors in the Disability Determination Process: A Logistic Approach, Social Security Bulletin 43, 11-16.

Morley, R. (1979), Profit, Relative Prices and Unemployment, The Economic Journal 89, 582-600.

Parsons, D.O. (1980), The Decline in Male Labor Force Participation, Journal of Political Economy 88, 117-134.

Praag, B.M.S. van and Halberstadt, V. (1980), Towards an Economic Theory of Non-Employability: a First Approach, in Roskamp, K.W. (ed.), Proceedings of the 34th. Congress of The International Institute of Public Finance, Hamburg, 1978, Paris.

Schechter, E.S. (1981), Commitment to Work and the Self-Perception of Disability, Social Security Bulletin 44, 22-30.

Social Security Administration (1980), U.S., Department of Health and Human Services, Social Security Programs Throughout the World 1979, Washington.

Water, P.N. van de (1979), Disability Insurance, American Economic Review 69, 275-278.

ARNE RYDE SYMPOSIUM ON SOCIAL INSURANCE
L. Söderström (editor)
© Elsevier Science Publishers B.V. (North-Holland), 1983

DISABILITY AND WORK EFFORT:
A PROBABILISTIC CHOICE ANALYSIS OF THE LABOR
SUPPLY DECISIONS OF OLDER MEN

Robert H. Haveman
and
Barbara L. Wolfe*

1. INTRODUCTION

Among the most notable social policy developments of the past decade in Western industrialized countries is the growth in the number of recipients in and the public expenditures on disability programs for working-age people. Most of this growth has been concentrated in disability income support programs. There has been much speculation on the causes of this growth, including the liberalization of income support benefits, the extension of in-kind benefits, the inclusion of labor market conditions and vocational considerations in eligibility criteria, and the poor performance of the economies.

Table 1 presents estimates of the growth from 1968 to 1978 in the primary disability income support programs in seven Western industrialized countries. The rates of increase in the number of disability income transfer recipients (column 2) are truly impressive for several of the countries. The Netherlands, for example, has experienced an average growth rate of over 11 percent per year. Even though the population growth rate in the Netherlands has been very low, the number of recipients increased from about 200,000 to nearly 600,000 over the decade. Italy and the United States have somewhat lower, though still substantial, rates of growth in the number of beneficiaries. The annual rates for these countries -- 7-8 percent -- are very large, given annual population growth rates of 1-3 percent.

This growth in number of recipients is reflected in the growth rate of real expenditures on these programs, shown in column 3. Of the seven countries shown, the real growth rate has exceeded 10 percent in three.

Accompanying this growth in benefit rolls is the increased incidence of "early retirement" - the cessation or substantial reduction of work prior to the standard retirement age. In the United States, for example, 11.5 percent of males aged 45-59 were not labor force participants in 1980, as compared to only 4 percent in 1956. In other Western countries, similar de-

Table 1. Patterns of Decrease in Older Male Labor Force Participation
         Rates and Disability Program Growth, Late 1960s to Late 1970s,
         by Country

	Percentage Change in Ratio of Older to Prime-Age Worker Participation Rates, 1960s to 1970s[a]	Annual Rate of Growth of Disability Program Recipients, 1968 to 1978	Annual Rate of Growth of Real Disability Program Expenditures, 1968-1978
France	- 7.4%	- 1.3%	- 1.3%
Italy	-15.5	8.1	12.7
Netherlands	-14.8	11.3	18.6
Sweden	- 9.5	5.2	11.7
United Kingdom	- .2	2.0	.5
United States	-12.5	7.0	6.3
West Germany	-15.4	2.5	5.3

[a] In general, the age range for older male workers is 45 to 64. However,
data for some of the countries includes older workers somewhat outside
this age range. Prime age refers generally to ages 18 to 45. The time
period is typically 1968-1978; however, in a few cases starting and
ending years deviate slightly from these.

creases in the labor force participation of older workers have occurred in
recent years. These decreases are shown in column 1 of Table 1.

The similar patterns of growth in the percentage of the older worker group
not in the labor market and the percentage receiving disability transfer
benefits suggests that the increasing generosity of this and other disability income support programs is responsible for at least part of this reduction in work effort. However, while a high percentage of those who have
left the labor force during past years do receive income support from disability transfer programs, that fact says little about the determinants of
these similar time-series patterns. Labor market opportunities may have deteriorated over this period for older workers; the incidence of work-related impairments may have increased; more spouses are working and
contributing to household income; eligibility standards may have been
applied more leniently; tastes for work may have deteriorated; or the generosity of the benefits of transfer programs may have attracted an
increasing number of potential beneficiaries out of the work force. All of

these are relevant hypotheses for explaining the growth in disability transfer recipiency and the reduction in labor force participation of older workers.

In this paper, we focus on one of these hypotheses -- that the attractiveness of disability income transfer options relative to labor market options has led workers with a health problem to leave the labor force in order to apply for and receive alternative sources of income, and that this choice has led to the growth of disability transfer programs. The framework is one of rational choice on the part of older workers in which economic position is maximized. We assume that each older worker compares two expected levels of economic well-being, one if he chooses to secure primary income support via working and labor market earnings, and the other if he chooses to rely primarily on disability income transfers, with little if any labor market activity. Essentially, then, the choice is between participating in the labor market and receiving the income flow associated with that option, and seeking disability-related transfers and receiving the income flow associated with that option.

We first briefly review the existing literature on the effect of disability transfers on labor supply. The main studies, we find, have important weaknesses. Then, in section 3, we set forth our model, which emphasizes the three primary determinants of the work effort choice of older workers: expected disability transfers, expected labor market income, and health status. In sections 4 and 5, we describe the data used, the models estimated, and the results obtained. Finally, in section 6, we relate our results to those of others, draw some conclusions, and discuss additional research needs.

2. THE WORK EFFORT EFFECTS OF DISABILITY TRANSFERS: A REVIEW

The rapid recent increase in expenditures on the recipients of disability income transfers suggests a causal relationship between the generosity and accessibility of this means of economic support and work effort. Because the bulk of the beneficiaries of these programs are older male workers, most studies have focused on this population. The most important studies in terms of both data and technique are very recent ones by Parsons (1980a; 1980b) and Leonard (1979). They are described in Table 2.[1]

Parsons´ study is an explicit work-status choice model in which the individual rationally compares the expected annual income streams associated with being in and out of the labor force (presumably as a proxy for the present value of income flows associated with each option) and chooses that option which maximizes his economic welfare. The expected income associated with being a labor force participant is proxied by the individual´s earlier wage rate, and that associated with non-participation is measured by an imputed value of Social Security Disability Insurance (SSDI) benefits to be received were the individual a beneficiary. Other factors affecting the work status choice are an index of disability status (the individual´s mortality experience in the years after the observation period), age, schooling, unemployment experience, expected non-disability transfer income, and marital status.

Parsons finds that the probability of labor force participation falls significantly as the "replacement rate" (the ratio of imputed SSDI benefits to the earlier wage rate) rises. While both of the estimated elasticities of

Table 2. Labor Supply Analyses of Disability Income Transfers

	Parsons (1980a, 1980b)	Leonard (1979)
Population Analyzed	Men, 48-62 (a) or 45-59 (b)	Men, 45-54
Data Used (all cross-sectional)	NLS, 1969 (a) or 1966 (b)	1972 SSSHWC merged with benefit and earnings records
Dependent Variable	Participation in work force	SSDI recipiency
Program Variables	Potential DI and prior wage	Expected DI benefits
Specification	Probit	Logit
Results	Elast. of non- participation w.r.t. replace- ment rate = 1.8 (1966) or 0.63 (1969)	Elast. of recipiency w.r.t. expected benefits = 0.35

NLS = National Longitudinal Surveys of Labor Force Participation.

SSSHWC = Social Security Survey of Health and Work Characteristics.

labor force non-participation with respect to expected disability transfers shown in the table are very large, one is triple the other (even though the same specification is applied to data of two different years). The disability status measure is a weak proxy for work limitations since numerous work-related impairments would appear to have little relationship to mortality. As modelled, Parsons' estimates presume that receipt of SSDI benefits is a matter of individual choice for all older workers -- no recognition is given to the fact that receipt of program benefits depends on the meeting of a set of program eligibility criteria involving the presence of a disabling condition expected to last for at least 12 months and enabling no "substantial gainful employment." Nor is any consideration given to disability-related transfers other than SSDI in the work effort choice. Moreover, the expected benefit value used in the estimation is that of the primary beneficiary alone, and neglects the benefits for dependents which accompany primary benefits. Finally, use of the replacement rate as the program variable confounds the roles of expected earnings and expected disability transfers, leaving the interpretation of the effect of benefit generosity on work effort unresolved.

The study of Leonard finds a strong relationship between expected SSDI benefits and the probability of being a recipient; he attributes somewhat more than 40 percent of the decline in older worker labor force participation since the late 1950s to increased benefit levels. In his study, the probability of being an SSDI recipient is taken to depend upon expected SSDI benefits (the product of benefits if eligible and the probability of being eligible), expected wages (proxied by a vector of background characteristics) and a disability status measure (based on a set of 27 binary independent variables reflecting the presence but not the severity of specific health conditions). Again, the estimation is carried out in a rational choice framework.

Like that of Parsons, Leonard's estimate of the elasticity of labor force participation with respect to expected SSDI benefits is very large. Again, several problems plague his results: the disability indicators give no indication of the severity of the impairment or the degree of functional limitation, the proxy for expected labor income is weak, issues of selection bias surround both the estimate of expected earnings and SSDI eligibility, no disability-related transfers are considered other than SSDI, and the identification of his system is problematic.

The results of both of these studies suggest that the decision of older workers to withdraw from the labor force is strongly conditioned by the availability and generosity of SSDI disability transfers. However, the size of the estimated elasticities and the methodological weaknesses which underlie them cast doubt on their reliability.

3. A MODEL OF WORK STATUS CHOICE

The model employed is designed to estimate the effect of potential disability benefits on the work effort choice of older men. It assumes that an older worker compares the economic benefits available in alternative work effort statuses and chooses that option in which he is best off. The level of economic returns in the various statuses is conditioned on the individual's characteristics, including his health status. In the dichotomous case of labor force participation and its complement, the opportunity cost of choosing one status is the income flow foregone by not choosing the other. When a person chooses to work, it is presumed that his reservation wage -- the monetary value of not working -- is less than the market wage.[2]

A simplified version of this framework is as follows: Assume that two work effort options are available to a worker. In the first option, the worker chooses work and labor earnings as the primary source of income, and foregoes the possibility of receiving disability-related transfers. In the second option, the individual seeks disability transfer recipiency at the cost of foregone labor market opportunities.[3] Given the choice to pursue one of the options, an expected income flow is observed. This flow is also conditioned on the person's health status, human capital, other socioeconomic characteristics, tastes for leisure, labor market conditions, and transfer program characteristics.

For the choice of the labor market option,

$$LE_\zeta = \underline{\beta}_1' Z_\zeta + \varepsilon_{1\zeta} \tag{1}$$

in which LE is the total annual income flow for the labor market option, Z_ζ is a vector of exogenous background characteristics related to expected income flows, $\varepsilon_{1\zeta}$ is the error term, $\underline{\beta}_1$ is the vector of coefficients to be estimated. By using an annual income stream as opposed to the present value of the stream of income associated with an option, it is presumed that the choice is not irreversible or that the annual flow is an accurate proxy of the present value of the lifetime expected flow.

For the choice of the disability transfer option,

$$DT_\zeta = \underline{\beta}_2'Z_\zeta + \varepsilon_{2\zeta} \qquad (2)$$

in which DT_ζ is the total annual income flow for the disability transfers option. $\varepsilon_{2\zeta}$ is the error term and $\underline{\beta}_2'$ is the vector of coefficients to be estimated. Since Z_ζ is assumed to be exogenous, $E(\varepsilon_{v\zeta}|Z_\zeta) = 0$ for $v = 1,2$.

If $Y_\zeta = LE_\zeta - DT_\zeta$, the income-maximizing individual will choose the labor market option when $Y_\zeta > 0$; the disability transfer option will be chosen if $Y_\zeta \le 0$. Hence, the sample selection equation is:

$$Y_\zeta = (\underline{\beta}_1 - \underline{\beta}_2)'Z_\zeta + (\varepsilon_{1\zeta} - \varepsilon_{2\zeta}) = \underline{\beta}_3'Z_\zeta + \varepsilon_{3\zeta} \qquad (3)$$

Since only self-selected samples are observed, direct estimation of (1) and (2) will not yield consistent estimates of $\underline{\beta}_1$ and $\underline{\beta}_2$. Following Heckman (1974, 1979), we assume that $\varepsilon_\zeta = (\varepsilon_{1\zeta}, \varepsilon_{2\zeta})$ has a bivariate normal distribution and that ε_ζ is independent of $\varepsilon_{\zeta'}$ for $\zeta \ne \zeta'$.

Given the selection rule and the normality assumption, the appropriate regression functions for (1) and (2) are:

$$E(LE_\zeta \mid \underline{Z}_\zeta, Y_\zeta > 0) = \underline{\beta}_1'\underline{Z}_\zeta + E(\varepsilon_{1\zeta} \mid \underline{Z}_\zeta, Y_\zeta > 0)$$

$$= \underline{\beta}_1'\underline{Z}_\zeta + E(\varepsilon_{1\zeta} \mid \varepsilon_{3\zeta} > -\underline{\beta}_3'\underline{Z}_\zeta)$$

$$= \underline{\beta}_1'\underline{Z}_\zeta + \frac{\delta_{13}}{\delta_{33}^{\frac{1}{2}}} \lambda_{1\zeta}(-\underline{\beta}_3'\underline{Z}_\zeta/\delta_{33}^{\frac{1}{2}}) \qquad (4)$$

$$E(DT_\zeta \mid \underline{Z}_\zeta, Y_\zeta < 0) = \underline{\beta}_2'\underline{Z}_\zeta + E(\varepsilon_{2\zeta} \mid \underline{Z}_\zeta, Y_\zeta < 0)$$

$$= \underline{\beta}_2'\underline{Z}_\zeta + E(\varepsilon_{2\zeta} \mid \varepsilon_{3\zeta} < -\underline{\beta}_3'\underline{Z}_\zeta)$$

$$= \underline{\beta}_2'\underline{Z}_\zeta + \frac{\delta_{23}}{\delta_{33}^{\frac{1}{2}}} \lambda_{2\zeta}(-\underline{\beta}_3'\underline{Z}_\zeta/\delta_{33}^{\frac{1}{2}}) \qquad (5)$$

where $\lambda_1(s) = \phi(s)/1 - \Phi(s)$ and $\lambda_2(s) = -\phi(s)/\Phi(s)$, where $\phi(s)$ is the density function and $\Phi(s)$ is the distribution function for a standard normal variable. The final equality in equations (4) and (5) is based on the formula for the mean of a truncated normal random variable.

The parameters in equation (4) and (5) are estimated in three steps. Let $D_\zeta = 1$ if $Y_\zeta > 0$ and $D_\zeta = 0$ if $Y_\zeta < 0$. Using equation (3),

$$P(D_\zeta = 1 \mid \underline{Z}_\zeta) = P(\varepsilon_{3\zeta} > -\underline{\beta}_3'\underline{Z}_\zeta \mid \underline{Z}_\zeta) = 1 - P\{\frac{\varepsilon_{3\zeta}}{\delta_{33}^{\frac{1}{2}}} < \frac{-\underline{\beta}_3'\underline{Z}_\zeta}{\delta_{33}^{\frac{1}{2}}}\}$$

$$= \Phi(\underline{\beta}_3'\underline{Z}_\zeta/\delta_{33}^{\frac{1}{2}}) \tag{6}$$

Performing the probit regression implied by (6), we obtain asymptotically consistent estimates of $\beta_3/(\delta_{33})^{1/2}$, denoted $\widehat{(\beta_3/(\delta_{33})^{1/2})}$. With $\widehat{\beta_3/(\delta_{33})^{1/2}}$, we next construct estimates of $\lambda_{\nu\zeta}(\cdot)$ (the inverse Mill's ratio), which we label $\hat{\lambda}_{1\zeta}(\cdot)$ and $\hat{\lambda}_{2\zeta}(\cdot)$. Finally, with the $\hat{\lambda}(\cdot)$ variables, the OLS regressions of LE_ζ on $(\underline{Z}_\zeta, \hat{\lambda}_\zeta(\cdot))$ and DT_ζ on $(\underline{Z}_\zeta, \hat{\lambda}_{2\zeta}(\cdot))$ are estimated over the appropriate subsamples. This procedure provides asymptotically consistent estimates of

$$\underline{\beta}_1, \; \underline{\beta}_2, \; \frac{\delta_{13}}{\delta_{33}^{\frac{1}{2}}}, \; \text{and} \; \frac{\delta_{23}}{\delta_{33}^{\frac{1}{2}}}.$$

In this model, disability transfer programs are viewed as influencing participation decisions through their impact on expected income flows. From (4) and (5), we obtain $\widehat{LE}_\zeta$ and $\widehat{DT}_\zeta$, which are estimates of expected income flows in the labor market and disability transfer options. These can be used to estimate the elasticity of the binary labor force participation variable with respect to disability program generosity.

$$P(D_\zeta = 1 \mid LE_\zeta, DT_\zeta) = \delta\widehat{LE}_\zeta + \eta\widehat{DT}_\zeta + \varepsilon_{4\zeta} \tag{7}$$

The framework in (1)-(7) implicitly reflects the fact that not all individuals choose and are successful in each option. This is so in that each $\widehat{LE}_\zeta$ and $\widehat{DT}_\zeta$ is based on a regression which includes age, health status, education, and other conditions reflecting conditions of access to income flows in each of the two options. Alternatively, the probability of an individual being successful in gaining access to income flows in either option if he sought them could be explicitly attached to estimates of the income which would be received in each option if successful. With this explicit probability of success framework, (1)-(7) would be modified as follows: Let $P(D = 1 \mid Z_\zeta)$ and $P(D = 0 \mid Z_\zeta)$ be the probabilities of success in gaining access to income flows in the labor market and disability transfer options, respectively. The product of estimated income in the labor market option (from (4)) and $P(D = 1 \mid Z_\zeta)$, both conditional on the individual's exogenous characteristics, yields the estimate of expected income if the labor market option is chosen,

$$E(LE_\zeta) = P(D = 1 \mid \underline{Z}_\zeta) \cdot E(LE_\zeta \mid \underline{Z}_\zeta, Y > 0). \tag{8}$$

In this formulation, then, we presume that the individual, with his characteristics, is best viewed as seeking entry to the labor market group, with some probability of success in earning income in this status. If he is successful, the level of income received depends upon his characteristics. Hence, knowing the individual's characteristics, and the nature of the labor market, his expected income in the labor market option is the product of the estimated probability that he will be successful in becoming a member of the labor market group and the expected level of income if in that group.

By the analogous procedure,

$$E(DT_\zeta) = P(D = 0 \mid \underline{Z}_\zeta) \cdot E(DT_\zeta \mid \underline{Z}_\zeta, \ Y < 0). \tag{9}$$

Equation (7) then becomes

$$P(D_\zeta = 1 \mid E(LE_\zeta), E(DT_\zeta)) = \delta \widehat{E(LE_\zeta)} + \eta \widehat{E(DT_\zeta)} + \varepsilon_{4\zeta} \tag{7´}$$

To implement this approach, estimates of the relevant probabilities of success in attaining income flows $(P(D = 1 \mid Z_\zeta); P(D) = 0 \mid Z_\zeta))$ are required. Ideally, these estimates would be obtained from probit equations estimated over samples of individuals who applied for employment income and disability transfers, respectively, in which the success or failure of observations was recorded in the data. In the absence of such application data for each of the options, an approximation is possible. From (6), the probability of being in the labor market group can be used as a proxy for $P(D = 1 \mid Z_\zeta)$. From a similar probit estimation, a proxy for $P(D = 0 \mid Z_\zeta)$ can be obtained.[4] In Section 5, estimates for both approaches, one without the explicit introduction of the probability of eligibility, the second with the eligibility proxy incorporated, are presented although interpretation emphasizes this latter approach.

A number of presumptions underlie this approach to modelling work status. First, by including income flows from various sources and programs in the expected value for each option, variation in the expectation of income flows is introduced. The resulting estimates of behavior in response to incentives can be used to infer the contribution of relative changes in income flows over time to observed work status. Second, because it is expected monetary values (possibly tempered by the stigma costs of not working) which are taken to determine the choice among work status options, we presume that work-related costs, benefits in the form of leisure, and non-monetary benefits (e.g., health insurance and other fringe benefits) do not significantly affect the work status choice.

4. DATA AND MODEL SPECIFICATION

The empirical analysis uses data from the Panel Study of Income Dynamics (PSID). While the choice of work status in the latest year -- 1978 -- is the focus of the study, the panel character of the data allows construction of variables related to past earnings, occupational change, and the duration of impaired status. (The specific variables employed are described in the Appendix.)

One of the central concerns in this study is the role of health status in the work choice of older workers. For 8 of the 11 years of survey data, respondents were asked whether or not they were disabled. In most years the extent of disability is also asked. From this information, we created disability measures which capture both the duration and the intensity of the impairment. These are appropriate measures for modeling the receipt of transfer benefits, such as those provided in the Social Security Disability Insurance program, which is designed to provide support for those unable to participate in "substantial gainful activity." The duration and intensity of health problems are also likely to influence earnings. Employers may be less willing to continue to hire individuals with intermittent, persistent, or long-term health problems. Similarly, the disabled person may perceive limited job or earnings potential because of his impairment. Thus, in modeling expected income flows in the two options, a cumulative measure of the severity of a health problem is utilized. In addition, income expectations are viewed as being dependent on the current extent of disability, which we measure with a variable indicating the percentage of lost functional capabilities.

The estimates which we present are based on a two-stage, reduced form probit model. A reduced form specification is chosen to avoid bias from incomplete or inappropriate modeling of the underlying structural model, the underlying composition of which is not fully understood. Moreover, the reduced form specification makes the two-stage probit specification consistent with a full maximum likelihood estimation, as demonstrated by Lee (1979). In the first step, probit equations corresponding to (6) are fit over observations in the full sample, in order to predict the probability of being in the labor market or disability transfer recipiency groups.[5] The labor market option was defined as either being a labor market participant (having earned income or unemployment benefits greater than zero) and having no disability-related transfers, or having disability transfers greater than zero and earnings in excess of \$3360.[6] The disability transfer recipiency option is defined as having disability transfers (except Workers' Compensation) greater than zero and earnings less than \$3360.[7]

The variables in these equations reflect those demand- and supply-side characteristics of both the labor market and the disability transfer recipiency "market" which are likely to affect expectations of income flows in either option. Past experience, including downward occupational change, education, and disability status capture the individual's perception of his potential work capacity and productivity, as does age. They also describe important determinants of eligibility for disability transfers. Marital status and the presence of children reflect the income requirements of the household. The unemployment rate and the region are demand-side factors which are included to reflect employment opportunities in the individual's labor market, and hence affect the likelihood both of obtaining a job and of gaining eligibility for disability transfers. Region of the country also proxies for the differential application of eligibility determination criteria. Veteran's status indicates eligibility for military-related disability benefits. Past usual occupation proxies for disability pension coverage and, in the labor market equation, for past earnings. Race enters the equations to capture the effect of potential labor market discrimination in constraining employment opportunities and as a determinant of eligibility for disability transfers. Religion is entered as a taste variable.

In the second step, the expected income flow in the labor market option and the expected income flow in the disability transfer recipiency option are estimated for each individual in the sample. OLS regressions correspond to equations (4) and (5) and include the inverse Mill's ratio to correct for selection bias. Estimates from these equations yield income estimates for each individual in the two options. The two probit regressions corresponding to equations (8) and (9) are employed to obtain estimates of the probabilities for each individual in the two options.

In the third step, we use these estimates in the two versions of our choice model (equations (7) and (7')). In equation (7) only the income estimates are used as the basis of choice; equation (7') tempers the estimated income

Table 3. Probit Equations for Predicting the Probability of (1)
         Disability Transfer Recipiency and (2) Labor Market Participation

Explanatory Variables	Disability Transfer Recipiency		Labor Market Participation	
CONSTANT	339.45	(0.9)	-330.65	(0.8)
Cum Dis Severe	3.73	(3.4)*	-3.03	(2.9)*
(CUMDSEV)^2	-0.96	(0.8)	0.32	(0.3)
PERDIS	1.67	(1.3)	-1.13	(1.0)
(PERDIS)^2	-0.30	(0.3)	-0.28	(0.3)
AGE78	-0.05	(0.5)	0.02	(0.2)
Age spline 52	-0.006	(0.006)	0.02	(0.2)
Age spline 59	0.35	(2.2)*	-0.35	(2.4)*
Educ	-0.45	(1.3)	0.26	(0.9)
Ed spline 8	-0.08	(0.6)	0.03	(0.3)
Ed spline 11	-0.10	(0.5)	0.04	(0.3)
DWHITE	-0.15	(0.6)	0.38	(1.6)
UnRate78	-0.01	(0.3)	-0.03	(0.6)
DPROT	1.06	(2.5)*	-0.50	(1.4)
DCATH	0.96	(2.0)*	-0.56	(1.4)
DJEW	0.51	(0.5)	-0.56	(0.8)
DSESDOWN	0.41	(1.7)	-0.11	(0.5)
NMARNK	0.93	(2.4)*	-0.71	(2.0)*
KIDS1878	0.01	(0.1)	0.002	(0.02)
DSPOUSEWK77	-0.23	(1.0)	0.31	(1.4)
D Par Wealthy	0.12	(0.3)	-0.15	(0.4)
Other household income	0.00002	(1.3)	-0.00002	(1.1)
DSOUTH	0.40	(1.2)	-0.55	(1.7)
DWEST	-0.006	(0.02)	-0.31	(0.8)
DNC	0.11	(0.3)	-0.35	(1.0)
DVET	0.43	(1.9)*	-0.27	(1.4)
Age ed	0.009	(1.5)	-0.006	(1.1)
DPROF	-68.68	(0.9)	67.12	(0.9)
DMANAG	-4.62	(1.0)	4.29	(0.9)
DClerical Sales	7.50	(0.9)	-7.05	(0.8)
DCRAFT	-45.18	(0.9)	44.19	(0.9)
DOPERATIVE	-35.13	(0.9)	34.37	(0.9)
DFARM	254.35	(0.9)	-248.80	(0.9)
DMISC	-38.18	(0.9)	37.65	(0.8)
OCCLIM	-29.06	(0.9)	28.41	(0.9)
Cumyr 73	0.0002	(0.01)	-0.006	(0.3)
MARNK	0.38	(1.3)	-0.31	(1.1)
2 x Log Likelihood Ratio	497.2		495.0	
No. of observations	967		967	

Note: t-statistics are given in parentheses.
* Significant at the .05 level.

Table 4. Ordinary Least Squares Regressions for Predicting Income Flows Under the Disability Transfer Recipiency (Equation (5)) and Labor Market (Equation (4)) Options

Explanatory Variables	Disability Transfer Recipiency		Labor Market Participation	
CONSTANT	24658.0	(2.2)	-8036.4	(0.5)
Cum Dis Severe	-2468.9	(0.7)	-7663.9	(0.7)
(CUMDSEV)^2	1381.1	(0.5)	32.1	(0.002)
PERDIS	8781.5	(1.8)	-3526.9	(0.6)
(PERDIS)^2	-6326.0	(1.5)	777.4	(0.1)
AGE78	-432.5	(2.0)*	235.9	(0.8)
Age spline 52	284.4	(1.0)	-198.1	(0.6)
Age spline 59	-462.6	(1.0)	-394.6	(0.5)
Educ	-2610.8	(2.6)*	2327.9	(2.3)*
Ed spline 8	158.7	(0.5)	-316.6	(0.5)
Ed spline 11	308.8	(0.5)	1990.7	(3.9)*
DWHITE	1436.1	(2.4)*	951.0	(1.0)
NMARNK	-2335.4	(2.3)*	-5653.6	(3.4)*
KIDS1878	-430.5	(1.7)	177.6	(0.5)
DSPOUSEWK77	84.6	(0.1)	-2251.3	(2.9)*
D Par Wealthy	2800.4	(2.4)*	3871.6	(3.4)*
Other household income	-0.009	(0.2)	-0.03	(0.5)
DSOUTH	-1529.7	(2.1)*	-1735.9	(1.7)
DWEST	-1772.5	(1.4)	-464.1	(0.4)
DNC	-268.4	(0.3)	525.1	(0.5)
DVET	437.3	(0.7)	363.4	(0.5)
Age ed	49.1	(2.7)*	-38.5	(2.2)*
DPROF	480.3	(0.3)	4696.9	(2.5)*
DMANAG	630.3	(0.5)	9267.5	(5.7)*
DClerical Sales	2742.6	(2.1)*	4584.3	(2.5)*
DCRAFT	1393.5	(1.5)	5490.1	(3.7)*
DOPERATIVE	2160.1	(2.5)*	4439.1	(3.0)*
DFARM	-1845.2	(1.2)	-2311.0	(1.0)
DMISC	4468.1	(3.0)*	6106.6	(1.8)
Cumyr 73	45.2	(1.1)	117.6	(1.2)
MARNK	-2335.3	(2.7)*	1299.2	(1.3)
λ	194.2	(0.2)	2397.8	(0.6)
No. of observations	119		837	
R^2	.62		.36	

Note: t-statistics are given in parentheses.
* Significant at the .05 level.

R.H. Haveman and B.L. Wolfe

Table 5. Probit Estimates of the Determinants of Work Status Choice [coefficient (t)]

	Equation 7		Equation 7'		$\bar{X}$	σ
	Simple Model	Extended Model	Simple Model	Extended Model		
Expected Labor Market Income [LE; E(LE)]	.19 (14.1)*	.10 (4.8)*	.17 (8.5)*	.18 (7.0)*	$14,340	$8,411
Expected Disability Transfer Income [DT; $\widehat{E(DT)}$]	-.23 (8.3)*	-.07 (2.1)*	-.31 (5.5)*	-.23 (3.5)*	$632	$1,600
PERDIS	—	1.71 (7.3)*	—	.47 (1.7)	1.7	.35
Age 78	—	-.05 (3.1)*	—	-.03 (1.5)	52.9	5.0
NMARNK	—	-.13 (.5)	—	.06 (2.2)*	.08	.27
Unearned Income	—	-.04 (2.0)*	—	-.06 (3.3)*	$1,538	$4,581
Constant	.14 (1.0)	3.91 (4.0)	.04 (1.9)	1.64 (1.6)		
(2 x Log Likelihood Function)	354*	421*	500*	515*		

Note: For the dependent variables: $\bar{X}$ = .867; σ = .34

*Significant at .05 level

by an expectation or eligibility term. In one estimate for equations (7) and (7ˉ), only the expected income streams are employed; in an alternative specification, we include factors affecting the stigma cost associated with not working -- the extent of disablement, age, the presence of dependents, and the volume of unearned non-transfer income.

The model is estimated over men aged 45-62 in 1978. We exclude workers older than 62 since most are eligible for Social Security early retirement at that age. Inclusion of this group of workers would further complicate the estimation problem and mask the role of disability transfers in the early retirement decision. Evidence suggests that the availability of disability transfers is less likely to alter the work status choice of men below 45 years of age. Other researchers have also focused on this older age group.

5. EMPIRICAL RESULTS

Tables 3 through 5 present our empirical results on the determinants of the work status choice of older workers, emphasizing the role of expected income flows in the two options.

The probit equations corresponding to (6) are reported in Table 3. They provide both the basis for imputing probabilities to each individual, and the inverse Mill's ratio for the regressions predicting income flows in the two options. The income regressions in Table 4 correspond to equations (4) and (5), and are estimated over the sample included in each work status group.

Income flows associated with presence in either group are predicted from reduced form, ordinary least squares equations estimated over observations in each group. The equations include the standard determinants of market income -- age, education, experience, disability status, and race. These variables are also judged to be related to income for those who are recipients of disability-related transfers. Other determinants of income flows in both options include attitudes, family background, region, and need. Usual occupation, as a proxy for prior earnings, is also viewed as a determinant of both market and transfer income. And, because some disability transfers (and, perhaps, market income) depend on veteran's status, that too is included.

The final step in the analysis corresponds to equations (7) and (7ˉ), and posits that the choice between the two work status options depends on expected income flows in the two options and the stigma costs of not working. Because the stigma costs of not working cannot be estimated directly, we use proxies which imply that these costs are greater the younger the worker, the less severe his current health problem, the greater the number of persons dependent on him, the smaller the volume of his independent asset income. The results of this estimation are presented in Table 5.

These final estimates indicate the role of disability transfers -- their accessibility and level -- in affecting the work status choice of older men. In the table, two versions of the model are shown. In the first, the presumption is that the older worker bases his choice on an expected income flow which reflects both the probability of success in securing an income flow in each status and the expected income flow in that status if he is successful. This version corresponds to equation (7ˉ) and is designated by

$(\overline{E(LE)}; \overline{E(DT)})$ in the table. The second version presumes that the choice is based only on the expected income flow in each status. This version corresponds to equation (7). The predicted income flows are based on the regressions in Table 4, with the coefficient on the Heckman term used in the estimation, but not in the predictions. These results are designated by $(\widehat{LE},\widehat{DT})$ in the table. Both versions are estimated in a simple and an extended form.

In both versions of the model, and in both the simple and extended forms, expected income in the disability transfer option is negatively related to the decision to opt for participation in the labor market. $\widehat{E(DT)}$ and $\widehat{DT}$ are statistically significant at the .05 level. All but one of the variables representing the stigma costs of not working have the correct sign and are in most cases statistically significant. The exception is being not married or having dependent children. The elasticities (at the mean of the extended equation) implied by the derivatives are small -- that for expectation-adjusted income in the disability transfer recipiency option ($E(DT)$) is -.004; for income in the labor market option ($E(LE)$) the elasticity is .003. (The corresponding values for $\widehat{DT}$ and $\widehat{LE}$ are .-005 and .007, respectively.)

Thus, while the response to the incentives implicit in disability transfers -- increased leniency in eligibility or more generous benefits -- are verified and statistically significant, their quantitative significance is not substantial. Indeed, based on the $E(DT)$ elasticity, a doubling of expected disability transfer benefits is likely to generate a decrease in the percentage of those choosing the labor market option of slightly more than one half percentage point.[8] This corresponds to a reduction in the labor force of approximately 130,000 older workers. This response is several orders of magnitude smaller than that of previous studies, and cannot justify attributing a major share of the observed decrease in labor force participation of older workers to the increased accessibility and generosity of disability-related transfers. However, the significant effect of expected disability benefits on work status does indicate that this factor is a partial explanation of the growth of disability transfer expenditures and the decrease in labor force participation.[9]

6. CONCLUSION

These estimates suggest that the increasing relative generosity and/or leniency of disability income transfer programs do have a statistically significant, though quantitatively small, effect on the work effort choices of older workers. Through this, the growth in these programs is also partially explained. Nevertheless, they leave many questions unanswered. No insight is gained into the relative contributions of several other relevant variables to the fall in labor force participation rates or the rise in the number of disability program recipients. While disability benefit generosity or leniency appears to have played a small role in explaining the reductions, the contributions of changes in tastes for work, changes in social expectations regarding early retirement, changes in the physical demands of occupations, changes in the incidence of impairments, and changes in income from spouses and other sources remain unexplained.

The deviation of our elasticity estimates from those of other researchers has been explored in Haveman and Wolfe (1982, 1983). The very large work status response to the replacement rate variable estimated by Parsons appears to be related to specification problems involving failure to account for selectivity, the confounding of wage and benefit effects in the replacement rate construction, and the neglect of dependent benefits in the numerator of the replacement rate. In addition, we have undertaken a variety of alternative specifications to those reported here. On the basis of these results, we are relatively confident that the response to increases in transfer program generosity or leniency is an important factor in the work status choice. However, it is quantitatively small. Further exploration of these important policy questions requires improvements in disability status measures,[10] the availability of longitudinal data, and information on the determinants of access to incomes in various options conditional on application.

APPENDIX: VARIABLES USED IN ESTIMATES

Disability Variables

Cum Dis Severe: negative exponential of years severely disabled 1968-1978, largest weight on 1978;

$(CUMDSEV)^2$: square of Cum Dis Severe;

PERDIS: percent currently disabled, from 0 for no disability to 1 for totally disabled;

$(PERDIS)^2$: square of PERDIS.

Dependents and Needs Variables

NMARNK: dummy variable = 1 if not married and no children under 18;

DMarried: dummy variable = 1 if currently married;

MARNK: dummy variable = 1 if currently married and no children under 18;

KIDS1878: number of children under 18 in 1978;

DSPOUSEWK77: dummy variable = 1 if spouse worked in 1977.

Other household income: household income not due to respondent ($000);

Unearned income: income from assets, rent, dividends, interest, and alimony ($000).

Tastes and Market Opportunities Variables

DPROT, DCATH, DJEW are dummy variables = 1 if person's religion is in each category, omitted category is no religion;

DWHITE: dummy variable = 1 if person is white;

DVET: dummy variable = 1 if person is a veteran;

DSOUTH, DWEST, DNC (North Central) are dummy variables = 1 if person currently resides in each area, omitted category is East;

OCCLIM: % of male labor force in usual 1 digit industry who are functionally limited;

DPROF, DMANAG, DClerical Sales, DCRAFT, DOPERATIVE, DFARM are dummy variables = 1 if usual occupation is in each category;

DMISC: usual occupation is armed forces or protective services;

AGE78: age in 1978;

Age spline 52: second piece of linear spline corner at 52;

Age spline 59: third piece of linear spline corner at 59;

UnRate 78: area-specific unemployment rate in 1978.

Human Capital Variables

Cumyr 73: years of work experience as of 1973;

Educ: years of education;

Ed spline 8: second piece of linear spline; corner at 8 years of education;

Ed spline 11: third piece of linear spline; corner at 11 years;

Age ed: age times education;

D Par Wealthy: dummy variable = 1 if parents well off when person growing up.

FOOTNOTES

*) The authors are, respectively, Professor of Economics and Associate Professor of Economics and Preventive Medicine, University of Wisconsin-Madison. Both authors are Staff Associates, Institute for Research on Poverty, which provided financial support for this research. Helpful comments of Gary Chamberlain, Sheldon Danziger, George Jakubson, Jacques van der Gaag, and an anonymous referee, research assistance of Steve Oliner, programming assistance of Yen Shan and Nancy Williamson, and typing of Nancy Rortvedt and Marie Goodman are gratefully acknowledged.

1) Nearly all of the empirical analyses of the work effort impact of disability transfers are for the United States. In addition to those in the table, there are a number of earlier studies using less adequate data and techniques. See Luft (1975); Scheffler and Iden (1974); Berkowitz, Johnson, and Murphy (1976).

2) This welfare maximization approach has been developed by Gronau (1974), Hall (1973), Hanoch (1976), and Heckman (1974, 1979).

3) As we will emphasize below, our empirical specification of this choice is more complex than this description. The specification reflects the fact

that the income stream available if one chooses the labor earnings option contains some transfer income. Similarly, the income stream expected if one chooses the disability transfer option may contain some earnings and nondisability transfers. These combinations of income in the two options reflect the presence of earnings limitations in disability programs which are greater than zero, but not substantial.

4) The difference between the probits is due to the exclusion of those who have not been successful in either option. Hence, the values of the effects of independent variables on the estimated probabilities will not be equal. The proxy probabilities from these probits deviate from the ideal to the extent that the probability of success in attaining income in either option conditional on application differs from unity.

5) Individuals can be in either work status choice or in neither. Of the full sample of 967 observations, 956 are classified as being "successful" in one of the options.

6) The $3360 cutoff was chosen because it is the annual equivalent of the monthly earnings limit in the dominant disability-related transfer program. Of the full sample, 838 are in this group.

7) Disability-related transfers are defined to include benefits from Social Security Disability Insurance, Supplemental Security Income (a program of income-tested benefits directed at the blind and disabled), veterans' disability benefits, other disability pensions, and, if disabled, a share of other welfare and help from relatives. Of the full sample, 119 are in this group.

8) This ratio is a close surrogate for the labor force participation rate.

9) To test the sensitivity of these results, we have estimated a variety of additional choice models -- some structural and some reduced form -- each representing a different view of the nature of the decision process. These include a set of structural equations which are used to estimate expected income of the labor market option and expected income if a disability transfer recipient. These are estimated as expected values, both using the estimated probability and not using the probability. In addition, in the final probit for both the structural and reduced form models, actual income streams are used for those individuals with observed values. Imputed values are used only for those without observed values. (This assumes that the observed values are the best predictor of income expectations.) Results from all of these are quite consistent with the reported results: the derivatives from the reduced form estimates using observed values are .0015 and .0005 for the labor market income streams (simple and extended) and -.0039 and -.0010 for the disability transfer income stream (simple and extended). These verify the generally significant but quantitatively small effects of the generosity of disability transfers on the work status choice. The structural estimates, based on a slightly different definition of the work status choice (labor force participation is the variable explained) show a similar pattern: the derivatives (using probabilities) are .0044 and .0022 for the labor market income stream. The results not using probabilities generally have somewhat larger (but still quite small) derivatives.

10) For example, Parsons (1979) indicates the sensitivity of results to

the nature of the disability status variable, and emphasizes the possible simultaneity of reported disability (on which our variables are constructed) and non-labor-force participation.

REFERENCES

Berkowitz, M., Johnson, W. and Murphy, E. (1976), Public Policy toward Disability, Praeger, New York.

Gronau, R. (1974), Wage Comparisons -- A Selectivity Bias, Journal of Political Economy 82, 1119-1144.

Hall, R. E. (1973), Wages, Income and Hours of Work in the U.S. Labor Force, in Cain, G. and Watts, H. (eds.), Income Maintenance and Labor Supply, Academic Press, New York.

Hanoch, G. (1976), A Multivariate Model of Labor Supply: Methodology for Estimation, Rand Corporation, R-1869-HEW, September.

Haveman, R., and Wolfe, B. (1982), Disability Transfers and the Work Effort Response of Older Males: A Reconciliation, Paper presented at a National Bureau of Economic Research Conference on Economic Incentives of Government Spending, November 1982.

Haveman, R. and Wolfe, B. (1983), The Decline in Male Labor Force Participation: A Comment, Journal of Political Economy, forthcoming.

Heckman, J. (1974), Shadow Prices, Market Wages and Labor Supply, Econometrica 42, 679-694.

Heckman, J. (1979), Sample Selection Bias as a Specification Error, Econometrica 47, 153-161.

Lee, Lung-Fei. (1979), Identification and Estimation in Binary Choice Models with Limited (Censored) Dependent Variables, Econometrica 47, 977-996.

Leonard, J. (1979), The Social Security Disability Program and Labor Force Participation, National Bureau of Economic Research, Working Paper 392.

Luft, H. (1975), The Impact of Poor Health on Earnings, Review of Economics and Statistics 57, 43-57.

Parsons, D. (1979), The Male Labor Force Participation Decision: Health, Declared Health, and Economic Incentives, Ohio State University, Mimeo.

Parsons, D. (1980a), The Decline in Male Labor Force Participation, Journal of Political Economy 88, 117-134.

Parsons, D. (1980b), Racial Trends in Male Labor Force Participation, American Economic Review 70, 911-920.

Scheffler, R. and Iden, G. (1974), The Effect of Disability on Labor Supply, Industrial and Labor Relations Review 28, 122-132.

U.S. Department of Health and Human Services, (1980), Public Health

Service, Office of Health Research, Statistics, and Technology, National Center for Health Statistics, Selected Health Characteristics by Occupation, United States, 1975-76, Vital Health Statistics, Series 10, Number 133, May, U.S. Government Printing Office, Washington, D.C.

ARNE RYDE SYMPOSIUM ON SOCIAL INSURANCE
L. Söderström (editor)
© Elsevier Science Publishers B.V. (North-Holland), 1983

FINANCIAL INCENTIVES AND RETIREMENT
IN THE UNITED STATES

Richard V. Burkhauser
and
Joseph F. Quinn*

1. INTRODUCTION

Over the last three decades, the United States has witnessed a dramatic demographic phenomenon. Regular employment beyond age 65, once a common occurrence, has become rarer and rarer over the years. In 1947, for example, the United States labor force participation rate for men aged 65 and over approached 50 percent; by 1980 it was below 20 percent - a decrease of 60 percent in three decades. The move toward earlier retirement was not confined to this age group. Over the same period the participation rates of men 55 to 64 dropped from 90 percent to near 70 percent. Most of this change occurred after 1961, the year in which Social Security eligibility for men was lowered from age 65 to 62. Today, more than half of eligible Social Security recipients claim benefits before age 65.

The work experience of older women in the United States does not show similar trends. This is probably because it reflects the combined impact of two conflicting trends - earlier retirement, as documented above, and increased labor force participation among women, especially those married.[1] For women aged 65 and over, the two almost exactly cancel out, and the rate today is at the same 8 percent level it was just after World War II. For those women aged 55 to 64, however, the latter trend dominates, and an increase from 24 to 41 percent has occurred.

In aggregate, however, the trend has definitely been toward earlier and earlier retirement, and its magnitude has been substantial. Recent uncertainties about the future caused by persistent recession and inflation appear to have slowed or even reversed the rate of change. Nonetheless, we clearly live in a very different retirement environment than we did even two decades ago. These changes have important effects on the macroeconomic economy (labor supply, consumption demand and savings) and on the levels of well-being of the individuals involved. Not surprisingly, these trends have been the subject of considerable research effort in the United States.

2. DETERMINANTS OF THE RETIREMENT DECISION

Research on retirement has grown sufficiently to have spawned a number of
surveys of the literature. (See, for example, Campbell and Campbell (1976),
Clark, Kreps and Spengler (1978) and Mitchell and Fields (1982).) According
to Campbell and Campbell, many early discussions of the retirement decision
put primary emphasis on the importance of personal health. In this sce-
nario, one continued to work until health deterioration (or perhaps
mandatory retirement) dictated retirement. One then turned to whatever retirement income sources were available, like savings, Social Security or
employer pensions. These income sources were not thought to induce retirement, but rather to soften the financial blow when it occurred. These conclusions were drawn largely from a series of Social Security Administration
surveys in which retired respondents were asked why they retired. The
overwhelming response was always health.

More recent analyses of retirement, mostly by economists, have concentrated
not on why people say they retired, but on their objective circumstances at
the time of the decision. In these econometric studies, retirement income
sources always play a major role. Eligibility for Social Security and other
pensions, the size of the benefits for which one is eligible, and the rules
and regulations concerning changes in benefits over time all appear to be
important determinants. As Clark, Kreps and Spengler have made clear, the
importance of these financial factors does not exclude other explanatory
variables. Health remains important in nearly all the retirement studies,
despite problems in finding objective measures. Studies have also found
that wage rates are important, both on the current job and in alternative
employment (see Gustman and Steinmeier, 1981), as are mandatory retirement,
economic characteristics of the community and other demographic characteristics of the individual, such as sex, race and marital status.

The empirical literature on retirement in the United States has burgeoned
for three reasons. First, public interest and discussion of retirement
issues have increased dramatically due to the tremendous growth of Social
Security expenditures. Political pressure concerning any of the proposed
solutions (lower or later benefits or increased taxes) has spurred government interest in these issues and considerable government-sponsored research. Second, two superb data sets have recently become available
offering microeconomic detail previously unavailable. These are the National Longitudinal Surveys (NLS), funded by the Department of Labor, and the
Retirement History Study (RHS), undertaken by the Social Security Administration. Both involve large sample sizes, extensive questionnaires, and are
both cross-sectional and longitudinal in nature. The RHS, which we utilize
below, also includes the entire internal Social Security earnings record of
each respondent. And finally, significant advances in economic theory
relating to the retirement decision have occurred. (For an excellent review
of recent theoretical and empirical research, see Danziger, Haveman and
Plotnick (1981) and Mitchell and Fields (1982).) Simple one period explanations have been expanded into life cycle models, optimal control theory has
been introduced, and many of the institutional details of the Social
Security and pension systems have been incorporated.

3. THE MEASUREMENT OF RETIREMENT INCENTIVES

Our research has concentrated on the description of the financial incentives imbedded in the American retirement income system and on the estima-

tion of the impact of these incentives on individual behavior. The sophistication of the treatment of Social Security and pensions has grown dramatically in the last decade.

The earliest characterizations of retirement plans used simple eligibility dummies (e.g., Gordon and Blinder, 1980, or Quinn, 1977). This is unsatisfactory for a number of reasons. It does not differentiate between eligibility for full and reduced benefits, and ignores the wealth stored in these systems before the day of first eligibility. In addition, the dummies ignore the size of the benefits, obviously an important characteristic.[2] Since benefits are usually related to earnings, this last omission biases the wage coefficient towards zero, since the coefficient must pick up both the earnings effect, which discourages retirement, and the benefit impact, which encourages it.

Later, attempts were made to estimate the size of the annual Social Security and pension benefits for which the individuals were eligible (e.g., Boskin, 1977, and Burtless and Hausman, 1980). Such attempts either relied on estimates supplied by the survey respondents, which were marred by unacceptably high "don´t know" or "no answer" responses for any single question, or on the Social Security earnings records, which were appended to the RHS. These variables, used either as explanatory variables on their own or combined with earnings to form a one-year replacement rate, represent a significant improvement. But they neglect an extremely important aspect of the incentive structure - how the benefits would change if one were to continue to work. Obviously the financial rewards are quite different for two individuals eligible for identical annual retirement benefits if one person´s benefit would rise during an additional year of work while the other´s would not. As Mitchell and Fields point out, "The independent variables...must be expressed as streams and not just in terms of their current levels. Models without this feature are fundamentally flawed."[3]

The breakthrough on this front involved viewing retirement rights as a stream of future incomes. The size of the stream is conveniently summarized by its present discounted value - pension or Social Security wealth. This concept was introduced in macro research by Feldstein (1974) and at the micro level by Burkhauser (1979). It is now generally accepted, and can be seen in the current work of Burtless and Moffitt (1981), Gordon and Blinder (1980), Hamermesh (1981), Hurd and Boskin (1981), Kotlikoff (1979), Pellechio (1978) and us.

This asset or wealth characterization of retirement rights improves the empirical work in at least three ways. First, the impact of these rights on labor supply is not contigent on current eligibility. The wealth exists anytime after vesting (and even beforehand if vesting is anticipated) and could induce retirement before eligibility if the individual is able to dissave or borrow to finance consumption in the interim. Second, the issue of inflation protection after retirement can be addressed. As explained below, whether the benefits are indexed for inflation affects the discount rate used. The same initial benefit corresponds to very different wealth equivalents depending on whether the amount is fixed in nominal or real terms (see Quinn, 1982). Finally, and most important in our research, we can consider changes in wealth contingent on current work-retirement decisions. In most pension plans (including the United States Social Security system), the asset value of the streams depends upon when the individual claims it. During some periods (for example, before eligibility) the asset value grows as one continues to work. After some point, however, it

begins to fall, as future increments no longer compensate for current benefits foregone. In other work (Burkhauser and Quinn, 1983), we have treated
these wealth changes as increments or decrements to earnings, and have
argued that true earnings, comprehensively defined, actually fall for older
workers because of this. In this paper, we describe the measurement and
magnitude of these effects, and their impact on the retirement decision.

There are a number of important issues in the measurement of Social
Security and pension wealth, including the discount rate, the lifespan,
contributions to the retirement system and the rules determining the size
of benefits. The last issue is particularly troublesome for employer pensions, since there are tens of thousands of pension plans in the United
States. They all have their own calculation rules, and these rules are not
included in current microeconomic data sources. The assumptions we have
used to address this problem are outlined below.

Pension (or Social Security) wealth in our work is defined as follows:

$$\text{WEALTH(S)} = \sum_{i=0}^{N} \frac{B_i(S) \times P(i|i-1)}{(1+r)^i} \tag{1}$$

where B (S) is the annual benefit amount in year i of a pension claimed
      in year S;
   P(i|i-1) is the probability of living through year i
      having lived through year i-1;
   r is the discount rate; and
   N is the number of years until age 100.

We define DELTA, the change in wealth term, as

$$\text{DELTA} = \text{WEALTH(J+1)} - \text{WEALTH(J)} - C(j) \tag{2}$$

where C(j) is the employee contribution to the retirement plan
during year j.

Defined in this way, a positive DELTA denotes a gain in wealth. The issues
behind these definitions are discussed below.

A dollar today is preferred to a dollar in the future for a number of reasons. If there is inflation, tomorrow's dollar will buy less. Even without
inflation, today's dollar can be invested and grow, at the real rate of interest, to more than a dollar in the future. And even if the real rate of
interest were zero, so that investment and growth were impossible, personal
utility functions would probably dictate a preference for today.

The appropriate choice of a discount rate (r) is not obvious. Real rates of
return and inflation vary considerably over time. Our approach has been to
experiment with a range of discount rates - 2, 5 and 10 percent.

Inflation is included in the discount rate when the initial pension amount
is fixed in nominal terms, as in the case for many private sector pensions.
When pensions are fully indexed, only the real component is appropriate.
For pensions which are only partly indexed (e.g., the adjustment is
capped), as in the case for many state and local government pensions in the
United States, only the unindexed portion of inflation is included. In this
paper, government workers are excluded, and we are left with private sector

pensions (often unindexed) and Social Security (fully indexed, previously by frequent Congressional action and now by law). Since inflation and inflationary expectations were certainly not zero in the era of our data (early and mid 1970s), different discount rates are appropriate for pensions and Social Security. In the behavioral equations below, we use the 5 percent figures for Social Security wealth and 10 percent values for employer pensions.

Variations in life expectancy can be treated in two ways. The discrete approach is simply to use the average life expectancy for the demographic cell (defined by sex and age) into which the individual falls. For example, for a specific person, pension benefits might be assumed to last for 17.5 years, then cease. Alternatively, one might take a probabilistic approach, and multiply each year's benefit by the probability that the respondent will live through that year. Empirically, it makes very little difference. We have adopted the latter approach, and arbitrarily limited the maximum age to 100.

Certain employer pensions provide the option of survivor's benefits for the spouse if the spouse outlives the primary recipient. In our pension data, we do not know for whom this option exists, nor if the respondent took it. We have assumed, therefore, that there are no survivor's benefits. With Social Security, this is definitely not the case, since survivor's benefits are an integral part of the insurance. Our definition of Social Security wealth therefore includes the probability that the spouse will outlive the primary recipient and receive a survivor's benefit.

Pension plans differ with respect to employee contributions. In calculating the change in wealth following an additional year's work, we want to consider the employee contributions $C(j)$ during that year. Again, we do not know the details of the individual pension plans. Since employee contributions are relatively rare in the private sector, we have assumed all pension contributions are made by the employer and that $C(j)$ equals 0. (See Quinn (1982).) For Social Security, we use the statutory employee contribution rate.

The most difficult issue is the benefit calculation rules. These are key in determining the change in wealth over time. Annual benefits can rise with additional work for two reasons. If benefits are based on total pension contributions, years of service or average earnings over some time period (and these are the most common determinants), the parameters in the calculation formula will usually change. In addition, there may be an actuarial supplement to compensate the recipient for foregone benefits.

For Social Security, we can calculate the wealth change precisely since we know the entire earnings record, the Social Security benefit calculation rules, and the contribution rate. In considering a hypothetical additional year of work, we assume annual earnings the same as in the previous year, which we know. The additional year changes the average monthly earnings (AME), which changes the primary insurance amount (PIA), which determines the benefit. The additional actuarial adjustment for delayed retirement was about 7 percent per year at ages 62 through 64, and 1 percent per year beyond that.[4]

For pensions, we know only an annual benefit expected or being received. We do not know how this would change if the individual worked for another year, since we do not know the calculation rule nor whether an additional actuarial adjustment exists. We have adopted two sets of assumptions (A and B) about these unknown parameters, and calculated DELTA values under each.

A: i)   The yearly benefits described by the workers do not
          include a joint and survivor provision;

    ii)   Once a worker is eligible to collect full benefits
          (as described by the respondent), annual benefits
          do not increase at all when postponed;

   iii)   If a worker is eligible to collect reduced benefits,
          annual benefits increase when postponed by a given
          percentage based on a broad industry-wide average; [5]

    vi)   All increases in benefits due to additional
          contributions or years of service are ignored.

Under this set of assumptions, the DELTA values for all eligible respondents turn out to be negative (wealth loss). For those already eligible for full benefits, this is obvious since we assume no increased benefits in the future. In fact, since C(j) is assumed to be 0 for employer pensions, the DELTA equals the annual benefit foregone. The full benefit is lost if one continues on the job, and there is no reward for this later on. For those eligible for reduced benefits, positive DELTAs (wealth gain) are possible, but do not occur because of the low average actuarial adjustments by industry.

Under the second set of assumptions, we assume that years of service is the key determinant: specifically,

B: i)   The yearly benefits described by the workers do not
          include a joint and survivor provison;

    ii)   The annual benefit amount is based on years of service,
          so that an additional year of work increases the benefit
          by 1/n, where n is the number of years with the firm;

   iii)   Those currently eligible for full benefits enjoy no
          additional actuarial adjustment; and

    iv)   Those currently eligible for reduced benefits do enjoy
          an additional actuarial adjustment equal to the
          industry-wide average (see footnote 5).

As is seen below, these assumptions yield a wide range of DELTA values, and both positive and negative amounts.

4. THE SIZE AND IMPACT OF RETIREMENT INCENTIVES

The retirement incentives we are considering here are the wealth values of Social Security and pension rights, and the changes in these values that would occur during an additional year of work. To demonstrate that these magnitudes are large and that they influence labor force behavior, we have drawn a sample of workers nearing retirement age from the Retirement History Study (RHS).[6] Our sample includes men aged 62 to 64 who were employed in 1973. They are observed again in 1975, and the labor force behavior refers to this two-year transition period. Since we do not observe the respondents between 1973 and 1975, we assume that they all remain employed until 1974, and then make the decision we observe. The tables below describe the financial incentives they face in 1974, when they are aged 63 to 65.

Table 1 shows the distribution of pension wealth for this sample, using three different discount rates. Because most private sector employer pensions are not automatically indexed, the 5 and 10 percent rates, reflecting inflationary expectations, are the most relevant. In our sample, over half have pension wealth on their current or previous jobs. The median values for those with pension wealth are $17,610 (5%) or $12,970 (10%) in 1974 dollars. Around these medians, there is wide dispersion. With the 5 percent discount rate, for example, 25 percent of those with pension wealth (and 14% of the overall sample) have wealth exceeding $30,000, and 9 percent (5 percent of the total) have pension wealth over $50,000.

In Table 2 are analogous Social Security figures. There are a number of striking differences. Since Social Security is fully and automatically indexed for inflation, the lower real discount rates (2 and 5%) should be used. The coverage of Social Security is almost universal in this sample (which excludes government workers), and therefore only a very small fraction (5%) have no Social Security wealth. The median values are much higher than for pensions - either near $70,000 (2%) or $50,000 (5%), and the dispersion is much narrower. At the lowest discount rate, 55 percent of these men have between $70,000 and $90,000 in Social Security wealth.

When expressed in these terms, the magnitude of these retirement income rights becomes clear. In fact, these sources of wealth are far more important for this age cohort than all the other sources of traditionally measured wealth, with the possible exception of equity in the home (see Quinn, 1983).

Unlike other forms of wealth, the values of pension and Social Security income streams depend critically on when the benefits are claimed. The changes in wealth (DELTA) that would occur over an incremental year of work (1974-1975) are shown in Tables 3 and 4. Here we drop the 2 percent discount rate, which we argue is too low for the calculation of these DELTAs - for pensions, because of inflation and for Social Security, because of a quirk in the legislation at that time.[7] We disaggregate the sample by age in these tables to illustrate how these incentives change at different ages, and especially at age 65. For Social Security, at age 65 the actuarial adjustment changed from about 7 percent per year to 1 percent. For pensions, the effect is less dramatic, but 65 is an age at which many employees become eligible for "full" pension benefits. Under both of our sets of assumptions, this decreases the value of the DELTAs and we predict, increases the disincentives to work.

Table 3 shows pension DELTA values for both sets of assumptions - A and B. Notice that a higher proportion of workers are in the "no pension" column here than in Table 1, since DELTAs only apply to pensions earned on the current job. We assume that pension rights from previous jobs are unaffected by current labor supply decisions.

Under both sets of assumptions, the DELTAs display a wide range of values. They are considerably lower (larger wealth losses) under assumptions A, since the years of service effect is ignored.[8] These assumptions give no

Table 1. Percentage Distribution of Pension WEALTH for Employed Men Aged 63 to 65, by Discount Rate - 1974

Discount Rate	No Pension on any job	1- 10,000	10,000- 20,000	20,000- 30,000	30,000- 40,000	40,000- 50,000	50,000- 75,000	75,000+	Median[a]
2	45	11	14	10	6	4	6	3	$22,300
5	45	15	15	10	5	4	4	1	$17,610
10	45	22	16	8	5	2	1	1	$12,970

[a] Median of those with positive pension WEALTH. Medians calculated on intervals of $2000. Sample size with good pension data = 934.

SOURCE (for all tables): Retirement History Study, 1969 through 1975.

Table 2. Percentage Distribution of Social Security WEALTH, Employed Men Aged 63 to 65, by Discount Rate – 1974

Discount Rate	0	1-30,000	30,000-40,000	40,000-50,000	50,000-60,000	60,000-70,000	70,000-80,000	80,000-90,000	Median[a]
2	5	4	6	9	7	13	39	16	$72,338
5	5	10	11	13	44	17	0	0	$53,519
10	5	25	40	30	0	0	0	0	$36,125

[a] Calculated on intervals of $2000. Sample size = 1047.

Table 3. Percentage Distribution of Pension DELTAs[a] for Employed Men Aged 63 to 65, by Age and Discount Rate - 1974

Age	No Pension on Current Job	-5000 and below	-4000 to -5000	-3000 to -4000	-2000 to -3000	-1000 to -2000	-1 to -1000	0[b]	1 to 1000	1000 to 2000	N	Median[c]
Assumption A Discount Rate = 5%												
63	57	2	1	4	5	8	7	16	0	0	407	-$650
64	58	2	2	5	9	12	9	2	0	0	328	-$1,778
65	61	4	2	5	9	8	9	2	0	0	252	-$2,031
Assumption A Discount Rate = 10%												
63	57	2	2	4	6	6	7	16	0	0	407	-$850
64	58	3	2	4	9	12	8	2	0	0	328	-$1,806
65	61	4	2	5	8	10	8	2	0	0	252	-$2,042
Assumption B Discount Rate = 5%												
63	57	1	0	1	3	4	13	0[c]	18	3	405	-$59
64	58	1	1	1	7	10	16	0	5	1	326	-$964
65	61	2	2	2	9	10	10	0	4	0	251	-$1,389
Assumption B Discount Rate = 10%												
63	57	2	0	2	4	8	10	0[c]	16	1	405	-$354
64	58	2	1	3	7	12	13	0	4	0	326	-$1,271
65	61	3	2	2	8	10	10	0	4	0	251	-$1,594

a The difference in pension wealth when the pension is postponed one year from 1974 to 1975.

b See text.

c Median of those with a pension on the current job. Median calculated on intervals of $250.

pension credit for work prior to the age of earliest eligibility. For these workers, the DELTA values are 0, since additional work results in no loss in current benefits and no gain in future benefits. Where the latter assumption is inaccurate, our DELTA values underestimate the true value and thus exaggerate the work disincentive in the pension rules.

Under assumptions A, the median pension wealth loss is in the $2000 range by age 65. Since the median earnings for this group is about $9,000, this is the equivalent of a substantial pay cut. We argue below that this is a significant disincentive to work.

Under the second set of assumptions (B), the rewards for continuing work are higher, since an additional year of seniority is added in the pension benefit calculation. For those eligible for a pension on the current job, the DELTA values will never be zero, unless the calculation rules were actuarially fair to the dollar. The zero values under assumptions A have moved to positive values (work incentives) under B. Here the median loss is about $1500 by age 65. At the 10 percent discount rate, 18 percent of those with pensions on the current job lose $3000 or more, and 8 percent lose over $5000.

The age effect is much more dramatic with Social Security as can be seen in Table 4. At a 5 percent discount rate, the Social Security rules provide a subsidy to the median worker in our sample at age 63 or 64 - future benefit increments more than offset the current loss. At 65, however, this reverses completely, and virtually everyone loses Social Security wealth if they continue to work. These losses are high - over $3000 for nearly half of this sample. At the higher discount rate, the losses are more severe, and the median worker loses at all three ages.[9]

That these financial incentives exist and are substantial does not necessarily mean that they influence behavior. We used the longitudinal nature of the RHS data to test whether they did. Between 1973 and 1975, about half of our sample stayed on their 1973 job and half left.[10] Of those who left, most withdrew completely from the labor force. A few switched jobs, but we do not differentiate between the two here. We hypothesize that the probability of leaving one's job increases with size of the financial incentives to do so incorporated in pension and Social Security DELTAs and WEALTHs. Other things equal, the probability should be lower the higher the reward to work - the annual earnings (for 1973) which accrue from the job. Since health is always found to be an important determinant in decisions at this age, we included a dummy variable which is on if the individual's health deteriorated over the two year interval.[11] Finally, we included a marital status dummy to test whether this affects the decision. In summary, the model of quit behavior is

QUIT = f(Health, Marital Status, Earnings, Pension DELTA, SS DELTA,
        Pension WEALTH, SS WEALTH).

Initial health status (described either as health relative to peers or the presence of a health condition limiting the type or amount of work the respondent could do) and other assets were also included, but were consistently insignificant and are not reported in the paper. We suspect that initial health is unimportant because of the sample we have chosen - workers employed in 1973. Those with poor health at this age were likely to be out of the labor force already, and hence excluded from our sample. The "other assets" variable may be picking up two offsetting effects - an eco-

218   *R. V. Burkhauser and J. T. Quinn*

Table 4. Percentage Distribution of Social Security DELTAs[a] for Employed Men Aged 63 to 65, by Age and Discount Rate - 1974

Age	-5000 to -6000	-4000 to -5000	-3000 to -4000	-2000 to -3000	-1000 to -2000	-1 to -1000	0	1 to 1000	1000 to 2000	2000 to 3000	3000 to 4000	4000 to 6000	N	Median[b]
DISCOUNT RATE = 5%														
63	0	0	0	0	1	12	5	25	19	34	3	1	435	$1,345
64	0	0	0	0	6	17	4	33	18	20	2	0	342	$612
65	5	12	26	30	19	3	4	1	0	0	0	0	266	-$2,727
DISCOUNT RATE = 10%[c]														
63	0	0	0	1	22	33	5	35	3	0	0	0	435	-$175
64	0	0	0	8	33	32	4	21	1	0	0	0	342	-$714
65	7	23	27	31	6	1	4	0	0	0	0	0	266	-$3,181

a Social Security DELTA is the change in Social Security wealth if receipt is postponed one year from 1974 to 1975, minus employee Social Security taxes paid during that year.
b Medians calculated on intervals of $250.
c See footnote 7.

nomic effect inducing retirement and a "missing variable" effect - the impact of an unmeasurable taste for work that results in large asset holdings from hard work in the past and a reluctance to retire today. The "other assets" variable also suffered from a high proportion of "don´t know" responses.

The QUIT equation was estimated with both ordinary least squares regression and with logit techniques. In both cases, the two alternative sets of assumptions for the pension DELTA calculations were used. The results appear in Table 5.

As expected, the financial variables are highly significant. Workers with high earnings are more likely to continue on the job; those with large work disincentives (wealth losses) are less so. The point estimates in the regressions suggests that each $1000 in wealth loss (Social Security or pension) increases the probability of quitting by 3 to 4 percentage points. Given that Social Security and pension DELTAs under -$3000 range are not uncommon at age 65, this effect can be substantial.

The choice of assumptions behind the pension DELTA calculations makes little difference. Under assumptions A, when years of service are ignored, the coefficient is higher and more significant. With the B assumptions, the coefficient estimate is still significantly different from 0.

Even if the pension systems were actuarially fair, and the DELTA values therefore 0, one would expect the wealth value of Social Security and pension rights to influence the retirement decision, just as any source of wealth should. Our results are mixed. Under B, pension wealth is a significant determinant, and each $10,000 in such wealth is associated with an increased quit probability of about 3.4 percentage points. When the A assumptions are used in the DELTA calculations, the wealth coefficients are small and not quite statistically significant at the 5 percent level. Pension wealths and DELTAs are correlated ($r = .6$), and this sample size is inadequate to resolve clearly their independent effects. Social Security wealth, on the other hand, is never significant. It may be that the missing variable explanation applies here as well - those who are predisposed to continue working have always been hard workers, and so have earned relatively high Social Security benefits.

Of the other two variables, only the health term is significant. Health deterioration during the transition period increases the probability of leaving one´s job by nearly 10 points.

The logit specification is more appropriate in the case of a dichotomous dependent variable, as we have here, since the predicted probabilities are automatically constrained to the (0,1) range, and the impacts of the explanatory variables taper off as these extreme values are approached. Unfortunately, the logit coefficients are not partial derivatives, and have no intuitive interpretation.

The logit estimates also appear in Table 5. They are reassuring, since the signs and significance levels are almost identical to the regression results. The main difference is that both pension DELTA and pension wealth are significant in both equations. We conclude from this empirical work that retirement income wealth and changes in this wealth as one ages are important determinants of the retirement decision, as are earnings potential and changes in health.

Table 5. Quit equations, Employed Men aged 63 to 65 in 1974
(Dependent variable = 1 if respondent leaves his 1973 job by 1975.)
(t-statistics in parentheses)

Variable	Regression 1		Regression 2		Logit 1		Logit 2	
Health Deterioration (1973-75)	.097	(2.39*)	.010	(2.40*)	.393	(2.22*)	.314	(1.75*)
Married in 1973	.071	(1.30)	.068	(1.22)	.287	(1.19)	.287	(1.17)
Earnings previous year ($000)	-.010	(2.72*)	-.009	(2.58*)	-.038	(2.32*)	-.038	(2.30*)
Pension DELTA (Assumptions A) ($000)	-.041	(2.93*)			-.210	(2.99*)		
Pension DELTA (Assumptions B) ($000)			-.030	(1.88*)			-.219	(2.66*)
Social Security DELTA ($000)	-.036	(4.12*)	-.036	(3.95*)	-.183	(4.50*)	-.171	(4.15*)
Pension WEALTH ($0000)	.023	(1.58)	.034	(2.36*)	.117	(1.73*)	.132	(1.97*)
Social Security WEALTH ($00000)	-.002	(0.16)	.002	(0.13)	.020	(0.36)	.025	(0.45)
Constant	.474		.461		-.203	(0.72)	-.148	(0.51)
F value	7.54*		6.53*					
Likelihood ratio index					54.24*		48.46*	

*significant at 5 percent level (one sided)

5. SUMMARY

The recent trend toward earlier and earlier retirement among American men has been dramatic. The reasons for this behavioral change are undoubtedly many and varied. We have argued that an important factor has been the retirement incentives built into the American Social Security and pension systems. These systems have grown in coverage and in benefit levels over the past 30 years. In addition, the Social Security age of earliest eligibility was dropped form 65 to 62 (in 1956 for women; in 1961 for men). Although we have not analyzed the changes in the retirement incentives over time, we have established that retirement incentives do exist, can be substantial and are statistically significant variables in explaning interpersonal differences in retirement behavior.

Other writers have emphasized the growth in retirement income wealth over time (e.g., Hurd and Boskin, 1981). This is particularly true for Social Security. Every cohort retiring up to now has received benefits far in excess of what their contributions would have earned in bank accounts, stocks or bonds (see Burkhauser and Warlick, 1981). This windfall wealth increase is undoubtedly partially responsible for the earlier retirement patterns, although the effect does not show up in our empirical work. We have emphasized another aspect - how the asset values of the retirement income rights vary with receipt at different ages, and have shown that after some age they begin to fall for most workers. Our empirical work suggests that workers understand this and respond to it. Those with larger work penalties are less likely to continue to work than others.

As our society became wealthier, it was perfectly reasonable for workers to spend part of this additional wealth consuming more leisure. As we move into the next century, however, well-established population trends appear likely to make such leisure increasingly costly. In the United States the debate has already begun over how the retirement system should adjust to this coming crisis. Across-the-board reductions in Social Security or pension wealth will increase work effort and reduce the costs of the retirement system. But we argue that many of the anti-work aspects of our current retirement system must also be changed if social policy dictates that older workers stay longer in the work force than they now do.

FOOTNOTES

*) Vanderbilt University and Boston College, respectively. This research was partially funded by a grant from the Labor Management Services Administration, U.S. Department of Labor. We would like to thank Irene Powell and Richard Fendler for research assistance.

1) While the labor force participation rates rose from 50 to only 59 percent for single American women, and from 37 to only 41 for those widowed, divorced or separated, they more than doubled for the married population, from 20 to 45 percent. These labor force participation rates are all taken from the Employment and Training Report of the President (U.S. President, 1981).

2) The size of retirement benefits were very difficult or impossible to obtain in the early waves of the Retirement History Study. The Social Security earnings records were not appended until later, and questions concerning expected Social Security benefits went largely unanswered. With

regard to pensions, "don´t know" responses were a problem (though less so) as were skip patterns that bypassed certain respondents. When the earnings histories were added, and as additional waves of data increased the sources of pension benefit information, it became possible to deduce these values for the vast majority of the sample.

3)   Mitchell and Fields (1982) p. 1.

4)   The 1 percent per year actuarial adjustment for delayed receipt beyond age 65 applied in 1973-1975, the years of our data. In 1982, this adjustment was increased to 3 percent, still far from actuarially fair. The recent National Commission on Social Security has proposed raising it further, to 8 percent per year of delay.

5)   These broad industry averages were provided to us by the Urban Institute (1982) from data in the Bureau of Labor Statistics Level of Benefits Study.

6)   The Retirement History Study is a ten-year study of the retirement process undertaken by the Social Security. Over 11,000 men and nonmarried women aged 58 to 63 were initially interviewed in 1969, and then reinterviewed at 2-year intervals through 1979. The data include detailed information on labor force status and history, earnings, retirement benefits and mandatory retirement, income sources, assets and debts, attitudes and expectations about the future, social activities, expenditures, health, and work status and experience of the spouse, where applicable. Our research is based on the first 4 waves of data, through 1975, on a subsample of the approximately 8600 respondents who completed these 4 interviews. For more detail on this suberb data source, see Irelan (1976).

7)   From 1961 to 1977, the absolute dollar cost of living increases given to Social Security recipients who retired early, with actuarially reduced benefits, were the same as the increases to those who claimed benefits at age 65. The penalty for early retirement was therefore a constant dollar amount (which dwindled in real terms over time), not a constant percentage. One discounts a constant dollar amount with the nominal rate of interest (including an inflation component), not with the real rate used in calculating Social Security wealth. For the Social Security DELTA calculations, therefore, we use the 5 and 10 percent rates. For more detail on this issue, see Burkhauser and Turner (1981).

8)   For many workers, this is the appropriate assumption after "normal" retirement age (usually 65) has been reached. A recent estimate indicated that perhaps half the employers in the United States do not add to one´s pension or credit additional years of service after retirement age (see Bettner, 1982). Unfortunately, we do not know what rules apply to the individual RHS respondents.

9)   The method of adjusting Social Security benefits has changed substantially since 1974. The quirk in the law mentioned in footnote 7 has been eliminated and the 1 percent actuarial adjustment at age 65 has been increased to 3 percent. Both these changes reduce the disincentives to work caused by the system. On the other hand the new method of averaging benefits and the increased number of years used increases the disincentives by decreasing the impact of an additional year of earnings in the benefit calculation. See Warlick and Burkhauser (1982) for a more detailed discussion of current rules.

10) The sample used in the equations of Table 5 exclude those with mandatory retirement during the two year transition period, 1973-1975. These workers did not have a choice whether to leave that job; we analyzed the behavior of workers who did.

11) The specific question is "How would you say your health today compares with your own health two years ago? Is it better, worse or the same?" The health deterioration variable is on for those who responded "worse."

REFERENCES

Bettner, J. (1982), Will Your Pension Work Beyond 65 If You Do? Surprise - The Odds are Just 50-50 It will, Wall Street Journal, April 5.

Boskin, M.J. (1977), Social Security and Retirement Decisions, Economic Inquiry, January.

Burkhauser, R.V. (1979), The Pension Acceptance Decision of Older Workers, Journal of Human Resources.

Burkhauser, R.V. and Quinn, J.F. (1983), The Effect of Pension Plans on the Pattern of Life-Cycle Compensation, in Triplett, J. (ed.), The Measurement of Labor Cost, NBER Conference Series on Research in Income and Wealth, University of Chicago Press.

Burkhauser, R.V. and Turner, J. (1981), Can Twenty-Five Million Americans Be Wrong? A Response to Blinder, Gordon and Wise, National Tax Journal, December.

Burkhauser, R.V. and Warlick, J. (1981), Disentangling the Annuity and Redistributive Effects of Social Security, Review of Income and Wealth, December.

Burtless, G. and Hausman, J. (1980), Individual Retirement Decisions Under an Employer Provided Pension Plan and Social Security, Unpublished paper, November.

Burtless, G. and Moffitt, R. (1981), Social Security and the Retirement Decision: A Graphical Analysis, Unpublished paper, December.

Campbell, C.D. and Campbell, R.G. (1976), Conflicting Views on the Effect of Old-Age and Survivors´ Insurance on Retirement, Economic Inquiry, September.

Clark, R., Kreps, J. and Spengler, J. (1978), Economics of Aging: A Survey, Journal of Economic Literature, September.

Danzinger, S., Haveman, R. and Plotnick, R. (1981), How Income Transfers Affect Work, Savings, and the Income Distribution, Journal of Economic Literature, September.

Feldstein, M. (1974), Social Security, Induced Retirement, and Aggregate Capital Accumulation, Journal of Political Economy, October.

Gordon, R.H. and Blinder, A.S. (1980), Market Wages, Reservation Wages, and Retirement Decisions, Journal of Public Economics, October.

Gustman, A. and Steinmeier, T. (1981), Partial Retirement and the Analysis of Retirement Behavior, unpublished paper, Dartmouth College, April.

Hamermesh, D.S. (1981), A General Empirical Model of Life-Cycle Effects in Consumption and Retirement Decisions, unpublished paper, Michigan State University, June.

Hurd, M.D., and Boskin, M.J. (1981), The Effect of Social Security on Retirement, NBER Working Paper No. 659, April.

Irelan, L.M. (1976), Retirement History Study: Introduction, in Almost 65: Baseline Data from the Retirement History Study, Social Security Administration, Office of Research and Statistics, Research Report No. 49, Government Printing Office, Washington, D.C.

Kotlikoff, L.J. (1979), Testing the Theory of Social Security and Life-Cycle Accumulation, American Economic Review, June.

Mitchell, O.S. and Fields, G.S. (1982), The Effects of Pensions and Earnings on Retirement: A Review Essay, in Ehrenberg, R. (ed.), Research for Labor Economics, JAI Press.

Pellechio, A.J. (1978), The Effect of Social Security on Retirement, NBER Working Paper No. 260.

Quinn, J.F. (1982), Compensation in the Public Sector: The Importance of Pensions, in Haveman, R. (ed.), Public Finance and Public Employment, Wayne State Press.

Quinn, J.F. (1983), The Importance of Pension and Social Security Rights in the Wealth Portfolios of Older Workers, in Garbacz, C. (ed.), Economic Resources for the Elderly: Prospects for the Future, Westview Press.

Quinn, J.F. (1977), The Microeconomic Determinants of Early Retirement: A Cross-Section View of White Married Men, Journal of Human Resources, Summer.

U.S. President, (1981), Employment and Training Report of the President, 1981, Government Printing Office, Washington, D.C.

Urban Institute (1982), Financial Retirement Incentives in Private Pension Plans, Report to the U.S. Department of Labor (Contract No. J-9-P-0-0163), January.

Warlick, J.L., and Burkhauser, R.V. (1982), Raising the Normal Retirement Age Under Social Security: A Life-Cycle Analysis, Conference on Social Accounting for Transfers NBER, Madison, WI, May 14.

ARNE RYDE SYMPOSIUM ON SOCIAL INSURANCE
L. Söderström (editor)
© Elsevier Science Publishers B.V. (North-Holland), 1983

INFLATIONARY EFFECTS OF UNEMPLOYMENT INSURANCE
- AN INTERNATIONAL SURVEY

Peder J. Pedersen*

1. INTRODUCTION

Much of the recent debate on disincentive effects from UI has concerned the question of induced unemployment and UI effects on participation rates.[1] In this literature the question of an UI effect on wages appears only in an indirect way. It is a standard result in search models that, for exapmple, an increase in the benefit-wage ratio induces an increase in the acceptance wage of an unemployed searcher. The main interest, though, has been the resulting longer periods of search unemployment, not the wage effect. Contract theory has been used to explain the existence of temporary layoffs in UI systems without perfect experience rating.[2] In this line of theory UI has no inflationary effects on wages. On the contrary, a main point in this type of models is the stickiness of wages.

There have been hints in the literature and claims in the public debate that more generous UI systems in recent years have had an inflationary effect. The purpose of this paper is to explore whether this has actually been the case. A UI system contains a number of parameters but practical considerations restrict the empirical section below to use of the benefit-wage ratio as a catch all variable. Section 2 presents some rather weak theoretical reasons to expect an inflationary effect. In Section 3 the data are briefly discussed. They consist of two sets of benefit-wage ratios for a number of OECD countries. One set has been collected from the literature and is mainly maximal or marginal benefit-wage ratios in the sense that benefits are computed for eligible workers. The other set is computed from ILO data on total benefit expenditures. The implicit benefit-wage ratios calculated from these data are interpreted as average ratios catching the effects of variations in coverage, eligibility rules, waiting periods and maximum benefit duration. The main contents of Section 4 are the results from expanding standard Phillips curves with the two types of benefit-wage ratios mentioned above. Finally some concluding comments are found in Section 5.

2. THEORETICAL ELEMENTS

The potential inflationary effects of UI can be related to a number of different theoretical approaches. One obvious possibility is an expanded
version of the standard, non-accelerationist, Phillips curve.[3] The expansion in this case consists of the inclusion of UI-variables in a standard
Phillips curve. We take as a point of departure the partial equilibrium
model used by Spindler and Maki (1979) to illustrate UI effects on the registered rate of unemployment, cf. Figure 1. Spindler and Maki make a
distinction between effective and apparent supply of labour. Effective supply, S_E, is taken to be a function of disposable wage income, net of UI
contributions, while apparent supply, S_A, is determined by expected disposable income, i.e. wage income + UI benefits during spells of unemployment.
Effective demand, D_E, is a function of labour costs net of employer contributions to UI. Initially it is assumed that D_E and S_E "clear" the market at
the wage rate w. At the initial value of the benefit-wage ratio this is
accompanied by a registered unemployment of the magnitude ab all of which
is UI induced. An increase in the benefit level means a shifting to the
right of S_A to S_A' and a shift to the left of S_E to S_E' as an increase is
assumed to be followed by increased contributions. At the same time D_E is
shifted to the left to D_E' as employers too have to contribute more.[4] The
alleged effect of the increase in the benefit-wage ratio is thus an in-

Figure 1. Effect of An Increase in UI Benefits

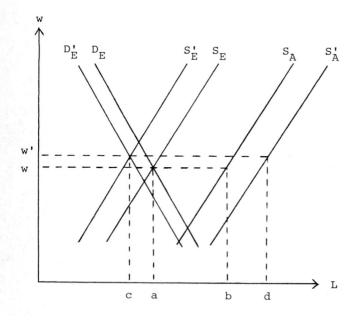

crease in the number of registered unemployed to cd. The effect on the wage level is normally neglected in empirical studies using this approach to UI induced unemployment.[5] It is seen from Figure 1 that the supply wage rises and the demand wage falls. We are consequently not able to predict whether the wage rate is going to fall or rise. To make sure that the wage rate will rise we must assume either that employers do not contribute (at least marginally) to UI or that increased employer contributions are neutralized by effects on aggregate demand from higher UI benfits. In the case that the new equilibrium wage rate is higher the immediate effect from higher benefits is to create a situation with excess demand ($D\bar{E}>S\bar{E}$ at the going wage rate). The Spindler-Maki analysis can then be related to Lipsey´s (1960) classical analysis of the theoretical foundations of the standard Phillips curve. In Lipsey the rate of change of wages is a function of relative excess demand. Excess demand for labour is assumed to be functionally related to the registered rate of unemployment resulting in the standard Phillips curve. Introduction of UI complicates matters as the registered rate of unemployment now is influenced both by standard demand and supply factors ($(S_E-D_E)/S_E$) and by UI ($(S_A-S_E)/S_E$). An increase in the benefit-wage ratio will shift the Phillips curve to the right if we assume that the change in induced unemployment dominates the change in "effective" unemployment.

Another approach is founded in search theory. Mortensen (1970) derives a Phillips relationship where the rate of change of wages, besides the rate of unemployment, changes in the rate of unemployment and the expected rate of inflation, is determined by the average probability per period of an unemployed worker finding a job. This probability is determined among other things by the benefit-wage ratio through the influence from this ratio on the level of the acceptance wage. An increase in the benefit-wage ratio decreases the probability of locating a job leading in Mortensen´s model to an increase in the rate of change in wages as long as the economy is out of long run equilibrium at the natural rate of unemployment.

Blomgren-Hansen and Knøsgaard (1980) use a simple search model with the purpose of testing empirically whether UI has an inflationary impact. It is assumed that an unemployed worker knows the normal wage for his type of skills and the rate of unemployment in his local labour market. It is further assumed that the unemployed worker maximizes the expected utility of his income one period ahead

$$E(U) = f(w,u)U(w) + (1 - f(w,u))U(d) \qquad (1)$$

where w and d are his reservation wage and unemployment benefits relative to the normal wage. The probability of finding an acceptable job is assumed to be a function f(w,u) of his reservation wage and the relevant unemployment rate. Maximizing (1) with respect to w yields

$$U´(w)/(U(w) - U(d)) = -f_w´(u,w)/f(u,w) \qquad (2)$$

determining the optimal reservation wage. To make (2) operational, specific assumptions must be made about the utility function and the probability function. Blomgren-Hansen and Knøsgaard choose a logarithmic utility function[6] and specify the probability function as

$$F(u,w) = (1 - u)^{w^k} \qquad (3)$$

This specification is arbitrary but it is argued that (3) has a number of desirable a priori qualities.

Inserting (3) and a logarithmic utility function in (2) and isolating lnw
gives the fundamental estimation equation[7]

$$\ln w = -\frac{1}{k}\ln k - \frac{1}{k}\ln u - \frac{1}{k}\ln(\ln(w/d)) \tag{4}$$

With semi-annual Danish data for the period 1957-78 a significant effect is
found from d to w. The relationship between the rate of change in wages and
the benefit-wage level implied by (4) can be found by differentiating

$$\dot{w} = -\frac{1}{k}\dot{u} - \frac{1}{k}(\ln(\dot{w}/d)) \tag{5}$$

i.e. the rate of change in wages is a function of the relative change in
unemployment and the relative change in the logarithm to the inverse benefit-wage ratio.

Quite another approach to the question of an inflationary impact from UI is
the potential effect on temporary layoff unemployment. UI without full experience rating subsidizes temporary layoffs as a way of smoothing the effects of random shifts in sales.[8] In contract theory UI has been used to
rationalize temporary layoffs and sticky wages at the firm level. On the
aggregate level the story might be different. Increased use of temporary
layoffs at the firm level increases the pools of labour attached to firms
at a given average level of aggregate production. This is the same as a reduction of supply in the "open" labour market which most probably leads to
an increase in the wage level affecting also the "closed" pools of attached
labour. Burdett and Mortensen (1980) integrate search and contract theory
in a model which has an interesting result in relation to the problem considered here. Both in search theory and contract theory considered in
isolation the effect on registered unemployment from higher UI benefits is
an increase. In the integrated model the total effect on unemployment is
indeterminate whereas the effect on the wage level is positive.

In both these cases higher benefits have a positive effect on the equilibrium level of wages. The arguments for an effect on the rate of change in
wages are the same as in the Spindler-Maki case, i.e. the effect is only
present as long as the economy is out of equilibrium.

A final possible mechanism of an inflationary impact could be called the
fact of overlapping distributions. The distributions are respectively of
benefits and of wages. As long as the benefit-wage ratio is low none or
only few persons have benefits higher than anybody´s wage-income. As the
ratio increases the area of overlapping increases too. In other words there
is an increase in the number of people who experience that their pay from a
full-time job falls short of the unemployed neighbour´s benefits. If altru-
ism is in short supply this might induce a cost push inflation. Another
possible effect from overlapping distributions[9] is that the main impact on
unemployment from an increase in the benefit-wage ratio is a composition
and not a size effect, i.e. that it has an effect on who becomes unemployed
but not on the total stock of unemployed persons. A side effect of this
would be that part of measured wage increases reflects increase in average
productivity among those who stay in employment.

None of the approaches discussed in this section provide a solid theoretical basis for an inflationary impact from the benefit-wage ratio to the
rate of change in wages. The main impact - in equilibrium - seems to run

from changes in the level of benefits to changes in the level of wages. An impact from the level or from changes in the benefit level on the rate of change in wages is consequently a disequilibrium effect. Because of the weak theoretical foundations of an inflationary impact the main motivation of the empirical sections below is to test the inflationary claims made in public debates with a number of rather ad-hoc specifications. Both the level and changes in the benefit-wage ratio are tried as explanatory variables in wage-change relations.

3. BENEFIT-WAGE RATIOS IN OECD COUNTRIES

As mentioned in the introduction, two sets of benefit-wage ratios are used. Table 1 shows a set of marginal or maximum benefit-wage ratios for a number of countries. A more detailed description of sources and methods is given in the notes to Table 1. They are mainly computed as benefits due to an eligible worker relative to average wages in industry. In some cases a crude tax-correction has been performed to make comparisons possible between countries with different tax treatment of UI benefits. Also some countries have made benefits taxable at some point of time in the period under consideration making a tax-correction necessary.[10] The unweighted average of the benefit-wage ratios for the years where observations exist for all the countries in Table 1 shows near constancy until 1966 followed by an increase of about 10 percentage points from 1967 to 1973. The greatest increase occurs in Great Britain where the level of the benefit-wage ratio nearly doubles.[11] The other extreme is Sweden where the ratio falls by 10 percentage points from 1957 to 1973.[12] For the rest of the countries the increase is moderate and the ranking about the same in 1973 as in 1957.

In Table 2 a set of average benefit-wage ratios is shown. They are mostly calculated as actual benefits paid out per unemployed[13] relative to average wages in industry. As in Table 1 a crude tax-correction has been performed in a number of cases for countries where benefits are tax-free and for countries where the tax-status of benefits has changed under the period. A more detailed description is found in the notes to Table 2. The idea behind this set of directly calculated ratios is that changes in UI coverage, in eligibility demands, in waiting periods etc. might more or less invalidate the "imputed" ratios in Table 1. Furthermore, Table 2 brings estimates for a number of countries not found in Table 1.[14] The overall impression from Table 2 is the same as from Table 1, i.e. great variation between countries.[15] and an increasing average benefit-wage ratio from the mid sixties to the beginning of the seventies.

Two further points should be noted. First if we compare the series for countries appearing in both tables some striking differences occur. For Canada, the series track each other quite well until the 1971-reform after which the average benefit-wage ratio (BA) jumps up significantly more than the marginal (BM2). In Italy a difference of the same type is seen for the first years of the period. The most striking difference though is found for Great Britain. This is obviously of some interest as quite a number of studies of the hypothesis of UI induced unemployment have been performed with British data.[16] The difference between the DM-series and the DA1-series (Sawyer, 1979) stems from the fact that Sawyer uses National assistance + 20% for rent paid as a more attractive alternative than flat rate UI benefit up to 1966. The consequence of this is to smooth out the violent jump in the BM-series following the introduction of earnings related supplementary benefits in 1966. The other - more dramatic - difference is be-

Table 1. Marginal Benefit-Wage Ratios for Unemployed Workers (BM)

Country	A	B	C		EI	D	H	I	S	UK		US	Average[1]
Year			1	2						1	2		(un-weighted)
1950	21.6	–	31.4	–	–	39.2	–	–	–	–	–	–	–
1951	17.6	–	29.3	–	–	41.9	–	–	–	–	–	–	–
1952	30.6	–	30.1	–	–	39.6	57.3	–	–	37.4	–	–	–
1953	29.1	–	31.5	34.5	–	43.8	57.4	–	–	40.9	43.6	37.7	–
1954	27.7	53.0	31.2	34.2	23.6	40.7	54.8	–	–	38.6	40.5	38.8	–
1955	25.9	51.9	30.3	33.1	25.8	37.3	56.1	35.9	–	37.3	43.7	37.3	–
1956	24.7	51.2	29.2	32.0	24.6	39.9	56.2	31.9	–	38.8	41.2	39.0	–
1957	31.0	51.8	30.8	33.9	24.1	44.0	56.1	28.2	58.8	36.7	39.2	39.4	40.4
1958	30.1	53.9	30.2	32.9	23.4	46.2	58.5	30.3	57.5	37.6	46.6	41.4	41.2
1959	27.9	61.4	28.8	31.5	22.5	45.8	59.6	28.4	55.0	43.5	46.0	39.6	41.5
1960	26.6	59.7	29.4	32.5	21.8	45.1	57.7	30.4	56.3	41.3	42.9	40.1	41.2
1961	29.7	57.8	30.5	33.7	23.9	45.2	51.7	34.4	55.0	40.7	47.6	42.2	41.4
1962	32.5	59.7	30.0	33.1	23.5	45.4	50.4	35.8	52.5	44.1	46.5	41.9	41.9
1963	30.9	58.9	29.3	32.4	26.0	44.9	51.3	37.4	50.0	44.1	51.1	41.6	41.8
1964	28.8	54.8	28.4	31.7	26.9	43.2	50.7	35.1	47.5	46.7	47.8	40.1	40.6
1965	27.6	55.2	27.0	30.2	26.3	41.5	54.8	31.3	50.0	45.7	52.6	40.2	40.3
1966	25.9	54.5	25.5	29.1	28.7	43.4	58.4	29.5	51.3	54.1	73.5	40.9	41.6
1967	24.4	55.5	24.7	28.9	28.5	49.3	66.4	32.1	53.8	69.7	78.0	41.1	45.0
1968	22.9	53.8	24.2	28.4	29.6	51.8	68.4	32.2	53.8	73.1	75.6	42.8	45.7
1969	26.2	53.0	27.2	32.5	30.7	52.0	69.1	33.0	57.5	72.4	73.3	43.1	47.0
1970	24.3	48.9	27.7	33.6	31.5	50.2	70.3	32.1	53.8	71.4	73.5	44.1	46.0
1971	25.8	47.8	28.6	34.8	31.8	49.3	70.1	32.6	51.3	73.9	79.9	44.4	46.2
1972	37.6	59.5	41.3	41.3	31.6	49.3	72.6	33.3	52.5	76.6	74.9	45.8	50.0
1973	38.6	58.1	42.7	42.7	32.9	48.5	72.7	31.8	48.8	72.9	70.1	45.1	49.2
1974	42.6	57.4	42.1	42.1	40.2	47.8	–	36.6	46.3	70.5	69.2	47.2	–
1975	–	–	–	–	50.7	51.2	–	–	–	69.5	–	–	–

Notes: <u>Australia</u> (A) Benefit for a married man with one child relative to average earnings. Holden & Peel (1979, Table 6, p. 614). <u>Belgium</u> (B) Average daily unemployment compensation relative to average daily wage net of taxes. Holder & Peel (1979). <u>Canada</u> (C) (1) Average weekly benefit payments to insured persons relative to gross average weekly earnings. Holden & Peel (1979). (2) Column (1) corrected for taxes. Benefits were taxable from 1972. For the years 1953-1971 the numbers in column (1) have been divided by (1-t) where t = (direct taxes on income + direct taxes not elsewhere classified + social security contributions)/current receipts of households. t is calculated from OECD National Account Statistics. <u>Ireland</u> (EI) Weighted average of unemployment compensation relative to average net earnings. Walsh (Grubel & Walker (eds.), 1978, Table A2, p. 196). <u>Germany</u> (D) Average unemployment compensation relative to average weekly wages net of taxes. König & Franz (Grubel & Walker (eds.), 1978, App. B, p. 259). <u>Netherlands</u> (H) Average weekly unemployment benefits relative to gross weekly earnings of male workers in industry over 24 years with two children. (Benefits are taxable in the Netherlands). Holden & Peel (1979). <u>Italy</u> (I) Unemployment benefits relative to gross income. Holden & Peel (1979). Primary source is the Italian Embassy, London. No detailed information is given on the principles of the calculation. <u>Sweden</u> (S). Average benefit per day relative to average wage per hour for male workers in industry. Ståhl (Grubel & Walker (eds.), 1978, Table E, p. 141). In Table 1 Ståhl´s series has been corrected for the introduction of taxation of benefits in 1974 by dividing through with (1-t) for the years 1957-1973. For t see the note on Canada. Furthermore Ståhl´s series is transformed to the usual format for a benefit-wage ratio by assuming an 8 hours´ working day for the whole period. <u>United Kingdom</u> (UK) (1) Standard rate of benefit plus earnings related supplementary benefit relative to average earnings net of taxes for a married man with two children. Spindler & Maki (1979, pp. 163-64). (2) Unemployment benefits and family allowances to a married man with two children relative to gross average weekly earnings + family allowances. Holden & Peel (1979). Corrected for taxes, cf. Canada. <u>USA</u> (US) Average weekly benefit check relative to average weekly wages. Holden & Peel (1979). In Table 1 the series has been corrected for taxes by dividing through with (1-t). For t see the note on Canada.

1. Exclusive of C(1) and UK(2).

232 P.J. Pedersen

Table 2. Average Benefit-Wage Ratios (BA)

Country	A	C	DK		I	J	N	Ö	S	UK		US	Average[1]
Year			1	2						1	2		(un-weighted)
1950	-	-	-	43.4	-	-	-	-	-	47.7	-	-	-
1951	-	-	-	40.4	-	-	-	-	-	47.3	-	-	-
1952	-	-	-	40.6	-	-	-	-	-	54.3	-	-	-
1953	-	-	-	42.4	-	-	-	-	-	54.5	-	-	-
1954	-	-	-	44.0	-	-	-	-	-	51.3	-	-	-
1955	-	-	-	41.5	-	-	-	-	-	49.8	-	-	-
1956	-	44.0	52.7	40.8	-	-	-	-	-	49.9	-	22.1	-
1957	30.8	39.8	53.2	39.4	-	43.3	-	50.9	65.1	48.4	-	24.5	-
1958	30.8	38.5	48.5	44.2	12.8	41.8	-	44.3	39.7	51.2	22.7	25.6	-
1959	29.0	35.8	48.0	40.1	15.4	40.6	-	44.2	59.2	51.8	19.3	20.6	-
1960	18.8	34.2	49.1	40.8	20.1	41.8	-	43.7	60.5	53.8	17.3	25.2	-
1961	33.0	32.5	46.0	40.7	30.7	44.5	49.1	45.2	52.7	53.9	19.3	23.0	36.3
1962	32.0	31.3	49.7	39.0	29.4	46.0	47.1	51.6	53.4	54.0	21.6	19.7	36.2
1963	31.4	30.0	49.2	41.7	26.0	47.7	41.7	51.7	46.2	56.7	22.2	18.3	34.7
1964	22.8	30.4	48.4	41.8	24.7	48.2	38.3	49.0	41.0	54.7	19.5	16.8	32.3
1965	27.4	29.8	49.9	41.3	27.3	48.8	39.3	54.9	50.8	60.1	24.1	15.5	34.8
1966	28.0	28.8	49.6	42.4	19.5	49.5	43.2	50.8	46.2	59.8	36.5	17.9	35.2
1967	27.1	28.8	68.2	42.9	18.6	48.3	49.1	48.9	65.1	68.7	33.1	17.7	37.0
1968	21.3	28.5	66.6	58.8	31.6	47.3	47.1	49.6	65.1	72.6	33.1	18.3	39.1
1969	16.9	30.6	68.9	60.0	20.4	45.8	48.1	53.0	59.2	72.4	28.6	19.4	37.1
1970	20.3	30.0	73.1	60.9	18.9	42.2	56.0	54.6	74.2	74.1	17.7	23.9	39.7
1971	33.6	39.8	83.8	63.6	36.0	43.0	53.0	63.5	71.0	70.1	27.0	24.5	44.1
1972	49.9	56.5	92.4	68.6	25.1	42.9	52.0	63.2	54.7	71.8	24.1	19.0	44.2
1973	52.7	53.5	96.4	73.1	29.1	40.9	55.5	75.0	48.2	-	23.4	19.9	45.4
1974	-	-	-	74.9	42.5	-	52.0	109.4	49.5	-	-	-	-
1975	-	-	-	73.4	-	-	-	-	-	-	-	-	-

Notes: General description. Total benefits (for most of the series) are from ILO. The Cost of Social Security (Geneva, 1979, 1976, 1972, 1967, 1964, 1961). The number of unemployed is from ILO. Yearbook of Labour Statistics (different years). A measure of benefits paid per unemployed is found by division. In a number of cases breaks in the unemployment series necessitate an index linking. Average wages in industry are from ILO. Yearbook of Labour Statistics. The benefit-wage ratio is found as benefits paid per unemployed relative to average wages. Country notes. Australia (A) Total benefits. ILO. Unemployed benefit receivers 1957-1967. From 1968-1973 number of unemployed from sample surveys. Average hourly wages for males. 1920 working hours assumed per year. Canada (C) Total benefits. ILO. Unemployment from sample surveys. Average weekly earnings in industry. 48 benefit weeks assumed per year. Tax-corrected, cf. note to Table 1. Denmark (DK). (1) Average weekly benefits paid out relative to average weekly wages in industry. (2) Total benefits. ILO. Number of insured unemployed. Average hourly wages in industry net of a number of additions to wages. 1920 working hours assumed per year. Italy (I). Total benefits. ILO. Number of unemployed from sample surveys. Hourly wages in industry. Tax-corrected. 1920 working hours assumed per year. Japan (J) Total benefits. ILO. Number of unemployment beneficiaries. Monthly wages in industry. Tax-corrected. 12 benefit months assumed per year. Norway (N). Total benefits. ILO. Number of registered unemployed. Average hourly wages for males in industry. Tax-corrected. 1920 working hours assumed per year. Austria (Ö). Total benefits. ILO. Number of unemployed from Employment Office Statistics. Average monthly wages in industry. 12 benefit months assumed per year. Tax corrected. Sweden (S). Total benefits. ILO. Number of insured unemployed. Average hourly wages in industry. Tax-corrected. 1920 working hours assumed per year. United Kingdom (UK). (1) 1953-1966 National assistance plus 20% for rent paid relative to average earnings net of taxes for a married man with two children. 1967-1972 in principle calculated as UK (1) in Table 1. Sawyer (1979, p. 139). (2) Total benefits. ILO. Number of registered wholly unemployed. Average weekly wages for males in industry. Tax-corrected. 48 benefit weeks assumed per year. USA. Total benefits. ILO. Number of uenmployed from sample surveys. Average weekly wages in industry. Tax-corrected. 48 benefit weeks assumed per year.

1. Exclusive of DK(1) and UK(1).

tween the BM-series and the BA2-series, cf. Table 2. BA2 is based on ILO data on total benefits paid relative to the number of registered wholly unemployed. Not only is the level much lower than for BM, but the profile over time is quite different as the increase in 1966 is followed by a decline in the following years to a level not very different from that prevailing at the beginning of the period.[17] The difference on the level most probably reflects the fact that only part of the registered unemployed receive National insurance benefits, cf. Atkinson and Flemming (1978, p. 81) showing that only 42% of the registered unemployed were receiving National insurance benefits in November 1977. Furthermore, this proportion has been declining. In 1968 well over 50% were receiving Unemployment Benefits while only 38% did so in 1978. Over the same period the proportion of the unemployed receiving only Supplementary Benefits increased from around 25% to over 40% (Disney, 1981, p. 170). Finally for the USA one notes that the increasing trend in BM is not found in the BA-series showing a constant/declining level over time.

The other point to note from Tables 1 and 2 is the obvious fact that a quasi-constant benefit-wage ratio is a bad candidate as a contributor in explaining variations in the rate of wage increases. Italy, Japan[18] and Norway are clearly suspect cases on this score. Belgium, Germany, Great Britain and USA are "dubious" cases. In Belgium and Germany the series show some changes over time but no clear trend. For Great Britain and USA the trouble is the lack of consistency between the BM and the BA-series.

4. SOME EMPIRICAL RESULTS

It is not a priori clear whether BM or BA is to be preferred as UI variable.[19] In this section both are tried in a number of relations. At a more disaggregate level one could argue that the relevant benefit-wage ratio is the one going to key groups in the labour market. If this is a sound argument BM is probably the most relevant of our macro ratios. On the other hand a great discrepancy between BM and BA could be interpreted as a situation of competitive pressure on the supply side of the labour market. This could be the case if the discrepancy reflected strict eligibility rules making for intensive job search among non-eligible unemployed. This argument points to BA as the most relevant variable.

Table 3 shows the results of expanding a standard, linear,[20] non-accelerationist Phillips curve with the benefit-wage ratio as a supplementary variable to the rate of unemployment and the rate of increase in consumer prices. The regressions in Table 3 are run on the whole period for which data are available in the different countries. Table 4 presents the same regressions run for comparable periods on the same countries as in Table 3. The immediate impression from Table 3 is a strong denial of the inflationary impact hypothesis. Only for Denmark is a strongly significant positive coefficient found to the benefit-wage ratio. For Austria the coefficient approaches positive significance at the 5% level. It appears from Table 3 that many of the regressions are influenced by multicollinearity. This is predominantly a collinearity between the constant term and the coefficient to the benefit-wage ratio which is not very surprising as a number of the benefit-wage series is near constant, cf. the discussion in Section 3. Again in Table 4 a significantly positive coefficient is found for Denmark. Positive coefficients approaching significance at the 5% level are found for the Netherlands, and with some good will, for Belgium and USA (BM). Again the regressions are influenced by collinearity mainly between the constant term and the coefficient to the benefit-wage ratio.

Experimenting with lagged values of the benefit-wage ratio does not change the picture emerging from Tables 3 and 4. The same is true when the rate of unemployment is excluded for the countries for which no significant impact is found from this variable in estimates of the standard Phillips curve.[21]

Finally, as an attempt to reduce simultaneity problems the rate of change in import prices was tried as a substitute for consumer prices. Significantly positive coefficients to the benefit-wage ratio were found for Australia (BA), Canada, Denmark, Ireland, Austria and the USA (BM). But the presence of quite strong autocorrelation in many of the relations renders the results somewhat dubious.

A number of experiments have been performed to probe a little more deeply into the relationship between the rate of unemployment and the benefit-wage ratio. This has implications for the Phillips curve approach used here but at the same time it throws some light on the debate on UI induced unemployment with an international data set.[22] A relationship where the benefit-wage ratio is used as left hand side variable and the rate of unemployment and a time trend as explanatory variables is dominated by significantly positive coefficients. But the regressions of this relation are so heavily influenced by collinearity and autocorrelation that no firm conclusions can be drawn. Instead an Okun-type relation is tried where changes in unemployment are explained by current and one year lagged values of the rate of change in real GNP and by the change (in percentage-points) in the benefit-wage ratio. Compared with the relations hitherto used in macro tests of the induced unemployment hypothesis the relationship used here lacks a labour supply variable. On the other hand the discussion of recent British results[23] seems to indicate that a supply variable introduces one extra trend dominated variable in a macro-relationship already heavily influenced by strong trends in the variables.[24]

Table 5 shows the results from regressions on the relationship

$$\Delta U_t = \alpha_0 + \alpha_1 \dot{GNP}_t + \alpha_2 \dot{GNP}_{t-1} + \alpha_3 \Delta BM_t (\Delta BA_t) + \varepsilon_t \qquad (6)$$

Induced unemployment does not seem to be supported strongly by the results.[25] For Australia, Belgium, Ireland, the Netherlands and USA we get significantly positive coefficients to changes in the benefit-wage ratio. In the light of recent debates it is interesting to note that no effect is found for Great Britain with either of the benefit-wage ratios. The significantly negative coefficient for Norway presumably reflects the fact that this country has been blessed with full employment in the regression period. The only strong result from Tables 3 and 4, for Denmark, does not seem to be influenced by induced unemployment.

Instead of entering the change in the benefit-wage ratio as in (6) the level could be used. The hypothesis in this case would be that the outflow from the unemployment register is lower as the level of the benefit-wage ratio is higher. With the same countries and periods as in Table 5 the results from testing this hypothesis are utterly negative. Ireland is the only country for which a significantly positive coefficient is found for BM.

Referring to the discussion in Section 2 it is not a priori clear in which dimension the benefit-wage ratio should be entered in the Phillips curve. A

Table 3. Benefit-Wage Ratio in Standard Phillips Curve. (Maximum Periods).
(Dependent variable: rate of increase in average hourly wage in industry).

Country	Period	Constant	BM	U	$\dot{p}$	$\overline{R}^2$	DW	F	mc
A	1950–71	0.54 (0.2)	-0.07 (-0.6)	1.11 (1.6)	1.23 (10.2)	.84	1.68	++	+
B	1954–74	5.49 (1.0)	0.04 (0.4)	-1.48 (-3.3)	1.28 (9.0)	.88	1.51	++	++
C¹	1953–74	3.41 (1.1)	0.04 (0.4)	-0.38 (-1.3)	0.99 (6.0)	.73	1.26	++	+
EI	1954–75	4.60 (0.7)	0.10 (0.3)	-0.77 (-1.0)	1.28 (3.4)	.86	2.08	++	+
D	1950–75	13.30 (2.0)	-0.14 (-1.0)	-0.27 (-1.1)	0.76 (4.1)	.41	1.20	++	++
H	1952–73	8.27 (1.3)	-0.00 (-0.0)	-1.94 (-1.6)	1.14 (3.3)	.54	2.18	++	+
I	1955–74	-0.74 (-0.1)	0.32 (0.8)	-1.00 (-1.7)	1.06 (4.6)	.69	1.35	++	++
S	1957–74	11.49 (1.6)	-0.06 (-0.4)	-1.39 (-1.2)	0.61 (2.9)	.45	1.62	++	++
UK²	1952–75	1.52 (0.8)	0.04 (0.8)	0.13 (0.1)	0.96 (7.3)	.83	1.87	++	++
US	1953–74	0.22 (0.0)	0.16 (1.1)	-0.70 (-3.2)	0.45 (3.0)	.75	1.31	++	++

Country	Period	Constant		BA		U		$\dot{p}$		$\bar{R}^2$	DW	F	mc
A	1957–73	0.40	(0.2)	0.08	(1.1)	-0.51	(-0.6)	1.01	(3.3)	.73	1.98	++	
C	1956–73	3.97	(1.9)	-0.01	(-0.1)	-0.20	(-0.6)	1.10	(3.9)	.53	1.24	++	
DK[3]	1948–75	-2.18	(-0.9)	0.20	(3.9)	-0.32	(-0.9)	0.59	(2.8)	.68	1.86	++	
I	1958–74	20.81	(2.3)	-0.18	(-0.9)	-3.05	(-2.0)	1.17	(4.3)	.68	1.11	++	+
J	1957–73	46.14	(2.0)	-0.64	(-1.7)	-7.96	(-1.7)	1.05	(2.0)	.64	1.38	++	++
N	1961–74	9.59	(1.1)	0.05	(0.3)	-6.03	(-1.3)	0.62	(1.9)	.52	2.12	+	+
Ø	1957–74	6.27	(1.9)	0.14	(1.8)	-1.95	(-2.1)	-0.39	(-0.5)	.61	1.63	++	+
S	1957–74	7.22	(2.8)	0.02	(0.6)	-1.75	(-1.8)	0.66	(3.7)	.45	1.75	++	+
UK[4]	1949–72	-3.34	(-0.9)	0.13	(1.4)	-0.08	(-0.1)	0.82	(3.2)	.48	1.54	++	+
UK[5]	1958–73	5.39	(1.4)	-0.18	(-1.4)	0.89	(0.6)	1.31	(3.3)	.56	2.21	++	
US	1956–73	3.11	(2.8)	-0.04	(-0.6)	-0.07	(-0.3)	0.94	(7.6)	.82	2.05	++	

Notes: 1. C – BM2. 2. UK – BM1. 3. DK – BA2. 4. UK – BA1. 5. UK – BA2.

Symbols: U, $\dot{p}$. Rate of unemployment and rate of change in implicit deflator for private consumption.

Source: E.S. Madsen & M. Paldam (1978). t-ratios in bracket. An F-value between 95% and 99% is indicated with +, while significance over the 99% level is indicated with ++. An mc-score of + indicates that at least one of the correlations between the estimated coefficients is above 0.8, while ++ indicates correlation over 0.95.

P.J. Pedersen

Table 4. Benefit-Wage Ratio in Standard Phillips Curve. (BM-regressions 1957-73, BA-regressions 1961-73).
(Dependent variable: rate of increase in average hourly wages in industry).

Country	Constant	BM	U	$\dot{p}$	$\bar{R}^2$	DW	F	mc
A	1.73 (0.5)	-0.06 (-0.4)	0.33 (0.4)	1.32 (4.7)	.70	2.16	++	+
B	-1.24 (-0.2)	0.15 (1.4)	-1.86 (-2.6)	1.61 (5.8)	.84	2.08	++	+
C[1]	3.82 (1.0)	0.02 (0.1)	-0.29 (-0.5)	1.04 (2.9)	.53	1.19	++	
EI	2.83 (0.2)	0.21 (0.6)	-0.99 (-0.9)	1.34 (3.0)	.74	1.76	++	+
D	15.24 (1.7)	-0.15 (-0.8)	-0.82 (-0.9)	0.57 (1.4)	.11	1.22		++
H	-0.48 (-0.1)	0.22 (1.8)	-4.91 (-3.3)	0.85 (2.9)	.62	1.68	++	+
I	-6.33 (-0.2)	0.41 (0.6)	-0.68 (-0.5)	1.44 (4.0)	.63	1.27	++	++
S	12.82 (1.7)	-0.09 (-0.6)	-1.39 (-1.2)	0.71 (3.0)	.42	1.92	+	++
UK[2]	1.24 (0.4)	0.01 (0.2)	0.72 (0.4)	1.12 (2.4)	.50	2.10	++	
US	-4.81 (-1.1)	0.21 (1.6)	-0.28 (-1.4)	0.69 (3.8)	.86	2.38	++	++

Country	Constant	BA	U	$\dot{p}$	$\overline{R}^2$	DW	F	mc
A	0.72 (0.3)	0.09 (0.8)	-0.55 (-0.5)	0.97 (2.3)	.70	1.86	++	
C	3.20 (1.1)	-0.00 (-0.0)	-0.03 (-0.0)	1.05 (2.5)	.46	1.09	+	
DK[3]	2.88 (0.7)	0.14 (2.2)	-1.40 (-0.8)	0.70 (1.2)	.39	2.36		
I	25.99 (1.7)	-0.05 (-0.2)	-5.87 (-1.6)	1.36 (3.1)	.54	.99	+	+
J	48.45 (1.9)	-0.72 (-1.7)	-5.26 (-0.6)	0.77 (1.2)	.36	.88		+
N	4.37 (0.7)	0.13 (1.3)	-3.03 (-1.0)	0.29 (1.3)	.51	1.96	+	+
Ø	8.66 (0.7)	0.13 (0.8)	-3.29 (-1.1)	-0.24 (-0.3)	.37	1.60		
S	6.49 (2.9)	0.04 (0.8)	-1.10 (-0.8)	0.55 (2.5)	.28	2.63		+
UK[4]	2.47 (0.6)	-0.11 (-0.8)	0.87 (0.6)	1.50 (3.4)	.65	2.84	++	+
US	2.51 (2.1)	-0.14 (-1.4)	0.35 (1.3)	1.11 (7.4)	.88	2.22	++	

Notes: 1. C – BM2. 2. UK – NM1. 3. DK – BA2. 4. UK – BA2.

Symbols and sources, see notes to Table 3. t-ratios in bracket.

P.J. Pedersen

Table 5. Effects of Changes in Benefit-Wage Ratio in the Unemployment Relationship (6).

Country	Period	α_0	α_1	α_2	$\alpha_3(\Delta BM)$	$\bar{R}^2$	DW	F	mc
A	1958-74	1.45 (2.3)	-0.14 (-1.9)	-0.16 (-2.2)	0.06 (1.1)	.33	2.30	+	+
B	1958-74	0.60 (2.1)	-0.13 (-2.6)	0.00 (0.0)	0.06 (2.0)	.46	1.19	+	
C^1	1958-74	1.86 (3.1)	-0.30 (-3.0)	-0.08 (-0.9)	0.05 (0.6)	.35	2.02	+	
EI	1958-75	-0.06 (-0.2)	0.03 (0.6)	-0.07 (-1.2)	0.20 (3.6)	.38	3.19	+	
D	1958-75	0.80 (3.5)	-0.13 (-4.7)	-0.02 (-0.8)	0.02 (0.4)	.65	1.87	++	
H	1958-73	0.56 (1.5)	-0.09 (-2.1)	-0.02 (-0.5)	0.10 (2.7)	.42	2.30	+	
I	1958-74	1.03 (2.0)	-0.08 (-1.2)	-0.15 (-1.8)	-0.07 (-1.3)	.42	.90	+	
S	1958-74	0.48 (2.0)	-0.11 (-2.8)	-0.02 (-0.4)	0.00 (0.1)	.25	1.44		
UK^2	1958-75	0.72 (2.9)	-0.16 (-3.0)	-0.08 (-1.3)	0.02 (0.9)	.42	1.61	+	
US	1958-74	0.64 (1.8)	-0.16 (-2.7)	-0.07 (-1.2)	0.34 (2.2)	.57	1.45	++	

Country	Period	α_0	α_1	α_2	$\alpha_3 (\Delta BA)$	$\bar{R}^2$	DW	F	mc
A	1958–73	1.08 (1.3)	−0.10 (−1.1)	−0.12 (−1.7)	0.06 (2.0)	.47	1.50	+	+
C	1958–73	1.96 (3.3)	−0.34 (−3.3)	−0.05 (−0.6)	0.04 (1.0)	.40	2.20	+	+
DK[3]	1958–75	1.78 (4.3)	−0.26 (−4.6)	−0.18 (−2.7)	0.02 (0.6)	.60	1.65	++	
I	1959–74	1.39 (3.0)	−0.09 (−1.4)	−0.20 (−2.7)	−0.01 (−0.6)	.42	1.12	+	
J	1958–73	0.54 (3.7)	−0.04 (−4.0)	−0.02 (−1.7)	−0.02 (−1.0)	.57	2.06	++	
N	1962–74	−0.04 (−0.1)	−0.03 (−0.8)	0.04 (1.0)	−0.03 (−2.5)	.23	1.55		
σ	1958–74	0.23 (0.7)	−0.06 (−1.3)	−0.02 (−0.3)	0.01 (1.0)	−.03	2.20		
S	1958–74	0.33 (1.3)	−0.10 (−2.7)	0.01 (0.2)	−0.01 (−1.2)	.32	1.30	+	
UK[4]	1959–73	0.67 (2.4)	−0.12 (−1.9)	−0.10 (−1.4)	−0.02 (−0.6)	.19	1.76		
US	1958–73	1.31 (3.3)	−0.23 (−3.2)	−0.14 (−2.0)	0.07 (1.0)	.49	2.14	+	

Notes: 1. C – BM2. 2. UK – BM1. 3. DK – BA2. 4. UK – BA2.

Symbols and sources, see notes to Table 3. t-ratios in bracket.

potential inflationary impact might as well stem from changes in the benefit-wage ratio as from the level of this variable. Looking, for example, at
the model in Burdett and Mortensen (1980) it is changes in the level of
benefits that induce changes in the level of wages. Taking this approach
gives significantly positive coefficients to changes in the benefit-wage
ratio for Australia and Canada. The results are shown in Table 6.[26] Both
Australia and Canada are characterized by a moderate initial level of the
benefit-wage ratio combined with a significant increase under the period.
Note that none of the countries with significantly (or near-significantly)
positive coefficients in the level-regressions of Tables 3 and 4 appear in
Table 6.

Table 6. Effects of Changes in Benefit-Wage Ratios

Country	Period	Constant	ΔBM	U	$\dot{p}$	$\bar{R}^2$	DW	F	mc
A	1957-74	2.55(1.9)	0.25(2.1)	-0.49(-0.9)	1.02(8.9)	.86	2.29	++	+

				ΔBA					
A	1958-73	2.21(1.1)	0.13(1.9)	-0.44(-0.7)	1.10(4.9)	.76	2.32	++	+
C	1957-73	5.50(3.0)	0.19(3.0)	-0.48(-1.6)	0.96(4.9)	.72	1.82	++	+

Notes: Symbols and sources, see notes to Table 3. t-ratios in brackets.

Up to now it has been assumed that a possible inflationary impact is independent of the level of unemployment. Marston (1975) concludes that the
disincentive and inflationary effects of UI increase with the rate of unemployment. A liberal or generous UI reduces the number of discouraged
workers as unemployment increases making it rational to stay in the labour
force at least for the maximum duration of benefits. The inflation reducing
effect of an increasing rate of unemployment might be absent or weakened as
high benefit-wage ratio and/or long benefit duration makes for high and
slowly declining reservation wages. Okun comments (1975) that Marston´s two
points go against each other. Keeping more people attached to the labour
force will weaken the inflationary impact. Okun´s point seems to depend on
whether those who stay on in the labour force instead of retiring as discouraged workers are actively looking for jobs or choose - rationally - UI
benefits instead of a less attractive early pension scheme. If the latter
is the case, Marston´s two points can be kept separate.

Marston´s point has been tried with the following specification

$$\dot{w} = \alpha_0 + \alpha_1(U \times (1 - B)) + \alpha_2\dot{p} \qquad (7)$$

The marginal impact of an increase in the benefit-wage ratio increases with
U and the marginal impact of an increase in U decreases with increases in
B. No strong effects are found in regressions on (7).[27] Significantly nega-
tive estimates of α_1 are found for Belgium, the Netherlands, Italy,
Austria, Sweden and USA. But except for Italy either U or B both are
already found to have significant coefficients in Table 4. Furthermore re-

gressions on (7) do not lead to significant increases in $\bar{R}^2$ compared with the results in Table 4.

An alternative approach to single country time series regressions would be to estimate cross-country models. Some examples are given below. The cross-country approach is seemingly attractive but gives rise to a number of problems. Assume we have a data set for N countries in T years consisting, in the most simple case, of one dependent variable y_{it} and one explanatory variable x_{it} ($i = 1, \ldots, N$ and $t = 1, \ldots, T$). In the single country time series model used above we estimate the relation $y_{it} = \beta_{0i} + \beta_{1i}x_{it}$, i.e. the coefficients are assumed constant over time but different between countries. In a cross-country approach one could postulate either the relation $y_{it} = \beta_{0t} + \beta_{1t}x_{it}$ or the relation $y_{it} = \beta_0 + \beta_1 x_{it}$. In the first case the structure is assumed to be the same across countries but changing over time. In the second case the pooled time series-cross-section approach assumes the structure to be the same both across countries and over time.[28]

Both cross-country approaches are theoretically more ambitious than the time series approach as they assume the same structure in the labour markets of quite different countries.[29] Further, even though great care has been taken to make variables comparable across countries, it is inevitable that differences in the methods of measurement - especially for the rate of unemployment and the benefit-wage ratio - will distort the results in cross-country approaches.[30]

With those reservations in mind, Table 7 reports the results from a number

Table 7. Regressions on Country-Average Values

	$\bar{R}^2$	DW
$\dot{w} = 0.79 - 0.15U + 1.80\dot{p} + 0.02BM$ $(0.2)\ (-0.3)\ (2.6)\ (0.3)$	0.35	1.50
$\dot{w} = 1.80 - 0.26U + 1.91\dot{p} - 0.03\Delta BM$ $(0.6)\ (-0.8)\ (2.7)\ (-0.5)$	0.37	1.55
$\dot{w} = -7.12 + 0.68U + 2.89\dot{p} + 0.04BA$ $(-1.5)\ (1.2)\ (4.1)\ (0.9)$	0.75	2.21
$\dot{w} = -4.82 + 0.45U + 2.88\dot{p} - 0.01\Delta BA$ $(-1.1)\ (0.8)\ (3.8)\ (-0.1)$	0.72	1.95
$U = 10.3 - 0.66G\dot{N}P - 0.10BM$ $(4.2)\ (-1.6)\ (-3.1)$	0.50	1.69
$U = 5.46 - 0.03G\dot{N}P - 0.07BA$ $(3.5)\ (-0.2)\ (-2.2)$	0.25	2.39

Note: In regressions with BM or ΔBM country averages for 1957-73 are used. In regressions with BA or ΔBA country averages for 1961-73 are used.

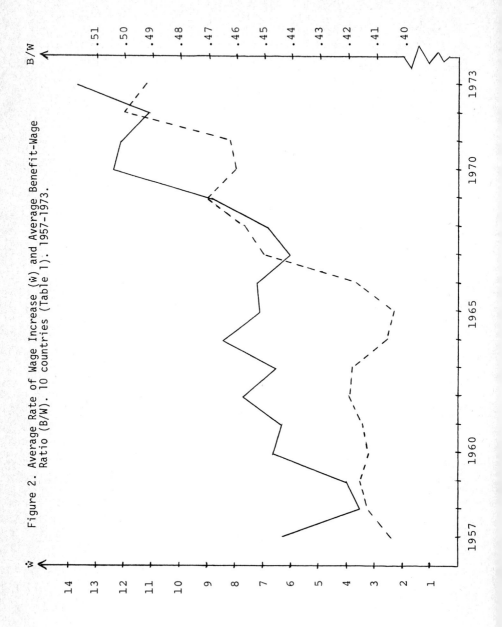

Figure 2. Average Rate of Wage Increase (ẇ) and Average Benefit-Wage
Ratio (B/W). 10 countries (Table 1). 1957-1973.

of cross-country regressions. The regressions have been run on country-averages of the variables for two different periods (1957-73 for BM and 1961-73 for BA). They are consequently rather crude variants of pooled time series cross-section regressions. In the first and the third regressions we test the hypotheses that countries with high benefit-wage levels have had higher increases in wages. In the second and fourth regressions the hypothesis is that increases in the benefit-wage ratio have had an inflationary impact. Finally the two last regressions test the hypothesis of induced unemployment, i.e. whether countries with on average higher benefit-wage ratios also have on average had a higher rate of unemployment. All the hypotheses are strongly refuted with cross-country data. In the unemployment relations we find a reverse Maki-Spindler effect, i.e. the higher the level of the benefit-wage ratio the lower the rate of unemployment. This should not be given any behavioral interpretation as the result reflects roughly the division between a set of (European) countries with high benefit levels and low unemployment and a set of countries with the opposite characteristics.

5. CONCLUDING REMARKS

An inflationary impact from liberalization of UI has been suggested by a number of authors, Arndt (1973), Mortensen (1970), Feldstein (1976) and Cubbin and Foley (1977). The conclusion in the present paper seems to be a refutation of this hypothesis at least with the kind of data and methods used here.

On the other hand the development in average benefit-wage ratios and the average rate of increase in industrial wages shown in Figure 2 exhibits the same broad pattern, i.e. an increase in the pre-OPEC stagflation years. But we know from Section 3 that while the acceleration in wages is a common phenomenon, this is not so for the benefit-wage ratio. Consequently a common UI-explanation for the individual countries of the stagflation years is not to be expected.

A priori one would expect an inflationary impact to be strongest in countries with either a high level of the benefit-wage ratio and/or a spectular increase.[31] Looking at the results in Section 4 we find significantly (or near significantly) positive coefficients in the level regressions for Denmark, the Netherlands and Austria. For Australia and Canada significantly positive coefficients were found to changes in the level of the benefit-wage ratio. These countries have in common a significant increase in the benefit-wage ratio during the period. In four countries, Belgium, Germany, Norway and Sweden, the level of benefits to wages is high but no significant change takes place during the period. Consequently no inflationary effects could be identified. Finally we get mixed evidence for Great Britain and for USA. Different estimates of the benefit-wage ratios show quite different developments over time. Consequently no reliable estimate of a potential inflationary effect can be found for these countries.

Summing up, UI does not seem to be the villain in the inflation drama. On the other hand no final answer can be given with the crude data and methods used here.

FOOTNOTES

*   University of Aarhus. Comments are gratefully acknowledged from J. Fitzgerald, J.H. Gelting, F. Kirwan, K.G. Löfgren, M. Paldam, S. Sharir, I. Ståhl, J. Taylor, P. Zweifel and an anonymous referee. I have benefited greatly from very competent research assistance by Niels Eberhardt and by access to Erik S. Madsen & Martin Paldam´s data bank.

1)   E.g. Feldstein (1973), Grubel & Maki (1976), Grubel & Walker (eds., 1978), Maki & Spindler (1975).

2)   Azariadis (1981).

3)   Cf. the suggestion in Feldstein (1976, p. 955) of UI as the cause of the shifting standard Phillips curve.

4)   The macroeconomic effects of increases in the benefit-wage ratio (that are not fully financed by increased contributions) are normally kept out of the analysis.

5)   Cf. Hatton (1980) for a critical discussion of this point in relation to Benjamin & Kochin´s (1979) explanation of interwar unemployment in Great Britain.

6)   Choice of a specific functional form is of no great importance if the benefit-wage ratio exceeds a level of about 0.50.

7)   Only wage-drift is explained in (4). A number of other variables are tried besides u and d.

8)   Feldstein (1976).

9)   Mentioned as a hypothesis by Junankar (1981).

10) This is the case for Canada and for Sweden.

11) This probably explains why the debate on UI effects has been more intense in UK than in most other countries, but see below for quite different estimates of the UK benefit-wage ratio.

12) Ståhl (1978) suggests a number of explanations for this decrease. The principal point is the special difficulties in Sweden of isolating UI from other labour market policy instruments. The fall might reflect that a growing number of the unemployed have received partial pensions.

13) Registered number of unemployed or number of unemployed from sample surveys.

14) For a number of countries calculations of average benefit-wage ratios produced unacceptable results, i.e. ratios over 100 or extreme swings from year to year. This is the case for Belgium, Finland, Germany, Ireland, The Netherlands and New Zeeland.

15) Comparisons between countries are difficult because of differences in the way the number of unemployed is calculated.

16) Maki & Spindler (1975), Cubbin & Foley (1977), Sawyer (1979), Spindler & Maki (1979), Benjamin & Kochin (1979), Junankar (1981), Hatton (1980).

17) BA2 resembles a series computed by Taylor (1977). Taylor has revised and updated the series to 1979 and finds a rather sharp decline in the benefit-wage ratio from the mid-seventies to 1979 (Private correspondence).

18) In the case of Japan matters are complicated by the choice of a series for the number of unemployed. In Table 2 the number of UI beneficiaries is used. Alternatively, one could use the number of unemployed from sample surveys. This gives a dramatic increase in the implicit benefit-wage ratio from 1957 to 1964 followed by an equally dramatic decrease. Behind this pattern lies the peculiar fact that the number of UI beneficiaries is significantly greater than the number of unemployed from sample surveys in the years 1962-1966.

19) Note that lack of data necessitates the suppression of a number of other relevant UI parameters.

20) Linearity might not be a sensible specification in cases where the benefit-wage ratio approaches 1. Further one could argue that the ratio should be truncated at some level as it is hardly conceivable that the low levels in some of the countries at the beginning of the period could have had any inflationary impact.

21) Australia, Canada, Ireland, Germany, Norway, and Great Britain. See Paldam (1980).

22) See fn. 16.

23) Cubbin & Foley (1977), Sawyer (1979), Spindler & Maki (1979).

24) A more pragmatic motive is the lack of yearly data on participation ratios for the majority of countries discussed here. Experiments with Danish data for the period 1948-78 yield significantly negative and insignificant coefficients to a labour supply variable contrary to the positive coefficient found by Maki & Spindler (1975) for the UK.

25) This test is only tentative. More conclusive evidence would be possible if data were available not only on changes in the stock of unemployed but on gross flows, i.e. quits and layoffs.

26) Significantly negative coefficients to ΔBM are found for Germany and Great Britain. For ΔBA significantly negative coefficients are found in Japan, Norway and USA. In all cases except Great Britain these are countries with near constant/declining wage-benefit ratios. The sign of the coefficient is thus no surprise.

27) For periods between 1957 and 1972/75.

28) Country-specific intercepts could be introduced through the use of country dummies.

29) A thorough discussion of the single country time series vs. the pooled time series-cross-section approach in a Phillips-curve and in an industrial conflicts context is found in Paldam (1981). The conclusion in Paldam's study is that the pooled time series-cross-section approach is inferior

compared to the single country time series approach.

30) Principles of measurement will also change over time in individual countries but usually the changes will be of a much smaller magnitude than the cross-country differences.

31) With the data and methods used here an inflationary impact could not be identified unless the benefit-wage ratio shows some movement over time.

REFERENCES

Arndt, H.W. (1973), Inflation: New Policy Prescriptions, The Australian Economic Review, 41-48.

Atkinson, A.B. and Flemming, J.S. (1978), Unemployment, Social Security and Incentives, Midland Bank Review, Autumn, 6-16.

Azariadis, C. (1981), Implicit Contracts and Related Topics: A Survey, in Hornstein, Z., Grice, J. and Webb, A. (eds.), The Economics of the Labour Market, HMSO, London.

Benjamin, D.K. and Kochin, L.A. (1979), Searching for an Explanation of Unemployment in Interwar Britain, Journal of Political Economy, 441-478.

Blomgren-Hansen, N. and Knøsgaard, J.E. (1980), Løn, Ledighed og Arbejds-løshedsunderstøttelse (Wages, Unemployment and Unemployment Relief), Na-tionaløkonomisk Tidsskrift, 16-36.

Burdett, K. and Mortensen, D.T. (1980), Search, Layoffs and Labor Market Equilibrium, Journal of Political Economy, 652-672.

Cubbin, J.S. and Foley, K. (1977), The Extent of Benefit-Induced Unemploy-ment in Great Britain: Some New Evidence, Oxford Economic Papers, 128-140.

Disney, R. (1981), Unemployment Insurance in Britain, in Creedy, J. (ed.), The Economics of Unemployment in Britain, London.

Feldstein, M.S. (1973), Lowering the Permanent Rate of Unemployment, A study prepared for the Joint Economic Committee, 93. Cong. 1. sess. GPO, Washington.

Feldstein, M.S. (1976), Temporary Layoffs in the Theory of Unemployment, Journal of Political Economy, 937-959.

Grubel, H.G. and Maki, D.R. (1976), The Effects of Unemployment Benefits on US Unemployment Rates, Weltwirtschaftliches Archiv, 274-298.

Grubel, H.G. and Walker, M.A. (eds., 1978), Unemployment Insurance. Global Evidence of its Effects on Unemployment, The Fraser Institute, Vancouver.

Hatton, T.J. (1980), Unemployment in Britain between the World Wars: A Role for the Dole? Discussion Paper No. 139, University of Essex.

Holden, K. and Peel, D.A. (1979), The Benefit/Income Ratio for Unemployed Workers in the United Kingdom, International Labour Review, 607-615.

ILO. 1961, 1964, 1967, 1972, 1976, 1979. The Cost of Social Security. (1949-57, 1958-60, 1961-63, 1964-66, 1967-71, 1972-74), Geneva.

ILO. Different Years. Yearbook of Labour Statistics, Geneva.

Junankar, P.N. (1981), An Econometric Analysis of Unemployment in Great Britain, 1952-75, Oxford Economic Papers, 387-400.

König, H. and Franz, W. (1978), Unemployment Compensation and the Rate of Unemployment in the Federal Republic of Germany, in Grubel, H.G. and Walker, M.A. (eds.), Unemployment Insurance. Global Evidence of its effect on Unemployment, The Fraser Institute, Vancouver.

Lipsey, R.G. (1960), The Relation between Unemployment and the Rate of Change of Money Wages in the United Kingdom, 1862-1957: A Further Analysis, Economica, 1-31.

Madsen, E.S. and Paldam, M. (1978), Economic and Political Data for the Main OECD-countries 1948-75, MEMO 78-9, University of Aarhus.

Maki, D. and Spindler, Z.A. (1975), The Effect of Unemployment Compensation on the Rate of Unemployment in Great Britain, Oxford Economic Papers, 440-454.

Marston, S.T. (1975), The Impact of Unemployment Insurance on Job Search, Brookings Papers on Economic Activity, 13-60.

Mortensen, D.T. (1970), Job Search, the Duration of Unemployment and the Phillips Curve, American Economic Review, 847-862.

Okun, A. (1975), Comment, (in Marston (1975)).

Paldam, M. (1980), The International Element in the Phillips Curve, Scandinavian Journal of Economics, 216-239.

Paldam, M. (1981), Technical Notes on the Use of Country Sets of Estimates for the same Equations, MEMO 81-4, University of Aarhus.

Sawyer, M.C. (1979), The Effect of Unemployment Compensation on the Rate of Unemployment in Great Britain: A Comment, Oxford Economic Papers, 135-146.

Spindler, Z.A. and Maki, D. (1979), More on the Effects of Unemployment Compensation on the Rate of Unemployment in Great Britain, Oxford Economic Papers, 147-164.

Ståhl, I. (1978), Unemployment Insurance: The Swedish Case, in Grubel, H.G. and Walker, M.A. (eds.), Unemployment Insurance. Global Evidence of its Effects on Unemployment, The Fraser Institute, Vancouver.

Taylor, J. (1977), A Note on the Comparative Behaviour of Male and Female Unemployment Rates in the United Kingdom, 1951-76, University of Lancaster, mimeo.

Walsh, B.M. (1978), Unemployment Compensation and the Rate of Unemployment: the Irish Experience, in Grubel, H.G. and Walker, M.A. (eds.), Unemployment Insurance. Global Evidence of its Effects on Unemployment, The Fraser Institute, Vancouver.